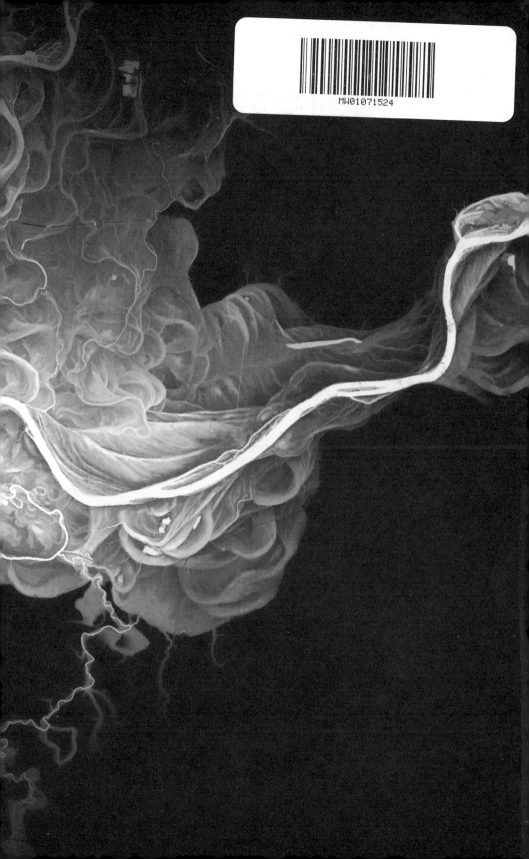

IS A RIVER ALIVE?

IS A RIVER ALIVE?

Robert Macfarlane

W. W. NORTON & COMPANY

Independent Publishers Since 1923

Copyright © 2025 by Robert Macfarlane

For information about special discounts for bulk purchases, please contact W. W. Norton Special Sales at specialsales@wwnorton.com or 800-233-4830

Manufacturing by Lakeside Book Company
Production manager: Delaney Adams

Endpaper image: *Willamette River Historical Stream Channels, Oregon*, by Daniel E. Coe, Oregon Department of Geology and Mineral Industries.

Cover: *Meander* © Stanley Donwood, 2024

ISBN 978-0-393-24213-3

W. W. Norton & Company, Inc.
500 Fifth Avenue, New York, NY 10110
www.wwnorton.com

W. W. Norton & Company Ltd.
15 Carlisle Street, London W1D 3BS

10 9 8 7 6 5 4 3 2 1

For the rivers and their guardians,
and Julia

i.m. Josef DeCoux (1951–2024)

*How can I translate — not in words but in belief — that a river is a body,
as alive as you or I, that there can be no life without it?*

Natalie Diaz (2020)

Dear broken rivers . . .

Alexis Wright (2019)

CONTENTS

PROLOGUE

The Springs

Twelve thousand years ago, a river is born.

In a hollow at the foot of a hill on which flints lie white as eyes, water rises for the first time from a crack in the chalk – and flows away. Rises and flows, rises and flows: for days, then years, then decades, then centuries, watched by a midsummer day-moon and a berry-red winter sun, watched in all weathers, watched by deer who stand six feet tall at the withers, watched by the sentries of hawk and fox, watched in sleet and hail, watched by aurochs eleven feet long from muzzle to tail.

This spring-water fell first as snow. It settled, melted, seeped slow through the bedrock, then surfaced here as a spring – a sleepless flutter of silver movement, rippling the pool it has made with its whispers and mutters.

The years below ground have clarified this water. It is transparent as glass and there is a blueness to it. North of here, the glaciers are in grudging retreat: vast crystal lobes and prows of ice, creaking as the warming climate hauls them back towards their last stand in the high places. The great ice-sheet leaves behind it scoured ground, scarred plains of bedrock, meltwater lakes and moraine. An immense weight has been lifted – and the land itself rises in relief. Trees stalk the glaciers northwards: first birch and hazel, then grey willow follows, filling the hollows. Down in the south, the frost has at last yielded its iron grip: water can soak deep into the earth, sate the aquifer – and cause this spring to flow at the foot of the hill.

Spring becomes stream becomes river, and all three seek the sea.

Now it is eight thousand years ago — the time of the linden tree. A wildwood of lime thrives, thronging right to the coasts and tight to the pool where the spring emerges. Rain-fed, the spring's stream surges seawards: gravity at work, or something like longing. The stream joins the river who winds in fat meanders to its mouth where at last — between bronze beaches — it reaches the ocean, and is havocked into waves by tide and wind's commotion.

Shadows shift between the trees around the spring: here are people for the first time, drawn to this place where water is born. The spring becomes a fixed point in their wanderings; a strange attractor in the loops and curls of their seasonal movements. Here they drink, eat, sleep, and use deer antlers to knap tools from knuckles of flint which are white without and dusky blue within. They haft blades to wooden shafts, craft awls and adzes, sharpen burins with which to engrave bone. They make cooking hearths from stones, leave them charred on the chalk. Their night-fires blaze in the great loneliness of this scarcely populated land, in the greater loneliness of the universe. One winter night, the aurora flickers across the heavens: shifting, radiant sky-rivers that flow and twine in currents, and pink-green light falls on the people's upturned, astonished faces — before all is once more swallowed in the immense dark.

History runs both fleet and slow, eddying back upon itself to shape spirals where flow meets counterflow. Life and death rise and fall — and the spring, as it has always done, organizes existence around itself, exerting something like will upon the land. Settlement begins: a cause-wayed enclosure is dug and fortified atop a hill overlooking the spring, big enough for ten families or so. Centuries pass. The enclosure is abandoned, overgrown, absorbed by green. New dead are buried in the old chalk, and grave goods with them: pots, beads, and the sweeping horns of an aurochs killed with a poleaxe that punched a hole in its skull right between its brimming eyes.

The magic lantern flickers fast and faster. Two thousand years pass: the chalk hills are a stronghold again – the site of a huge ring-fort, ditched and palisaded. In the little wood, more springs have risen: nine of them, filling two pools. Water carriers beat a path into the earth, treading back and forth from fort to springs to fort, over and over. Water-worship floods the wider land. Springs and streams become sacred places, where water speaks in voices that cannot be understood or denied. In this age, rivers are seen and named plainly as gods: Dana (later the Danube); Deva (the Dee); Tamesa (the Thames); Sinnann (the Shannon). But if the stream who flows from the springs who pulse at the white hill's foot is ever named, that name is lost to time.

Numberless nows become thens. The Pax Romana brings peace to the valley of the springs. Small farmers divide up the land. Their iron ploughs strike orange sparks from flints at dusk, shattering the stones so their sharp flakes lie indistinguishable from those knapped by human hand four thousand or five thousand years earlier. The Romans venerate the dryads of the trees and the naiads of the water. The water of each spring and stream is not interchangeable. Water's source *matters*. Its course *matters*. Each river is differently spirited and differently tongued – and so must be differently honoured. Far to the north, where glaciers once dragged their bellies, Batavian soldiers build a temple over a spring and dedicate it to the goddess Coventina, whose name they take from the Celtic word *gover*, meaning 'little stream'. Gifts are made to the water goddess, thousands of them: coins, beads of bone and lead and jet, a copper brooch of water serpents. As for the little springs with their lucid waters: each year a few legionaries turn from the straight and aggered road that runs a mile away, and come to lay down spear and dagger, slake their thirst and murmur prayers. They call the place Nona, after one of the goddesses of fate. In time, Nona will become Nine – Nine Wells. The springs of fate, where a river is born.

Time lapses, repeats, and the springs flow on, season after season. Blossom in succession: blackthorn, plum, hawthorn, dog rose, spindle.

Leaves with their different greens: hornbeam, hazel, oak and maple. In the wood around the springs, owls call from ash and beech, each to each, year on year. Someone fastens an iron ladle on a long chain to a tree at the pool's edge, so people can dip and drink the springs' cold water.

Centuries pass. Plague moves westwards from Europe in long-legged leaps, reaches the region. Sharp-toothed and hungry, it stalks the young city of Cambridge which is now growing near the springs – and devours its people. Half of the city dies. Half of Europe dies. An old thorn tree flourishes by the springs, and petitioners come to tie rags of cloth to its branches, hoping the life of the waters will protect them from death. But the buboes still fester in their armpits and groins. Some of the dead are buried alone and with care; others are heaped together in trenches dug in churchyards. Still the springs run on, still the river seeks the sea.

It is the 1530s. Henry VIII has broken with Rome and overthrown the authority of the Pope. The Reformation is under way, but it is not only altars that are stripped and rood screens that are smashed. A purging fury is visited upon the animate land as well, bent on exorcizing *that most detestable sin of idolatry*. Vigilante groups fan out across the country. Running water – with its power to heal, bless and act – attracts particular persecution. Holy wells are filled and capped. A chapel built by a saint's spring far in the west is destroyed, its attackers vowing to leave *not one stone thereof upon another*. Some of those who persist in making pilgrimages to springs and rivers are arrested and tried. Still people come, sometimes under darkness's cover, and still they leave offerings. To many, the authorities' suppression of spring sites simply confirms the numinous power of such water, welling mysteriously and wilfully from the earth as it does – as it has done for thousands of years.

Almost three centuries later a burningly handsome young poet with a limp, who is reputed to keep a bear in his university rooms, swims naked in a green pool of the river near the springs. Later he writes a poem describing a nightmare in which the sun was extinguished, and an icy Earth swung blind and blackening through space, and *the rivers, lakes and ocean all stood still, while nothing stirr'd within their silent depths.*

Horses give way to tractors on the slope of White Hill, as they now call the high ground beneath which the springs rise. War engulfs the world, threatens the land. The city's people turn out in their thousands to dig a seven-mile trench into which the Wehrmacht's tanks will supposedly plunge if they attack from the south. But the grey soldiers never make landfall, the trench is back-filled, and during the peace that follows a big new hospital arises near the springs.

The hardest winter on record comes in 1967: the springs freeze solid for six weeks, and tree branches break under the gathered weight of ice. The hardest drought comes in 1976: roads melt, scrub-fires rage and billions of aphids drift over fields and towns like plumes of green smoke. Drawn by the aphids, a plague of ladybirds swarms the south, settling in number upon people who suddenly find themselves shimmering with thousands of insects, as if they have grown their own elytra. The springs run dry for the first time since the retreat of the glaciers. And that August, at the height of the drought, a boy is born; he has very dark hair which soon turns flaxen.

The fast-growing city is thirsty for water: to flush, to wash, to drink. Boreholes are dug, the aquifer is tapped, and abstraction begins from stream and river. The water table drops as the crops, the taps and the hosepipes all take their share. Almost no one now comes to the springs, whose flow grows weaker and weaker. The stream falls into disregard, choked by algal blooms and duckweed. The river becomes slower, more polluted. The water company fears bad press if the springs run dry on their watch, so they send men with back-hoes and lengths of blue plastic piping to install an 'augmentation scheme': water from elsewhere in the system will be pumped into the springs to keep them alive.

Five hundred yards away in the hospital, scores of human bodies lie on ventilators, chests rising and falling to the steady rhythm of the pumps, the bleep of the heart monitors. Here in the little wood, the springs are also on life support.

The boy with flaxen hair, who is now a man, and a father for the first time, has moved to live on the edge of the city, a mile from the foot of White Hill. It takes him two years to discover the springs, forgotten as they have become, hidden as they are in a copse of beech and ash trees, tucked between fields of wheat and barley, close by the railway line. Quickly, the springs come to fascinate him. He starts to visit them often: walking, cycling or running up to the wood, sometimes three or four times a week. He likes to drink a handful of the spring-water; it feels round on the tongue and has the silky chill of stone. He discovers that the stream who flows from the springs is only one of around two hundred chalk streams in the whole world; that a spring-fed chalk stream is among the rarest habitats on Earth. He discovers that on current trajectories of pollution and abstraction, the entire English chalk-stream network is unlikely to survive into the second half of the century.

Ten more years pass. The man, who is me, has three children now. It is the summer of 2022, the hottest on global record – the summer when all the rivers nearly die.

~

The rainlessness begins in June. Dry days lengthen into weeks then months of drought. Crops brittle in the fields; soil cracks into stars. Fierce light frames curtains and shutters from dawn until what passes for dusk. I dream often of rain; we all do.

One morning we wake to find that southerly gales have carried a fine red dust up from the Sahara and left a powdery film on cars, windows and the leaves of plants. It gets in the mouth and tastes of exhaustion. The sun shines rust-orange through the haze, as in disaster movies or California.

Time falls out of joint. The mind fails to process the dissonance. The first of the year's two autumns comes in early August, when the trees begin to shed their leaves from heat stress. Oaks and beeches stand bare-branched. Asphalt melts glossy on the pavements and sticks to our soles like black chewing gum. Each new day brings the same old weather. We wear the heat like a suit of armour.

The rivers have it worst. The Po dead-pools. Sections of the Rhine are no longer navigable to the shallow-draughted barges that keep Germany's heartlands moving. In western Canada, spawning salmon are poached alive in gravel beds. On the banks of the Yangtze in Sichuan, parents sit their young children in buckets of water to keep them from heatstroke. In the borderlands of England and Wales, the run-off from giant chicken farms sickens the listless water of the River Wye.

The radio says: *The source of the River Thames has moved nine miles downstream.*

As water levels drop worldwide, things that have been hidden begin to surface and some of them are marvellous: medieval Buddhist statues; the 100,000-year-old skull of a deer; and a Bronze Age city that discloses itself on the banks of the Tigris River in Iraq. Archaeologists hurry to the site, where they wander and map the city's light-struck streets. They find five ceramic vessels containing more than a hundred unfired clay tablets, dense with script, and are astonished that these texts could have survived so long underwater.

Lake Mead on the Colorado River shrinks deep into its sandstone belly, leaving million-dollar speedboats beached at its margins. Wise-guy ghosts appear: a decayed body, dead from a single gunshot wound, stuffed into a fifty-five-gallon steel barrel and wearing sneakers from the early 1980s. Six other human corpses are also exposed; one is mistaken at first for the skeleton of a bighorn sheep. In nearby Death Valley, men film themselves frying eggs on the sun-scorched bonnets of Lamborghinis, and monetize the footage.

And along the edges of the Elbe, the drought stones appear: river boulders that are exposed when water levels are desperately low. They carry carved dates and inscriptions from earlier drought years: 1417, 1473, 1616, 1830. Near Děčín, close to the Czech–German border, a stone emerges that bears a warning:

Wenn du mich siest, danne weine.

If you see me, weep.

~

One day late in the long dry, I walk up to the springs with my younger son, Will.

I know what we will find that day and I cannot quite understand why we are going, but I hold hands with Will and together we cross the threshold between the hot light of the fields and the wood's cool.

Nightshade, magpie cackle, flies scribbling the same message over and over again in floating patches of sun.

The springs have almost perished. Over-abstraction from the aquifer and a series of arid summers have done their preparatory work – and now the drought has struck. I've never seen the main pool so low. The hollow is choked and rank with leaves. There's less than an inch of water in the stream-bed that leads from the springs, and no perceptible flow.

'Has the water died?' asks Will. He is only nine. It is painful for him to see this. He understands that there is something very wrong here, though he cannot name it. Something in the old power of this place, and its new injury, troubles him deeply.

'No, of course not,' I say, but my certainty is a deceit.

As we leave the wood we see an egret, white as a slice of snow, standing stone-still in the exhausted outflow channel, as if its patience might somehow summon back the water's life.

INTRODUCTION

Anima

We are searching for the boats we forgot to build.

Barry Lopez (2022)

This book is a journey into an idea that changes the world – the idea that a river is alive.

It explores the histories, people, places and futures of that idea and others in its family: that a forest might think, for instance, or a mountain remember. It asks what happens if we take seriously the idea of a river's aliveness. What does such a recognition mean for perception, law and politics? It is an attempt to imagine water otherwise.

Is a River Alive? unfolds across three main landscapes. First, an Ecuadorian cloud-forest named Los Cedros, the 'Forest of the Cedars', home to the headwaters of the Río Los Cedros, the 'River of the Cedars'. Second, the wounded creeks, lagoons and estuaries of the watery city of Chennai in south-east India. And third, the wild interior of Nitassinan, homeland of the Innu people, through which runs the Mutehekau Shipu, also known as the Magpie River, who makes sea-fall at the Gulf of St Lawrence, six hundred miles north-east of Montreal.

Each of these places has become a focus for revolutionary thinking about what the philosopher Michel Serres called 'the natural contract'. Each is a place where rivers are understood in some fundamental way to be alive – and in each place, too, the survival of rivers is under severe threat: in Ecuador from mining, in India from pollution and in Nitassinan from dams.

'Water is speaking,' noted the Scottish writer Nan Shepherd. But what is it saying? Everywhere I travelled, I asked people the same question: what is the river saying? This is an old-growth question; it has been around a long time. The answers I received were beautiful, cryptic, troubling and illuminating. What all share is a recognition that we live in a polyphonic world, but also one in which the majority of Earth's inhabitants – human and other-than-human – are denied voice. To be silenced is not the same as to be silent; to go unheard is not the same as to be speechless. No landscape speaks with a single tongue.

I wish to say plainly and early that this book was written *with* the rivers who run through its pages, among them the Río Los Cedros, the Adyar, the Cooum and the Kosasthalaiyar, the Mutehekau Shipu, the mighty St Lawrence, and the clear-watered stream who flows unnamed from the spring that rises at Nine Wells Wood, a mile from my house, and who keeps time across the pages that follow. They are my co-authors.

One morning when we were walking to school together, my son Will asked me the title of the book I was writing. '*Is a River Alive?*,' I told him. 'Well, duh, that's going to be a short book then, Dad,' he replied, 'because the answer is yes!'

Most of us, I think, once felt rivers to be alive. Young children are natural explorers of the vivid in its old sense: from the Latin *vividus*, meaning 'spirited, lively, full of life'. Young children instinctively inhabit and respond to a teeming world of talkative trees, singing rivers and thoughtful mountains. This is why in so much children's literature – from fairy tales to folk tales, across centuries and languages – a speaking, listening, convivial landscape is a given.

The language of hydrological governance refers to rivers, streams and lakes as 'waterbodies'. To the forty thousand recognized water-bodies in England, Wales and Scotland should be added another 65 million or so – for every human is, of course, a waterbody. Water flows in and through us. Running, we are rivers. Seated, we are pools. Our brains and hearts are three-quarters water, our skin is two-thirds water; even our bones are watery. We were swimmers before we were walkers, slow-turning like breath-divers in the dark flotation tank of the womb.

Urban planners speak of 'daylighting' streams and rivers. This is the practice of un-burying the watercourses over which many cities have been built, and which have been confined to drains and tunnels, flowing invisibly down in darkness. These imprisoned watercourses are sometimes known as 'ghost rivers': their voices are heard at street level, if at all, as whispers drifting from manhole covers or drain grilles.

London has more than twenty such ghosts. You could walk the streets of London for years and not know that each day you are crossing rivers other than the Thames, entombed beneath the asphalt: the Fleet, the Moselle, the Walbrook, the Tyburn and the Westbourne to the north of the Thames, and south of it the Quaggy, the Peck, the Neckinger, the Effra, the Falconbrook and others, their names now largely lost to concrete and culvert. The celebrated 1865 'Viele Map' of New York records the locations and routes of Manhattan Island's natural springs, streams and marshes. It shows New York once to have been a water-city. West Broadway was a wetland. At Madison Square Garden, three creeks converged like the tines of a trident, becoming one and meandering away. The Minetta Stream flowed from Fifth Avenue and 20th Street through Washington Square to its swampy mouth in what is now Greenwich Village.

'Daylighting' lets the water of buried streams meet the sun again. It is a means of bringing river ghosts back to life in towns and cities, of re-encountering rivers as friends and fellow citizens. In cities where daylighting has occurred, the results have often been socially transformative. In Seoul the Cheonggyecheon Stream was freed from the highway that had encased it: the public park created along its banks now draws ninety thousand pedestrians on an average day. Summer temperatures at the waterside can be five degrees cooler than surrounding areas, and air pollution levels along the stream's corridor have dropped by more than a third. In Seattle, Yonkers, Singapore, San Antonio and many other cities worldwide, daylighting projects have helped resuscitate rivers and revitalize neighbourhoods. When, in a visionary act of urban redesign, Munich freed the blue-watered River Isar from the canalized flood channels into which it had been confined, and instead let the river wander across a wider bed, the city too was changed. Grayling now fin in shallow-water shoals in the shadow of willows. Meadows slope down to the shifting, shingled edge of the Isar, where people come to sit, talk, walk, sunbathe, sleep, swim and dream. It is not that the city has bestowed life upon the river; rather that the river has enlivened the city.

In the pages that follow, I want to daylight long-buried ways of feeling about water, both in history and in us – and to see what transformations occur when rivers are recognized as both alive and killable.

~

If you find it hard to think of a river as alive, try picturing a dying river or a dead river.

This is easier. We know what this looks like. We know how it feels. A dying river is one who does not reach the sea. A dying river's fish float belly-up in stagnant pools. Swans in the upper River Thames now wear brown tidemarks on their snowy chest feathers, showing where they have sailed through sewage. In the 1930s and 1940s, the Don River in Toronto suffered such contamination from the oil refineries on its banks that it twice caught fire and burned. In the 1990s, Lake Ontario was so chemically polluted that it was possible to develop photographic film by dipping it into a bucket of lake water. In the autumn of 2023, a funeral was held for Lough Neagh, Northern Ireland's biggest waterbody: black-clad mourners bore a coffin to the shore of the lough, whose water was stinking and dog-killing from the toxic algal blooms that had spread across it.

Rivers should not burn. Lakes should not need funerals. How has it come to this?

'The conquest of nature,' wrote the American geologist, anthropologist and racist William John McGee in 1909, 'which began with progressive control of the soil and its products and passed to the minerals, is now extending to the waters on, above and beneath the surface. The conquest will not be complete until these waters are brought under complete control.'

In the century or so since McGee committed to 'conquering' the world's waters, a large-scale transformation of river perception and river management has occurred. The rich and varied natures of running waters have been simplified into an understanding of 'river' as limitless source and limitless sump: that which supplies and that which disposes. A hard boundary between 'life' and 'not-life' has been constructed and policed by a world view which decisively locates rivers on the 'not-life' side of the frontier. For those who, like me, have been largely raised on rationalism, to imagine that a river is alive in a way that exceeds the sum of the lives it contains is difficult, counter-intuitive work. It requires unlearning, a process much harder than learning. We might say that the fate of rivers under rationalism has been to become one-dimensional water. Rivers have been systematically stripped of their spirits and reduced to what Isaac Newton called 'inanimate brute matter'.

The drive for control over water's movements – first undertaken at scale along the middle Yangtze more than five thousand years ago, and accelerated by the dual invention in the nineteenth century of pourable, reinforced concrete (1849) and dynamite (1867) – has successfully converted many rivers to what the philosopher Martin Heidegger christened *Bestand*, usually translated as 'standing reserve'. Heidegger gave a riverine example to explain what he meant by this term. He noted that Germany's Rhine had been a wellspring of inspiration for the poet Friedrich Hölderlin, in whose verse the river possessed its own personality and agency. However, once a hydroelectric dam was built 'into' the river, even the colossal Rhine 'appears as something at our command', wrote Heidegger. In his account, hydraulic engineering – for all the miracles it brings – fundamentally transforms our orientation to the river, replacing its autonomous liveliness with a subdued servitude. This infrastructural reframing of the river, he argued, was symbolic of the broader consequences of technocracy's administrative effort to entrap nature 'as a calculable coherence'. Nothing is good in and of itself; everything must be good *for* something. The identity of 'river' is stabilized and singularized, rendered legible only in terms of flow-rates and megawattage.

The Three Gorges dam project on the Yangtze River in China impounded so much water that it has measurably slowed the rotation of the Earth. There are now fifty thousand dams in the Yangtze catchment alone. Europe has the most obstructed river system of any continent, with more than a million barriers fragmenting river-flow, and only a handful of free-running waterways remaining. If one walks to the end of the five-mile-long Oosterscheldekering dam in the Netherlands – an entire kingdom made possible by the genius of landscape-scale water governance – one finds inscribed on a block of concrete the phrase *hier gaan over het tij, de wind, de maan en wij*: 'here the tide is ruled by the wind, the moon and us'. Many of these dams have brought wonders in terms of human survival and flourishing, of course; dams have powered cities, quenched the thirsts of billions, made hearts sing as symbols of human hope, and united people as various as Jawaharlal Nehru, Woody Guthrie and Josef Stalin.

Meaning, as well as water, can be impounded: can still and settle behind dam walls of thought. The impounded meaning of 'river' is now one of 'service provider', an identity held in place by structures of the imagination as well as of the land. We have become increasingly waterproofed: conceptually sealed against subtle and various relations with rivers, even as they continue to irrigate our bodies, thoughts, songs and stories. Rivers run through people as surely as they run through places.

One of modernity's many vanishing tricks is to disappear the provisionality of its own conclusions. We now take it for granted that we take rivers for granted. It is unremarkable that flowing fresh water can be owned, for instance – can be privatized and sold, reduced to liquid asset – or to think that access to a river's banks may be tightly controlled or forbidden, rather than being part of a blue commons. It is normalized that a corporation, in the eyes of the law, is an entity with legal standing and a suite of rights, including the right to sue – but that a river who has flowed for thousands of years has no rights at all.

Our rivers are now tightly bound by logics of objectification and extraction. Strong forces will be required to release older, more complex river-meanings from their impoundment – and to reanimate our relationship with these vast, mysterious presences whose landscapes we share. But as the economist Erich Zimmermann's enduring one-liner has it, 'Resources are not, they become.' Which is to say – they can unbecome too.

In his strange, slender book *H₂O and the Waters of Forgetfulness* (1985), the Austrian social critic Ivan Illich explores how far we have 'forgotten' water. The story he tells is one of disenchantment and homogenization. Water has been rinsed of its complex social and metaphysical contents, Illich finds, and reduced to a 'cleaning fluid'. Turning a river metaphor back upon itself, he suggests that the West has drunk from the memory-erasing River Lethe, and thereby suppressed the waters 'of the deep imagination'.

In a haunting image, Illich imagines a possible antidote to this amnesia: 'Following dream-waters upstream, the historian will learn to distinguish the vast register of their voices.'

~

As the living world has been further distanced and deadened into 'brute matter', so language use which recognizes the liveliness of land and water – a 'grammar of animacy', in Robin Wall Kimmerer's celebrated phrase – has become rarer. We have largely lost a love-language for rivers.

Occasionally, these animate grammars can still be heard – and they deliver a jolt to the mind's ear. In April 2021, four women from an inter-tribal coalition wrote an open letter to Joe Biden, seeking his protection of their sacred lands of Bears Ears – the desert region in Utah which Donald Trump had sought to open for mining and drilling. The *New York Times* printed the women's letter. 'Our histories run deep,' they said:

> We relate to these lands who are alive. We know the names of the mountains, plants and animals who teach us everything we need to know to survive . . . We know these lands as a mother knows her child, as a child knows her mother. Indigenous women worldwide know where the sacred springs are; where the plants necessary for food and medicines are found; and the animals who instruct us.

'Who', not 'which'. *These lands* who *are alive*. Words make worlds. In English, we 'it' rivers, trees, mountains, oceans, birds and animals: a mode of address that reduces them to the status of stuff, and distinguishes them from human persons. In English, pronouns for natural features are 'which' or 'that', not 'who': the river *that* flows; the forest *that* grows. I prefer to speak of rivers *who* flow and forests *who* grow. In English, we speak of a river in the singular. But 'river' is one of the great group nouns, containing multitudes. In English, there is no verb 'to river'. But what could be more of a verb than a river?

'Grammar' is that which orders the relations between things. The word sounds dry, but it hides great power within itself: in Middle English, 'grammar' also meant 'magic' – a 'gramarye' was a book of spells or sorcery. A good grammar of animacy can still re-enchant existence. To imagine that a river is alive causes water to glitter differently. New possibilities of encounter emerge – and loneliness retreats a step or two. You find yourself falling in love outward, to use Robinson Jeffers's beautiful phrase.

In Māori, one might greet someone new by asking, 'Ko wai koe?', which literally translates as 'Who are your waters?' My waters are the River Dee, who rises on the Cairngorm plateau, bubbling out of the plateau granite at four thousand feet among ptarmigan, snow buntings and wintry sunlight; and that nameless stream who rises as a spring in that hollow at the foot of White Hill.

Hold the map of your country in your mind. Imagine it now entirely blacked out except for the rivers and streams: these alone are present. Let them glow in vivid colours – blue and green, scarlet and violet. A new topography leaps to the eye. The land is suddenly intricately veined. Ridgelines show as dark, wandering absences; catchments gather fine filaments of water, braid them expertly into threads, ropes. Tilt – and zoom in. The pattern repeats, then repeats again with each scale-shift: a fractal branching of tributaries and channels, fronds and stems. It resembles the vascular system. It resembles a neural network.

Everyone lives in a watershed.

~

In my country, England, a gradual, desperate calamity has befallen our rivers and streams. Existing laws and regulations have failed to protect them from harm. Existing ways of relating to flowing water have failed to stop the slow violence to which our rivers have been subjected.

'Shifting baseline syndrome' is the name given to the process whereby ongoing damage to the natural world becomes normalized over time, as each new generation measures loss against an already degraded benchmark. A person born in the 1970s will remember the car windscreens of their childhood spattered by countless insect impacts after a long journey. The windscreens of today's cars bear a fraction of those impact marks – but someone born in the early 2000s would not recognize this as signifying a drastic decline in flying insect populations, because they never knew the earlier abundance. The same effect is also sometimes known as 'generational amnesia', and it is a powerful force in terms of disguising and enabling further ecological harm.

Shifting baseline syndrome has masked the stages of our rivers' ruin. Clean rivers have become rivers you cannot drink from without falling ill, which in turn have become rivers you cannot swim in without falling ill. Almost too late, we have woken up to the catastrophe. Today, as the river defender Feargal Sharkey puts it, 'The simple truth of the matter is that every river in England is dying.' They are dying through inattention and they are being killed by design.

It doesn't have to be this way. Shifting baseline syndrome can also function in reverse. We can normalize betterment as well as decline, and then wish for betterment's increase: let us call it 'lifting baseline syndrome'. We can run the reel backwards, and create a future in which the expectation of children-to-come is that rivers flow free and clear.

Rivers are easily wounded. But given a chance, they heal themselves with remarkable speed. Their life *pours* back.

When the Lower Elwha Dam in Washington State was removed in September 2011, a century after it was constructed, the Elwha revived breathtakingly fast. Millions of cubic yards of sediment which had accumulated behind the dam were flushed to the estuary, where the river's new flow quickly built shingle banks and sandbars, protecting the shore from storms and creating complex new habitats. In the reservoir's drained bed, a young forest and understorey soon sprang up: saplings of maple, fir and cedar; vast purple swathes of lupin; cottonwood and willow bushes. Black bears and mountain lions criss-crossed the scrub and padded through the river. Dippers appeared, bobbing on boulders in their smart bib-and-tucker like attentive waiters. Below the surface, other miracles occurred. As the water cleared, migrating salmon – their route no longer blocked by dams – returned first in their hundreds then their thousands each year, driven by ancient compulsion to reach the upper river, spawn in its shallows and then perish, in the great, wild fatality of the salmon run – an annual drama as alien and thrilling as any Greek tragedy.

As the river brought the salmon back, so with them came the web of life they feed. Salmon are primarily ocean creatures; they carry marine nutrients far inland in their bodies when they come to spawn. In the upper Elwha watershed, scavengers dragged the carcasses of dead and dying salmon into the forest, stripped flesh and guts and discarded the skeletons to rot on the moss and leaves. Fungi reached up their white ghost-fingers, drew the bones down and decomposed them – then shared the goodness with the roots of the trees. By means of the river, the ocean fed the forest.

People returned too: hikers, families, paddlers, politicians – and members of the Lower Elwha Klallam Tribe, whose sacred land had been drowned by the reservoir a hundred years earlier, who had fought for decades to get the dams removed, and who then scattered by hand the tons of native seeds which would reforest the territory through which the Elwha now runs again.

Hope is the thing with rivers.

~

Ideas move in space and time. They swim like fish. They drift like pollen. They migrate like birds. Sometimes their movement carries them right around the world, and they find new niches in which to flourish.

One day in October 1971, a young academic called Christopher Stone was giving a seminar on property law at the University of Southern California in Los Angeles. It had been an intense class; the students were tired and distracted. Pens were being twirled, windows stared out of. Stone decided to have a last shot at regaining their interest. What he said then jolted the students upright – and it also surprised him. He hadn't been expecting to say it.

'So,' he asked hesitantly, 'what would a radically different law-driven consciousness look like? A consciousness in which . . . *Nature* had rights. Yes, rivers, lakes, trees, animals. How would such a posture in law affect a community's view of itself?'

There was uproar from the students! How could a river have rights?

How could a forest be a legal person? It would flood the courts with vexatious claims. It would be an affront to those humans who are still denied rights. Who would speak for the river in court – and how would they know what the river wanted? If a river could sue, could it be sued in return if it flooded a property? These were all good questions. One thing was for sure: Stone had got their attention.

Afterwards, Stone couldn't stop thinking about what had happened. Where had the idea come from? He couldn't say. But he realized he really meant what he'd said. Rivers *should* have rights. Forests *could* be legal persons. He just didn't know how yet. So he pulled out a yellow jotting pad and began to work it out.

Stone grew his idea fast: first into a 1972 paper called 'Should Trees Have Standing?' – an essay now seen as a landmark in jurisprudence – and then into a book of the same name, which remains in print more than fifty years on. His idea initially met not only resistance but derision. Judges and lawyers heaped scorn upon it. Stone didn't mind. He knew there was a price to pay – a phase of testing to be passed through – for any strong new notion. 'Each time there is a movement to confer rights onto some new "entity",' he wrote in his 1972 paper:

> each time the proposal is bound to sound odd or frightening or laughable . . . This is partly because until the rightless thing receives its rights we cannot see it as anything but a *thing* for the use of 'us' – those who are holding rights at the time.

Almost forty years after Stone first coined the notion of nature's rights, a Māori legal scholar called Jacinta Ruru read his work. It struck her that an affinity existed between Stone's young concept of legal personhood for natural entities, and the long-standing Māori relationship with rivers as living, sacred ancestors.

In 2010, together with her student James Morris, Ruru published an article entitled 'Giving Voice to Rivers'. 'Indigenous peoples throughout the world have strong connections to the flowing freshwater of rivers,' it begins, before turning to Stone's work and considering the relevance of nature's rights to the rivers of Aotearoa New Zealand. 'We argue that it is timely to consider the application of this concept in the specific context of [our] rivers,' they wrote, on the grounds that it could 'create an exciting link between the Māori legal system and the state legal system':

> The 'legal personality' concept aligns with the Māori legal concept of a personified natural world. By regarding the river as having its own standing, the *mana* (authority) and *mauri* (life force) of the river would be more likely to be regarded as a holistic being, rather than a fragmented entity of flowing water, river-bed and river-bank.

Only seven years later Morris and Ruru's synthesis found real-world form in an extraordinary piece of legislation called the Te Awa Tupua Act, the passing of which – in Parliament House, Wellington, on 20 March 2017 – was accompanied by songs, dances and tears of joy. That Act concerns the Whanganui River, who rises as meltwater on the snowy slopes of three volcanoes on the North Island, and then flows for around 180 miles through steep rainforest, deep gorges and bush country to reach the Tasman Sea at the town of Whanganui.

At the Act's heart is a radical claim: that the Whanganui River is alive, and an ancestor to the Whanganui *iwi* (tribe). The Act speaks unambiguously of the river as an 'indivisible and living whole', 'a spiritual and physical entity' with a 'lifeforce'. The Māori word that recurs in the Act when describing the river is *mouri*, synonymous with Morris and Ruru's term *mauri*, both of which translate as: 'life principle, vital essence . . . the essential quality and vitality of a being or entity'. The closest English cognate is 'anima', which means 'a current of breath or wind, the vital principle, life, soul', and which gives us 'animal', 'animate', 'animism' and 'animus' in the sense of 'mind'.

The Act also recognizes its principal subject as 'comprising the Whanganui River from the mountains to the sea, incorporating all its physical and metaphysical elements'. What a beautifully inclusive definition of a river this is! As a tree is not only its trunk but also its branches, leaves, roots, and the lives who thrive upon and with it, so here a river is recognized not only as its main channel, but also as its sources, tributaries, watershed, estuary – and what the Act calls the life and health of the 'communities of the River', human and non-human, who exist within its catchment and whose well-being is continuous with that of the river's. *Ko au te Awa; ko te Awa ko au*, runs the Whanganui proverb quoted in the Act: 'I am the river; the river is me.'

To its recognition of the river as alive, the Act adds a second dramatic innovation: the river is also recognized as a 'legal person', with the capacity to represent itself in court and to bear rights – the right to flow unpolluted and undammed to the sea, for example, and the right to flourish. The Act establishes a body of River Guardians known as Te Pou Tupua, who constitute the river's 'human face'. The Guardians' task is to speak with and for the river; their obligation is to promote and protect its life force.

The Te Awa Tupua Act was the outcome of around 180 years of conflict between the Crown and the Whanganui *iwi* over land and water rights. At the heart of this conflict was a struggle between two incommensurable ways of seeing the river.

The first is that of the Crown: a utilitarian perception which has always viewed the Whanganui River as resource and service provider, there to be manipulated and exploited as the state has seen fit, and to be anatomized into its notionally separable, commodifiable elements: the bed, the banks, the flow, the fish, the minerals that lie beneath it. Since first claiming the river in the nineteenth century, the Crown had deforested, blasted, mined, abstracted, polluted and re-routed the Whanganui, reducing it by the early 2000s to a weakened, sickened river.

The second way of seeing is that of the Whanganui *iwi*. 'We want . . . to begin with the view that [the river] is a living being, and then consider its future from that central belief,' said Gerrard Albert, lead negotiator for the Whanganui *iwi*. 'We have fought to find an approximation in law so that all others can understand that, from our perspective, treating the river as a living entity is the correct way to approach it, as an indivisible whole, instead of the traditional model . . . of treating it from a perspective of ownership and management.'

The passing of the Te Awa Tupua Act echoed like a gong-strike around the world. The recognition – at the highest legislative level of a modern democracy – of a 'Great River' as a rights-bearing 'living being' seized the global imagination.

It also supercharged the dynamic, disruptive current of ideas usually now known as the 'Rights of Nature movement'.

~

There are few things as powerful as an idea whose time has come. Over the past twenty years, energized by ecological emergency, the young Rights of Nature movement has repeatedly inspired new forms of future dreaming, and unsettled long-held orthodoxies by appealing to imagination as much as to law.

Case after case has been brought worldwide to test the anthropocentric foundations of existing legislation – and the drive to recognize the lives, rights and voices of rivers, mountains and forests has lit up activists, lawmakers, politicians, artists and campaigners. Much of the trailblazing has been done by what the Mexican activist Gustavo Esteva called 'those from below': 'grassroots groups . . . which transform the world in the here and now', chiefly local people and Indigenous communities, mobilized by shared experiences of threat and loss to their landscapes. Much of it has also been driven by women, who have time and again stepped forward as leaders in the field.

Rivers, above all, have become the focus for this movement. 'River rights' have become the commonest form of novel legal subjectivity in dozens of countries around the world, from Australia to Colombia, Canada to Bolivia. In Bangladesh the judiciary has enforced the closure of 231 unauthorized factories which were judged to be violating the rights of the Buriganga River. In England a local council in Sussex has acknowledged the rights and legal personhood of the River Ouse. A Universal Declaration of River Rights has been drawn up which recognizes rivers as living entities with fundamental rights, including the 'Right to Flow' and the 'Right to be Free from Pollution'.

The centrality of rivers to this profound reimagining process is unsurprising. Muscular, wilful, worshipped and mistreated, rivers have long existed in the threshold space between geology and theology. They give us metaphors to live by, and they decline our attempts to parse them. Unruly, fluid and utterly *other*, rivers are – I have found – potent presences with which to imagine water differently. We will never think like a river, but perhaps we can think with them.

I take the Rights of Nature movement at its best to be a kind of legal 'grammar of animacy': that is to say, an attempt to make structures of power align with perceptions of a world which is far more alive than power usually allows. 'The law,' as the Nyikina Warrwa scholar-activist Anne Poelina puts it, 'is being used creatively to train human beings to listen, pay attention to, and learn from, rivers.' Recognizing nature's rights is one means of trying to tell a different story about the living world: a very old story, given new expression. A story in which the world is 'not a machine after all', as D. H. Lawrence put it, but 'alive and kicking'.

On Midsummer Eve in that drought-struck summer of 2022, I joined about a hundred people on the banks of the Cam – the river who flows through my home city and who is fed by the springs that rise near my home. The light that hot afternoon was syrupy and golden, the grass tawny from weeks of hard heat. The air was kiln-dry, and it was obvious to us all that the river was sick. Sweat crawled down us and the river crawled by us, its water low and greasy. Weed trailed lankly along its surface like hanks of hair.

Together, we read aloud a Declaration of the Rights of the River

Cam — as if just saying might make it so: *We declare that the River Cam and its tributaries have the right to flow and be free from over-abstraction, the right to be free from pollution* . . . Partway through, I had to stop speaking. I was overwhelmed by hope and futility. It was a mixture of a potency I'd never experienced before — and it silenced me.

Our fate flows with that of rivers, and always has.

~

I began these river-journeys in doubt and uncertainty. I knew the question to which I wanted a response — the question of this book's title — to be a formidably hard one, even as I wished it to be as simple as my son found it.

How we answer this strange, confronting question matters deeply. Even the asking of it is a first step. How we answer it now is of great importance to our ability to know, love and live on this Earth in ways that will help us do it justice and abide with it. The years I have spent seeking answers to this question have been bewildering as well as revelatory. In the end, of course, it was a river who gave me the truest and most complex response.

During my travels, I met stolen, drowned and vanished rivers, and saw the ruthlessly executed power of companies, criminals and governments. I met many river defenders who are trying to redefine our sense of what 'life' is, sometimes at grave risk to themselves; people for whom despair is a luxury. I watched a woman of unaccountable powers healed by water, and witnessed two discoveries, one of which shifted slightly the whole story of life on Earth. As to what occurred at the Gorge, ten days down a wild river in the far north-east of Canada — the point and place to which, it turned out, everything had been flowing? Well, I am still very far from being able to take that in, let alone comprehend it. I think perhaps I will always be coming to terms with it.

My first journey was to a cloud-forest in northern Ecuador. It is a living forest, certainly, through which living rivers run like veins. It is a place where a version of the world's oldest written story is being retold – though this time with a different ending.

It's night, a few miles from the equator, high in that cloud-forest, many miles from any road.

Cool air, damp ground. The chatter and click of night creatures.

A young river sings on ceaselessly in a gorge below.

In a little clearing, a fire burns – a small light in a vast dark. Shadow and flame tiger the leaves that fringe the clearing. Beyond and in all directions spreads the immense forest, seamed by streams and seething with sound.

The eyes of the forest are watching.

The ears of the rivers are listening.

The eyes of the forest can see a handful of people huddled close round the fire.

The ears of the rivers can hear one of them crying.

PART I

The River of the Cedars

(Ecuador)

One way to stop seeing trees or rivers or hills only as 'natural resource' is to class them as fellow beings — kinfolk. I guess I'm trying to subjectify the universe, because look where objectifying it has gotten us.

To subjectify is not necessarily to co-opt, colonize, exploit. Rather it may involve a great reach outward of the mind and imagination.

Ursula K. Le Guin (2017)

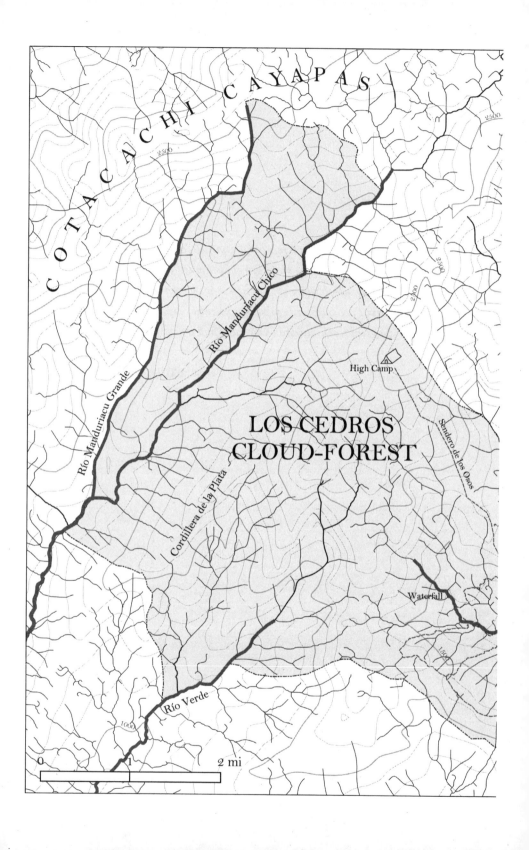

C O T A C A C H I   C A Y A P A S

2500

2500

2500

2700

Río Manduriacu Chico

High Camp

LOS CEDROS
CLOUD-FOREST

Río Manduriacu Grande

Cordillera de la Plata

Sendero de los Osos

Waterfall

1500

Río Verde

1000

0   1   2 mi

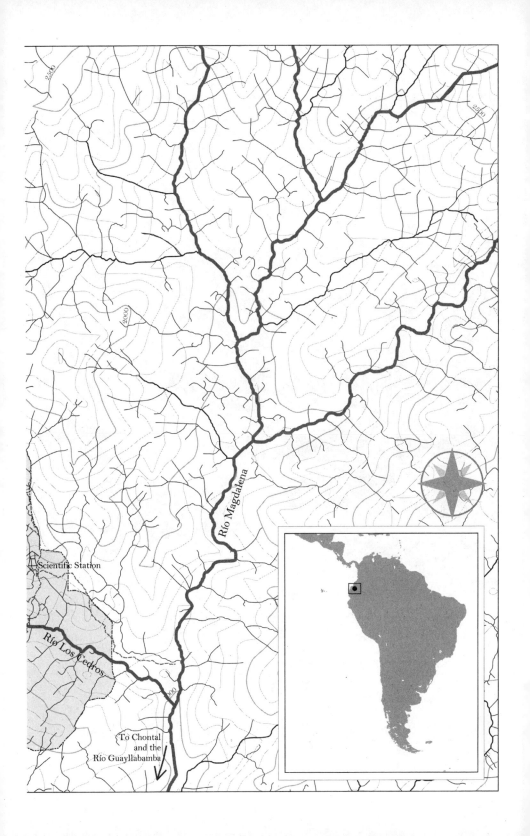

That first night at the high camp, the cloud-forest comes alight.

The fireflies start it, their orange diodes winking on and off as they drift. Then glow-worms in the understorey put tapers to their yellow lanterns. Then the red-ember eyes of kinkajous, bodiless in the dark, click on in the trees. They watch us from the branches with unblinking intent.

Far to our west, a storm slips along the Pacific coast. Blue-white sheet lightning silhouettes forested ridges. Thunder is muted by distance.

Far to our south, Cotopaxi erupts. Its magma chamber churns and slops. A seven-thousand-foot column of ash drifts in the still air.

From the spoil heaps of the mining district of Portovelo-Zamora in south-western Ecuador, mercury leaches slowly into the Puyango-Tumbes River, poisoning it for twenty miles downstream of the gold-processing centres.

In the gold futures markets, the spot price of a troy ounce climbs past $1,517.

We sit close round the fire in the little clearing, warmed by the blaze, comforted by each other's nearness. At night, at this height, the air is cold. Glimpsed through the cloud-forest canopy, the sky is blue-black clear and salted with stars. These equatorial constellations are odd to me in their orientations.

I have a strong sense of how very far we are from any road; of how deep into the forest we have come.

I realize Giuliana is crying quietly in the shadows. The sudden loss of her father remains so raw. *I am still in the house of death . . .*

Then she smiles a little through her tears. 'I'm crying from grief,' she says, 'but also out of happiness and relief at what's happened here in the forest, with the river, with you all. At what's been returned to me that I thought I might have lost for ever.'

A night-bird sings, trilling and liquid.

The fire burns down until it is no more than a rough circle of pulsing eyes.

¡Bosques sin Minería!: #JusticiaLosCedros, reads the text on a wall mural in Quito, Ecuador's capital: *Forests without Mining!*

¡La MINERÍA impulsa el Buen Vivir! reads a roadside advertisement for a copper company: *Mining promotes the Good Life!*

'Hola!' calls Giuliana suddenly. 'Head torches off! Look around!'

We kill our beams. Slowly, my night-sight simmers into focus – and I see that the trunks, stumps and fallen branches around us are all glowing with a light that is different in kind to any I have seen before. It's a yellow-silver brightness that comes from deep inside the object it illuminates, and it is heatless. I pick up a fragment of what feels like wood but looks more like radiant water. 'The light in this one seems to be rippling,' I say.

'That's because it's alive,' says Giuliana. 'That glow is mycelial. It's made by the miles of fungal hyphae that are growing through *this* wood *right* now, as the wood dies. That mycelium will, in the right season, produce bioluminescent mushrooms.'

I walk across to the rotting stump of a tree on the clearing's edge; the whole stump is shimmering with that water-light, as if a luminous river ran through it. In places the light is latticed; in others it is continuous. When I reach out invisible fingers to touch it, I find that I cannot – but nor can I occlude it. It is beautiful and eerie.

'What we have here this evening is nothing!' says Giuliana. 'If you hit the right night, in the right place, you can see *all* the veins of the forest lit up – you can see that *everything* is connected!' Then she murmurs, perhaps to herself, 'No one is without another.'

Under recessed ceiling spotlights in a Melbourne office building hailed by its owners as a workplace of unmatched distinction and surprise, a small team of in-house lawyers works through lunch to prepare paperwork for the final acquisition of a copper- and gold-mining concession in the cloud-forests of northern Ecuador.

On the eastern side of the Ecuadorian Andes, the scent of bitter almonds drifts through the forests of Zamora Chinchipe.

The rotting stump seethes, radiates. Cotopaxi slops and churns. The fireflies drift, wink. The River of the Cedars seeks the sea.

'If fungi were to speak,' says Giuliana, 'they would tell us what they show us, which is that really the death of an organism is the beginning of countless others; that there is no end to life, just a constantly shifting substrate.'

When we wake next morning in the clearing, the light of the mycelium is hidden by the greater light of the sun. The stump looks like any other stump, the branches like any other branches.

Mist fills the valley folds between distant ridges. Somewhere below us, two toucan barbets call out their counterpoint duet in smoky hoots – *hoo-ooh, hoo-ooh, hoo-ooh.*

Between the notes of the barbets, I can hear the high, trembling song of the River of the Cedars from down in the gorge, as it is born and born again.

~

I travelled to the mountains of northern Ecuador to seek a river, meet a forest and find two fungi – and because in 2008, this small country with a vast moral imagination changed the world.

In late 2006 the socialist democrat Rafael Correa won Ecuador's presidency – his election part of the so-called 'pink tide' of that period, which saw leftist governments elected across Latin America, from Chávez in Venezuela to Lula in Brazil and Morales in Bolivia. One of Correa's first steps in office was to initiate the process of designing and approving a new constitution for the country. A wave of reformist energy swept Ecuador, and by November 2007 a new Constitutional Assembly was convened – and given half a year to draft a new constitution.

That constitution, ratified by national referendum on 28 September 2008, was in many respects a startlingly progressive document. It identified drug use as principally a public health problem rather than criminal activity. Across fifteen sub-articles it guaranteed numerous rights and protections to Indigenous peoples in Ecuador. It also recognized water as a public good –'inalienable, imprescriptible, unseizable and essential for life' – prohibited the privatization of water, and declared a 'right to water', since 'its condition as an essential element for life makes it a necessary aspect for the existence of all living beings.'

The Ecuadorian Constitution's most radical aspect, though, was Articles 71 to 74: what have become known as the 'Rights of Nature' articles.

'Nature, or Pacha Mama, where life is reproduced and occurs,' states the first of these, 'has the right to integral respect for its existence and for the maintenance and regeneration of its life cycles, structure, functions and evolutionary processes.' The other three articles recognize nature's right to be restored when damaged, the relationship between the good health of nature and the 'good living' (*sumak kawsay*) of humans, and the obligation upon the state to restrict activities that might lead 'to the extinction of species, the destruction of ecosystems and the permanent alteration of natural cycles'.

It was a global first. The Rights of Nature – to exist, to regenerate, to be restored, to be *respected* – were enshrined at the highest level: among the fundamental principles by which a nation is governed. Nature's 'life' was recognized as requiring protection by the state. Crucially, the constitutional wording included human beings as 'an inseparable part' of 'Nature', rather than hiving humans off into a distinct, implicitly superior category. Ecuador's boldness of vision set the modern Rights of Nature movement in motion. So many subsequent developments in this field – including the recognition of the life and rights of the Whanganui River in 2017 – have their roots in this moment.

But how did this come to pass? Back in 2008, Rights of Nature thinking wasn't even at the fringes of modern political philosophy. A major part of the answer concerns the pressure brought to bear by Ecuador's Indigenous communities upon the drafting of the constitution. *Sumak kawsay* is a phrase from Kichwa, the most widely spoken Indigenous language in Ecuador: as noted above, it is usually translated as 'good living' or 'harmonious life'. Central to the 'good' of this 'good living' is an understanding – as the philosopher Carlos Larrea puts it – of 'all the beings around as living beings . . . the river is a living being . . . and the welfare of humans can only be understood and maintained in harmony with all the spirits of nature.' As the constitution was forged in part to uphold Indigenous human rights, so by extension it sought to support the Indigenous recognition of the lives and rights of rivers, mountains and forests.

In April 2008, shortly before the Assembly voted on whether or not to include the Rights of Nature in the draft constitution, the Uruguayan writer Eduardo Galeano wrote a short, fierce essay entitled 'La naturaleza no es muda': 'Nature is not mute'. 'The world is painting still lifes,' Galeano began:

> forests are dying, the poles are melting, the air is becoming unbreathable and the waters undrinkable – and at the same time Ecuador is debating a new constitution that opens up the possibility for the first time ever of recognizing the rights of nature . . . Nature has a lot to say, and it has long been time for us, her children, to stop playing deaf.

We might find it bizarre, Galeano continued, to think of a forest or river as having rights. Yet look how fully we have naturalized the idea that corporations have comparable rights to those of humans, 'as if companies could breathe'! How strange that we should assent to *this* legal fiction but be surprised – even outraged – at the notion that a river might be other than a 'piece of property'.

For Galeano, to carry forwards the great legal originality that was being attempted in Ecuador would be a significant step towards repairing the profound injuries that the wider Andean-Amazonian region had suffered since the Spanish Conquest, and which had devastated its rivers, land and people. Christian colonialism had systematically punished – with burning, hanging and killing – Indigenous perceptions of the landscape as inspirited. In the later fifteenth and early sixteenth centuries, Philip II's colonial administration had established a New World branch of the Inquisition dedicated to what it called 'the extirpation of idolatry'. Ecclesiastical tribunals were convened, which sentenced anyone found to have spoken to or with a river, or worshipped a stream, to a hundred lashes. The Spanish literally flogged animism out of their newly colonized subjects, and persecuted towards extinction the recognition of the forests and rivers as both central to life and themselves alive. Yet somehow, wrote Galeano – despite 'five centuries of prohibition and scorn' since the arrival of the Spanish, and despite 'the heavy legacy of racism, which . . . continues to mutilate reality and memory' in the region – the Indigenous communities of the Andes and Amazon had preserved these vital ideas of the entangled lives of rivers, forests, mountains and people.

Ecuador was at the time – as it still is – reeling from the consequences of decades of oil drilling in the Amazon, which had led to the discharge of billions of gallons of toxic wastewater and millions of gallons of crude oil into the waterways and ground of the region, with catastrophic consequences. That ongoing ecocide had become a wound in the national consciousness, and had compelled many in Ecuador to recognize the seemingly predatory intentions of multinationals, the fragile wonder of the country's forests and rivers, and the vulnerability of the people and creatures who lived among them.

Here was a chance, Galeano argued, to begin to heal such injuries and to prevent others like them from happening again. *Now* was the moment to move animist ideas into the centre of the state's own world view. There would be no comparable opportunity for decades to come – if ever.

Galeano was urged to write his essay by Alberto Acosta, the politician-intellectual who was appointed by Correa as President of Ecuador's Constitutional Assembly and placed in charge of drafting the new constitution. Acosta was already familiar with the philosophy of the Rights of Nature; he was also an active ally of CONAIE, the country's largest Indigenous organization, a group with an impressive record of fighting power and winning, especially over issues of land and water rights.

Knowing that the assembly vote on the Rights of Nature articles was imminent, elders and leaders (most of them shamans) from many of Ecuador's fourteen Indigenous nations – among them the Shuar, the Achuar, the Secova, the Waorani, the Chachi, the Cofán and the Sarayaku – travelled from all over the country to the town of Monte-cristi, where the assembly building was located. On the afternoon of 9 April, they gathered outside the building. Acosta joined them, and there the shamans held a public purification ceremony: singing, chanting and stamping, cleansing the air with bunches of leaves. On the ground they placed dozens of small clay vessels: pale pink and brown, four or five inches long, some with the heads of cockerels or turtles as their handles, others with human-like figures sitting inside them, arms folded. These vessels represented Air, Fire, Earth and Water. 'These elements,' a young Sarayaku leader called Juan Gualinga told Acosta and the gathered crowd, 'will bear witness to whether, in this great constitutional assembly, you will be sensitive to our feelings.'

That night, the Indigenous leaders and shamans met inside the assembly chamber. No one else was allowed access. The doors to the building were closed. The participants all ceremonially took aya-huasca, and then together they called for the spirit of Pachamama – Mother Earth – to be present in the voting chamber. In particular, they summoned the female spirit of the forested mountain which rose immediately behind the assembly building, and asked her to flood the space with her energy.

The next day – the day of the vote – the assembly members filed into the chamber which had been cleansed by the shamans, and into which the spirits of earth-beings had just been summoned. Acosta had also organized for a copy of Galeano's essay to be placed upon each seat; the essay was read aloud to the gathering by an assembly member. Shortly afterwards, the votes were cast. The assembly overwhelmingly backed the inclusion of the Rights of Nature in the constitution.

To the question 'Is a river alive?', Ecuador had answered a resounding 'yes'.

'We were moving forwards with ideas that seemed important to us,' Acosta recalled later of those weeks, 'although at the time we did not know their enormous significance. I had the feeling that we were already making history – but it was only later that we began to understand the huge import of what we had done.'

One of the regions whose future was to be determined by those events in 2008 was an area of rivers and cloud-forest in the north-west of Ecuador called Los Cedros.

~

The day we leave Quito for Los Cedros – long before the high camp in that fire-lit, firefly-haunted clearing – an altitude headache wakes me at dawn. It's a faint, distinctive pain, familiar from Alpine huts and Himalayan valleys but not from cities. We're at more than nine thousand feet here, though, and the air is thin for the newly arrived.

I lift the window-blind and see a hummingbird on the other side of the street, moving through a blue exhaust-haze raised by the backed-up traffic. The bird is jewel-bright. It's working the pink flowers on a line of pavement trees, dipping its long beak to sip nectar, while its body hovers motionless as a gyroscope and its wings blur the air. It moves between each blossom so fast it seems to teleport. *Blur, whir, dip, sip, slip.* I feel a nervous buzz in my stomach at what lies ahead. I have a bellyful of hummingbirds.

Coming with me to the cloud-forest are three people, each differently committed to the lives of rivers, forests and people: César, Cosmo and Giuliana.

César Rodríguez-Garavito is a Colombian lawyer who grew up in the bloodiest years of his country's civil war, when Pablo Escobar's kidnappings and killings were at their atrocious height. César was educated in a progressive Jesuit school in Bogotá, where he was taught liberation theology with a heavy emphasis on the 'option for the poor'; that is to say, the doctrine which holds that the moral test of any society is how it treats its most vulnerable members. He has since dedicated his life to social justice, and has spent many years in the trans-Amazonian region, fighting both for the rights of Indigenous people and those of the forests and the rivers – including the great, wounded Atrato River in his native Colombia. To César, there is no useful distinction to be made between human rights and the rights of nature; each is indissolubly merged with the other.

I think César, his dark curly hair turning pepper and salt at the sides, is in his early fifties, but it's hard to tell. He is neither stern nor severe, though he might be mistaken for both on first encounter. César radiates calm, itself a function of clarity of purpose. There is also a mystical side to César. He meditates daily and deeply. He loves being in forests, where the green soaks into him. He sees law as an extension of activism, and vice versa. Though he is a very serious person, with a slate-cleaving intelligence and flinty resolve that are vital for the work he does, there is a softness to César – a deep compassion, in fact. When he smiles, he really smiles. He reminds me a little of Chirrut Îmwe in *Rogue One* – the warrior-priest who is 'one with the force and the force is with him'. Like Îmwe, César seems unconcerned by the usual mortal distractions. In the cloud-forest, I will find, César somehow seems not to sweat, and his boots are never as muddy as mine. 'We live in an ongoing emergency, Rob,' he once said to me. 'I am tired of fighting the long defeat. I want *hope*. I thrive on it!' César is trying to generate and accelerate the ripples of Rights of Nature thinking worldwide. He has founded a group called the MOTH (More-Than-Human) Rights collective, of which I am a part. He is coming with me to Los Cedros to see what the Rights of Nature movement can do on the ground to help strengthen the forest's protection against the threat of mining.

Cosmo Sheldrake is, you might say, nine stone tall and six feet long – slender as a stem. He has an unruly mop of brown hair, and two sets of dimples bracket his mouth when he grins. Cosmo is all corkscrews and curlicues, a cosmic-comic Puck, impish and impious, ever ready to laugh at his own absurdity, or the universe's. He cherishes the double-selfie he once got with the world gurning champion: the champ with his lower lip folded up over his nose, Cosmo looking on with awestruck admiration. He is a brilliant musician and singer of perplexing versatility, who can play thirty or so different instruments and each year tries to learn at least one new instrument from somewhere in the world. The corners of his house are stacked with musical esoterica: horse-headed cello-like objects from Mongolia, torso-encircling sousaphones, and a flugelhorn from a Tyrolean valley. He seems to be able to make music with anything or out of nothing: belly bongos, beatbox cheeks and lips, a pair of spoons or bones, a yoghurt pot. Cosmo is also a listener. When he listens, he *really* listens. He enters another realm, becomes another person: wholly concentrated and dispersed into the sound-world. As a field recordist he has eavesdropped on the thriving life of a coral reef, used hydrophones to listen for the growls and croons of humpback whales, sung duets with nightingales and gathered the songs of birds – from the bittern's foghorn boom to the dawn chorus of an English oak wood. In Chile, Cosmo once placed contact microphones gently upon what is widely thought to be the oldest tree in the world, and could hear the slow pulse of its sap. He records life in all its beats and hisses – and he is coming to Los Cedros because he wants to 'hear the forest listening', he says.

And then there is Giuliana. Giuliana Furci is many things: a quadrilingual Chilean-Italian-British biologist-campaigner-filmmaker, daughter of a marriage between one of Pinochet's political prisoners and a handsome-as-hell Italian boy from a poor farming background. Above all, Giuliana is a mycologist: a hardcore scientist who has written two monumental field-guide volumes to the fungi of Chile – books born of hundreds of days on expedition in some of the wettest, coldest and windiest places on Earth – and who has helped drive global recognition of a third 'F', 'Funga', to set alongside 'Flora' and 'Fauna' in the taxonomy of conservation.

Late one day in March 2017, while driving a rough road through a monkey-puzzle and beech forest in southern Chile, with sleet spattering the windscreen, Giuliana suddenly screeched to a halt. She had seen something she later described as a 'fuzz in the matrix' on the exposed black earth on the left bank of the road. A difference; a *glitch*. She jumped from the car. There, growing among tree roots on the tangled bank, was a mushroom with a pitch-black cap flecked with small white scales. And another, *there*. And another. Six of them: six black-and-white mushrooms growing in that snowy undercut. A tingle of excitement rushed through her body. She knew immediately, knew *absolutely*, that these fungi were different from anything she or science had seen before. She instantly knew their genus too. *Amanita*, the genus which includes probably the most famous mushroom in the world – fly agaric (*Amanita muscaria*), the fairy-tale toadstool, renowned for its red and white-speckled cap. But the *Amanita* Giuliana found that afternoon had a night-black cap starred with white scales. Carefully, she photographed and collected two of the mushrooms. Genetic sequencing confirmed what Giuliana already knew in her bones to be true: the species was new to modern mycology. More than this, this *Amanita* species was old. Deep-time old: a Gondwanic species, in fact, which would have first flourished on the supercontinent that formed over half a billion years ago. That made it one of the oldest fungi still in existence, and likely to have been among the first to partner with plants in the inter-kingdom collaboration known as mycorrhizae – a mutualism first entered into some 400 million years ago, now popularly referred to as the 'wood wide web'. 'When I found it and looked into the black of the cap,' Giuliana said later, 'I *knew* I was looking into a very ancient, very deep night sky. So I called it *Amanita galactica*.'

Fungi are Giuliana's specialism, her vocation, her metaphysics and her style. Her forearms writhe with fungi tattoos: coralline and cup fungi, an *Amanita*, a webwork of mycelia and two earthstars, also known as spore-shooters – one of which is firing out both spores and the word *kairos*, meaning 'the right or opportune moment to act decisively'. Her WhatsApp status permanently reads: *En el bosque* ('In the forest'), and her WhatsApp handle consists of her name followed by two emojis: the red and white-spotted mushroom and the explosive flash. It's about as efficient a shorthand for her personality as could be: focused, fungal and dynamic. Hanging in the kitchen of her house in southern Chile, in sight of a restless volcano which puffs smoke-rings by day and spouts fire at night, is a neon-blue sign reading *Hongos Bar* – Bar Fungi. When I once asked Giuliana to describe the feeling she has when she's with fungi, she thought for a while before replying: 'Plenitude.' Her dark-brown hair is profuse and twirly, and shakes when she laughs, which is often. She's a very good person with whom to seek a river because she is a dowser, whose sensitivity to underground water is so great that she can sometimes estimate flow-rate as well as presence and location.

About the only way to annoy Giuliana is to demean fungi in some way.

And the only way to *enrage* her is to suggest that fungi are a kind of plant.

I don't intend to make either mistake.

Giuliana is the scientific lead on our expedition. She will be looking for two fungi in particular. In 2010, high in the Los Cedros cloud-forest, a mycologist called Bryn Dentinger made first collections of two small, brown witch-hatted mushrooms. Upon analysis, they turned out to be two previously unknown species of the *Psilocybe* genus: that is to say, the group of psychotropic mushrooms often called 'magic mushrooms' in English.

In the world of mycology, in order for a new species to be formally confirmed, a second, separate collection must be made. This second collecting is one of the aims of our journey. If Giuliana can find these fungi, and they're confirmed as new to science, it will be of major use in further protecting Los Cedros under Ecuador's Rights of Nature articles.

It is, though, unclear to me how Giuliana will locate two brown mushrooms, growing amid the cocoa-coloured leaf-litter and chocolatey rotting wood on the floor of an immense area of cloud-forest. Her task, which is also our task, seems the very definition of locating a needle in a haystack.

Giuliana's task has also been made vastly more difficult by the sudden death in Brazil, only a few weeks earlier, of her father. The shock, the grief and the grim aftermath – including the struggle she has faced simply to recover her father's body from the Brazilian authorities – have shaken her world. She is worried that grief has also attenuated her gift for finding fungi – of feeling 'the fuzz in the matrix'.

~

Giuliana, Cosmo, César and I help load up the back of the Hilux, throw a tarp over the cargo and rope it down tight.

There's a day-long journey ahead, first on roughening roads, then on foot along muddy trails – and up into the cloud-forest.

The northern highways out of Quito are snarled with traffic. It's a city unlike any I've seen before, long and thin and tentacular, as if it had been poured wet into the mould of the mountains and set there. Its urban planners are geology and geomorphology, river and time.

Marching up every hillside, thronging every patch of waste ground and steepling every ridge are eucalyptus trees. The eucalypts, an invasive species, are sinister in their number and power: a forest that eats other forests.

At last we get free of Quito's event horizon, and can gun the vehicle's big engine. Benzene-stink coils in through the windows. A two-lane highway leads through barren yellow hills with heavily grazed slopes. Debris spills from the mouths of small artisanal mines bored into the hillsides.

After two hours we stop at a gas station to refuel vehicles and humans. Cosmo acquires a bar of cannabis-infused chocolate and a quart-bottle of some clear spirit with a white-green label.

I raise an eyebrow. 'It's nine thirty a.m., Cosmo!'

He grins, takes a swig from the bottle, then offers it to me.

'The name of that spirit translates as "Seven Penises",' says Giuliana.

'I'll pass,' I say.

An hour later we are among wooded mountains, following the gorge-line of a river. The journey passes in flashes.

Two halves of a pig hung up by its trotters outside a butcher's shop; spine and ribs in cross section, a tight ball of flies glittering blue in one of its chest cavities.

Dogs asleep in the gutters, undisturbed by the tyres that thunder a few inches past their dream-twitching noses.

'Today is the first day I didn't wake up and cry about my father,' says Giuliana.

The roads become smaller, more pitted. A mottled cow is chewing the cud in the middle of the road ahead. As we approach, it swings its heavy head towards us, lazily knees itself upright and ambles to the verge.

'That's a zebu cow,' says Giuliana. '*Psilocybe* grows in their dung: that's a good omen!'

A security guard stands wide-footed and still outside a hardware store, pistol holstered on his hip, cradling his assault rifle like a baby. House martins weave in the air above him.

Lines of vultures hunch on fences, their shining black wings outstretched to burn off mites in the hot sun. A hummingbird with feathered legs flirts with a poster selling brightly wrapped chocolate.

'There's a giant Patagonian hummingbird species,' says Giuliana, 'and one of them came each year to visit the same eucalyptus tree that grows at our house by the sea in northern Chile. But then my father cut the tree down. We argued horribly about it. I didn't see the bird for years. Then when I at last got his ashes back to the house a fortnight ago – there was the giant hummingbird again, perched on another branch as if it had been waiting for us.' She pauses, then corrects herself. 'Waiting for me.'

Three hours later we cross the Río Guayllabamba. The metal of the bridge whangs and cracks as we clatter over it. The river's waters are deep and churning. The land rears up around us now. Colourful birds for which I have no name flee from roadside trees.

Early that afternoon we reach the end of the road. Three mules wait patiently on the dusty verge, shuddering within their gauze of flies. Behind a stand of bamboo, a bright stream bounces over boulders.

A thin footpath cuts diagonally from the roadside up between plantain trees. At the start of the footpath, nailed to a pole, is a lopsided sign, crusted with white and yellow lichens. Painted on it in an angular, Greek-style font are two words:

LOS CEDROS

~

A cloud-forest is a river-maker.

Cloud-forests form at higher altitudes than rainforests: typically between three thousand and eight thousand feet above sea level, in steep landscapes of peak, ridge and valley. The elevation means that cloud-forests are cooler than rainforests, and the drama of their topography means that their rivers are fast, shallow, clear and rock-bedded, compared to the muddier, slower rivers of rainforests.

Altitude and coolness co-create the cloud. Humid air is pushed upwards by the land, bringing the water it bears to condensation point, and forming the mist which cloaks such forests year-round. The mist also reduces direct sunlight, reducing transpiration from the trees and retaining more water within the forest system.

Because this drifting mist infiltrates the full volume of the forest – wandering from ground to canopy, between trunks, into every niche – the available surface area for condensation is maximized. And because cloud-forests are characterized by an astonishing density of 'air plants', or epiphytes (that is, plants which grow on other plants), this surface area is *immense*. Liverworts, mosses, ferns, orchids, lichens and bromeliads throng the trees of a cloud-forest; hundreds, sometimes thousands of plants can flourish upon a single big tree, in a proliferating density of floral life greater even than that of a rainforest.

Much as a bearded person walking through mist will find water droplets condensing upon the hairs of their beard as well as their skin, so the epiphytes of a cloud-forest act as collectors for the moisture suspended in the mist, which in time rolls and drips as water to the forest floor. This gentle, constant run-off is known by forest biologists as 'fog-drop', and it is what allows cloud-forests to maintain the flow of their streams and rivers even in dry periods. This is why an alternative name for a 'cloud-forest' is a 'water-forest'. This is why river and cloud-forest cannot be separated – for each authors the other.

The interior of a cloud-forest is a steaming, glowing furnace of green. To be inside a cloud-forest is what I imagine walking through damp moss might be like if you had been miniaturized. There, life thrives upon life upon life upon life in a seemingly endless *mise en abyme* that bewilders the imagination and opens a scale-slide of wonder into which the mind might plummet.

Cloud-forests are among the most biodiverse habitats in the world.

Although they account for less than half of 1 per cent of the Earth's land surface, they are home to around 15 per cent of known species. A cloud-forest can contain around four hundred species of tree in a single hectare; almost half as many as the number of native tree species found across the entirety of the contiguous United States. Among cloud-forests, the most biodiverse are generally agreed to be those of the Tropical Andes. There, a unique abundance and variety of life is created by the proximity of the Pacific and the Andes, which rise from sea level up to more than twenty thousand vertical feet in only a few hundred lateral miles.

But millions of hectares of Andean cloud-forests have been lost over recent decades to logging, farming, building and mining. Over 2 per cent of cloud-forest was destroyed globally between 2001 and 2018; in the Andean cloud-forests this rate reached 8 per cent. Existing legal protections have slowed but not stopped the loss – and much of that loss has happened in Ecuador.

Metal mining is the most catastrophic and terminal of cloud-forest interventions. For the gold and copper mining which now predominates in the northern Andes, the method of large-scale extraction is usually open-pit, which requires the digging of a series of vast stepped 'benches' to give heavy machinery access to the ore. The establishment of a pit first requires deforestation of the extractive zone, then the construction of a network of access roads for the heavy machinery. Dynamite blasts the bedrock, before large power shovels collect the shattered ore. Trucks transport the ore to the crushers, where it is ground to a fine consistency and mixed with water to make a slurry. The refining process then removes unwanted materials, separates out valuable by-products – and purifies the ore slurry to the desired concentrate.

In the case of gold mining, ore is typically piled into huge heaps for extraction by a technique known as 'cyanidation' or 'heap leaching'. The ore is sprayed with a dilute solution of highly toxic sodium cyanide, which filters down through the ore and forms a gas that smells of bitter almonds. Where it encounters gold, it dissolves it and carries it out. Because gold is widely disseminated in low-grade ore, large volumes of sodium cyanide and other solvents are necessary to leach it. Once deployed, these solvents theoretically require storage or safe disposal; the standard technique is to construct an impoundment dam, which retains the by-products in ponds or lakes. In practice, many smaller gold mines just let the solvents flow directly into nearby streams and rivers.

Thus the marrow of the mountain is cracked open, slurped out and sold; thus the cloud-forest and its rivers are poisoned and killed.

Among the most intact and miraculous cloud-forest regions of South America is the Cordillera de Toisán, a branch of the northwestern Andes which runs through the area of Intag, in the Cotacachi canton of Ecuador's Imbabura Province. In the western extension of the Toisán lies a small massif called the Cordillera de la Plata. And at the southern end of that massif – where earth-forces have rippled the terrain into steep-sided valleys and narrow ridges, and the ground rises to a pyramidal central peak of around nine thousand feet – is Los Cedros, a rugged and remote area of mostly primary cloud-forest, accessible only by foot, mule or helicopter.

The topographical map of Los Cedros is a beautiful document. It shows the green of forest veined with the blue of rivers and streams. It shows an intricate, lobed landscape, contoured into many small watersheds, each of which collects water from rain and fog-drop to create countless creeks and streams, who become the headwaters of the four main rivers flowing southwards out of the forest: the Río Manduriacu, the Río Magdalena Chico, the Río Verde – and the Río Los Cedros. It is the Río Los Cedros whose route I want to trace back towards its source in the upper gorges of the cloud-forest.

Los Cedros is a living *Wunderkammer*. It is the home of fabulous beasts, birds, plants and fungi who could have flown, crawled and grown straight out of Hieronymus Bosch's imagination: the spiny pocket mouse, the strangler fig, the white-headed capuchin, the devil's fingers fungus, the spectacled bear, the dwarf squirrel, the river otter, the jaguarundi, the golden-headed quetzal, the black-and-chestnut eagle . . .

Here lives a frog who can modify the texture of her skin at will, toggling from smooth to grainy in just a few minutes. Here live 'Dracula' orchids, whose purple, swooping petals resemble the Gothic cape of a vampire, and who mimic the smell of rotting meat in order to attract pollinating flies. Here live at least a dozen species of hummingbird, thimblefuls of molten metal who whir from flower to flower. Even their human names seem to have tumbled straight out of myth: the Andean emerald, the long-tailed sylph, the tourmaline sunangel.

Where the streams and rivers flow fast over rapids in Los Cedros, they are green-watered, and where they gather in pools they are blue as a glacier's heart. Pumas and spotted cats drink from them. White-throated dippers fish them.

It is not known exactly how old the area of cloud-forest now called Los Cedros is, and how many millennia of continuous flourishing it has performed. But according to the 'Dry Refugia' hypothesis – one of the two dominant paradigms for understanding the Pleistocene pasts of rainforests and cloud-forests in the neotropics – it is plausible that montane forest has existed continuously here throughout the glacial fluctuations of the Pleistocene; that is to say, for around 1.5 million years.

This is a forest who has self-regulated for an exceptionally long time.

~

As we load up the mules at the Los Cedros trail-head, Giuliana feeds them plantains and strokes their noses. They whicker their soft lips contentedly at her.

Swifts bank and hurtle: little crossbows hunting flies above the river. They return over and over to the same patch of air, circling it in helical loops like water spiralling an outflow.

A white car pulls up behind us. Two men get out. We have been expecting them, and I call out a greeting.

'Ramiro! Agustín!'

They are old friends. Both are in their fifties, both are legal scholars who have also served as Ecuadorian Constitutional Court judges – and together they form a high-contrast double act.

Ramiro Ávila Santamaría is flamboyant, loose-limbed, fearless and dramatic. He loves running, thinking and debating; he thrives on dialectic and gin. Agustín Grijalva Jiménez is shy, reserved and watchful – Abbott to Ramiro's Costello. In my mind, Ramiro's familiar is the howler monkey, the loudest mammal on Earth, and Agustín's is the armadillo: a quiet, blinking nocturnalist, possessed of a patient and terraforming power.

Both Ramiro and Agustín have played crucial roles in the story of Los Cedros – but they've never before been able to meet the cloud-forest in person, because their first involvement with it occurred during the pandemic years, when travel within Ecuador was severely curtailed. Now they're coming with us up into the mist – and they're excited.

Ramiro bobs around eagerly, helping load the mules. Agustín regards proceedings with a contented smile.

Giuliana has noticed me watching the swifts. 'Because you are a bird person, Rob,' she says, 'I must tell you before we get any further into the forest that I have a problem, which is that I can't look up as well as down – so birds always lose out to fungi.'

'I'm at ease with that. I can do the sky – you do the earth.'

'If I were *really* studying the fungi in Los Cedros,' she says, 'we'd move only a few metres each hour; a few hundred yards in a day. It would be the slowest of walks! Well, it would be a crawl, really.'

We make it perhaps ten yards up the trail when Giuliana cries out and drops to the ground. Has she been shot? No, she is greeting a fungus.

'Oh, hello! *Woo-hoo!* Come and meet her, everyone! Look – a

Pholiota! Can you see the scales on the pileus? Scales are the relics of the universal veil.'

'Surely that's a theological rather than a mycological proposition?'

'Just look at her floccose stipe, Rob!'

The pileus, she explains, is a mushroom's cap, the floccose stipe its woolly stalk – and the universal veil is what mycologists call the thin membrane that envelops certain mushrooms in their first, egg-like form.

Another fifty yards, another *woo-hoo!* from Giuliana. 'Look! Look, everyone! A witch's hat, s*ombrero de bruja*! That's a fine early find on the trail. Oh – and there's *Auricularia auricula-judae*. Jelly ear! Well, that's good news – I can guarantee we won't go hungry in the forest with that around.'

Her enthusiasm is contagious, her knowledge profound.

'Ah – leaf-cutter ants, running along our trail. Watch your feet, everyone!'

There they are, hundreds of shining black ants, each carrying a neatly trimmed triangle or trapezium of leaf. They resemble a tiny line of boats – green sails up, afloat. The ants have left their own path, an inch wide, beaten into the earth by the strike of millions of tiny ant feet. I kneel, lay my hand flat across their path. They continue without breaking stride, marching across my palm.

'Where's it all going? What's it for?' I ask. 'I didn't know ants ate leaves.'

'It's all about fungi again, Rob,' says Giuliana.

'Of course it is,' says César.

'It is! They're taking the leaf pieces to their huge subterranean nests, where the leaves are used to culture a fungus which is the *actual* food of the ants, or to be precise of their larvae. Leaf-cutter ants carry out arguably the first form of agriculture. The *fungus* is the crop. It's happening right here under our noses – and all over this forest.'

I watch the ceaseless, orderly procession of the ants: such organized diligence.

'So much biomass is being taken down into the nest. All day and all night this work continues, feeding the fungus?'

'Yes – and it's thought possible they somehow *weigh* it, to know exactly how much leaf tonnage is needed, and to streamline the efficiency of the workers.'

'We'll drop a microphone into a nest one day up in the forest,' says Cosmo. 'Extraordinary sound-world. You can hear them stridulating – that's how they communicate.'

'The ants also culture a mould that secretes chemicals which inhibit the reproductive phase of the main fungus,' says Giuliana, 'so it's always in asexual mode. I've been on expeditions in the Amazon to find and dig out abandoned fungus-farming ant nests. The fungus there is primarily a genus called *Pterula*. When you unearth them, they're brain-like in form and huge – like pale-white buried coral reefs.'

Giuliana is already giving me new eyes with which to see the life of the forest, and Cosmo is giving me new ears with which to hear it.

We walk on. The path is steep in places, and muddy underfoot; here and there we must pull ourselves up, using branches and roots as handholds. Sweat on the forehead. Salt in the mouth.

With every step we take up towards the Cedar Forest on that trail, the sense of the forest's activity thickens, steams, multiplies, teems. The forest's noise fizzes around us: hoots, buzzes, clicks, rasps, calls.

'This . . . *energy* of the forest is something else,' says Ramiro.

Mist is beginning to wisp the air between the trees, and bead on our clothes and eyelashes. I look at Ramiro. He is glistening.

'Oh, we're in it now for sure, Ramiro; deep in it – and more in it with every minute.'

~

The cloud-forest we are entering should not exist.

The slender path leading us into the mist should be a thirty-foot-wide access road, bulldozed up the ridgeline.

The trees among which we are walking, with their shaggy overcoats of epiphytes, should be stumped or burned off.

The smell of bitter almonds should drift through Los Cedros.

In 2017 a small Australian environmental non-profit called the Rainforest Information Centre discovered that a mining concession had been granted by the Ecuadorian government for the Los Cedros cloud-forest.

Where the cadastral map of the valley had once shown only the unbroken green of forest, there was now a large, diagonally hatched grid stamped in scarlet over the lower third of the forest, signifying the concession. The grid covered an area that included the headwaters of three of Los Cedros's rivers.

Worse was to come. It turned out that the permit for the concession had already been sold to a Canadian 'prospect generator' firm called Cornerstone Capital Resources. Prospect generator firms typically explore for ore-rich locations, then seek to acquire the 'social licence' – that is, government and community consent to mine – for sites they believe to have significant mineral potential. They then sell such knowledge and licences on to larger mining companies for fat profits, while also retaining a minority stake in the venture.

Los Cedros, one of the most biodiverse and bio-abundant places on Earth, was suddenly laid open for business. Cornerstone was to seek copper and gold in the cloud-forest, working in alliance with Ecuador's state mining company, ENAMI.

The Los Cedros concession was one of dozens of mining and drilling concessions secretively sold by the Ecuadorian government between early 2016 and mid 2017 to foreign mining companies – chiefly Australian, Canadian and Chinese. The concession areas ranged from cloud-forest to high plains to Indigenous lands in the Amazonian Andes. The silent fire-sale was organized during the last months of the rule of Rafael Correa, the president who had initiated the creation of Ecuador's visionary new constitution in 2008, but who had never been a keen supporter of either Indigenous rights or the Rights of Nature in the country. As his tenure proceeded, indeed, his extractivist agenda became increasingly open, and he began actively persecuting the Indigenous movement in Ecuador, and notoriously dismissed those advocating against mining and drilling as the 'infantile left'.

The main reason for Correa's mass granting of concessions in these highly sensitive areas was simple: cash. Ecuador was (and still is) held in a debt-noose by creditor states from the Global North, bonded into crushing sovereign debt service repayments. Then between 2014 and 2015 the barrel price of crude oil, one of Ecuador's major exports, fell by almost 50 per cent. Ecuador's economy was thrown into recession. Despite Correa's attempts to write off billions of dollars as 'odious debt', or to come to a 'keep-it-in-the-ground' arrangement whereby wealthy nations would pay Ecuador *not* to drill for oil, towards the end of his third presidential term his country's finances were shattered.

The cash injection from the concessions was a short-term fix. Correa knew that the majority of profit from the concessions, like the profits generated by other extractive industries in the country, would flee Ecuador in the form of international shareholder dividend and corporate wealth. 'Oil contracts,' he had said before his first election, 'are a true entrapment for the country. Of every five barrels of oil that the multinationals produce, they leave only one for the state and take four.'

As for the costs of opening these fragile regions to mining? Well, these would not fall at the doors of those multinationals or their shareholders, but would instead be borne, wrote one observer, 'by thousands of already endangered species in the world's most bio-diverse forests . . . borne by Indigenous people, and people who have lived for hundreds of years doing subsistence farming in the Andes . . . [and] borne by the rivers that will carry toxic heavy metals into the Amazon basin.'

In 2017, Cornerstone and ENAMI came with drills, maps and heli-copters to begin their surveying of Los Cedros. They would in due course bring the chainsaws, the feller bunchers, the log loaders and the de-limbers, to strip the forest of its trees and clear the ground for roads, camps and the open pit. After that they would bring the blasting teams, the excavators, the leachers and the river dammers. They came to kill the forest and its waters – and it seemed as if nothing could stop them.

But then on 10 November 2021, something remarkable happened. Something which could *only* have taken place in Ecuador.

That day a judgment was passed in the Constitutional Court in Quito. It deployed the political might of the constitutional articles guaranteeing the Rights of Nature – and it ruled that mining would violate the rights of Los Cedros: both the rights of its creatures and plants to exist, and the rights of the forest and its rivers as a system to 'maintain its cycles, structure, functions and evolutionary process'.

During the hearing, local people from the villages bordering Los Cedros had testified about the impact mining would have. It was often the rivers who were the focus of their testimonies. 'We have taken the pure water, the clean water, that comes from Los Cedros Forest,' said one witness, 'we are defending nature, the right to life, which is water.' 'I grew up here more than fifty years ago,' said another; 'when I was a child here, there was water at every step; today there are only rivers in the larger ravines, and if that which originates in the Los Cedros reserve is not defended now, what is going to happen tomorrow?'

The judgment wrapped a protective forcefield around Los Cedros – one so powerful that the mining companies were compelled to evacuate the area within weeks.

The chief judge who ruled on the case? That was wise, watchful Agustín Grijalva Jiménez. And his supporting judge was the extravagant and long-limbed Ramiro Ávila Santamaría.

'The forest helped us,' Agustín recalled to me later, in an openly animist account of how he and his colleagues had formed their judgment; 'the strong voice of life' proved a greater influence 'than even the legalistic framework'. He and his fellow judges felt 'the call of life' from Los Cedros; it 'swayed the bench'.

Agustín's deeply philosophical 124-page ruling found that the Rights of Nature, together with the human right to a healthy environment and to clean water, would be violated were mining to be permitted in Los Cedros. The mining companies were ordered immediately to cease all activities and to make good any damage, and the government was required to guarantee the rights to which Los Cedros was constitutionally entitled.

'A river [or] a forest,' wrote Agustín, are 'life systems whose existence and biological processes merit the greatest possible legal protection that a constitution can grant: the recognition of rights inherent to a subject'.

News of this thunderclap judgment echoed around the world. 'This ruling is as important to nature as Thomas Paine's Rights of Man were to our own species,' said Mika Peck, a field biologist who has worked in Ecuador since the 1990s. The British-Peruvian barrister Mónica Feria-Tinta described the Los Cedros ruling as comparable to 'the turning-point in the history of human rights of 1948'. In recognizing that nature could bear 'legal status and substantive rights', she said, it marked 'the law of the future'.

~

Step on steep step, the trail winds up.

The mist and the forest thicken around us, until we each move in a grey-green socket of softness.

The beginnings of rain now. Mosses mass on big trunks.

Our going is slow because Giuliana stops for every fungus, and this is one of the most fungally profuse places in the world – even now, at the end of the dry season. A heap of old mule dung sits in the centre of the path. Giuliana's eyes light up, and she crouches by it as if speaking to a child.

'Oh! *Parasola plicatilis. Woo-hoo!* Hello, my dear! Look! The pileus is already enveloped. These shit-loving fungi are just so gorgeous. This is a fungus that grows on dung, but most species that grow on mule dung won't grow on cow dung. So much fungal life is specific to its substrate.'

A dung beetle climbs patiently up one of the balls of dung, then falls off and lands on its back, showing its iridescent-blue belly armour and slow-pedalling its steel legs. I right it and we walk on.

A zigzag silver line of recently shed snakeskin, perhaps five feet long, is draped across a bank of earth. Individual scales of this serpent-ghost are still visible.

'Rob, Cosmo! *Wooo-hooo!* Come here – *Xylaria*! Look at those thin black fingers. *Xylaria* are more closely related to truffles than to mushrooms.'

I'm beginning to wonder if we will make it up into the forest by dark. Giuliana senses my concern. 'Trust me, Rob,' she says, 'I'm being *really* good. I'm filtering communications from the fungi, and trying my best to look up. I had to build my house in Chile on stilts, out of the woods and off the ground, as this was the only way to get some rest from the fungi.'

She plunges off to the right of the path. 'Oh – look! An exquisite *Marasmius*, decomposing the leaf!'

Two toucans call down from the canopy with honks and hoots. They are big, heavy-headed birds; bright-beaked carnival creatures. They peer down at us. They hop and reverse position on the branches, like rock climbers switching feet on a tricky pitch. Leaves nod in the rain. Thunder rumbles in the distance.

Bird alarm-calls are triggered by our presence, picked up by other species, and passed on in widening circles. 'I like hearing these ripples of information moving through the forest,' says Cosmo. 'In forest as thick as this, you can hear much further than you can see.'

After two more hours, the path flattens out. Suddenly there is infrastructure: a thickly mossed fence and, beyond it, a clearing with a small scatter of wooden cabins and buildings.

We have reached the Scientific Station: the one place in Los Cedros where human structures exist. For years, research scientists have used this as a base camp for fieldwork, as they try to fathom some aspect of the bewildering ultra-life of this forest.

César, Cosmo, Giuliana and I will spend a few days here with the judges, looking for fungi, tracking the river and meeting the forest; then the four of us will move up into the high forest to seek further fungi – and to find the source of the Río Los Cedros.

Ahead, I think I can identify two of the cedars which give the cloud-forest its human name. They are big trees, standing in clear ground, with pinnate leaves that remind me of the English ash. I can hear the muffled bronchial wheeze of a generator. Set into the fence is a rotting gate, and on the gate is a moss-eaten sign matching the one that marked the start of the trail:

LOS CEDROS

Beyond the gate, I can see into the first building. It's wooden, hexagonal in form and open-sided.

And in its shadows, something is stirring.

Out shambles a huge man – a bear emerging from his den. His hair is wild and white, his beard straggly, his clothes ragged at the knees, the ribs, the elbows. He lumbers towards us, unsmiling. I guess him to be in his seventies. A small dog skitters past him, snarling and snapping at us.

This bear is Josef DeCoux, who moved into Los Cedros in a tent in the 1980s – and who has lived here ever since, largely alone, protecting the forest against threat after threat down the decades. It was DeCoux who brought the Rights of Nature case against the mining companies.

He is not a man who tarries with small talk.

'Why the hell aren't you all in rubber boots like I told you?' he growls, jabbing a finger at our feet. 'You'll tramp mud all over the place. Get to that hosepipe and wash the filth off.'

Nice to meet you too, Josef DeCoux.

We hose the mud off our boots, and are grudgingly admitted to the hexagonal cabin, which is perhaps twenty feet across at its widest point. A thick vine the breadth of my forearm winds clockwise around the central rafter of the roof space.

There are two dogs. One is big, old, peaceful and drooling. One is yappy, tiny and aggressive: a chihuahua with an anger-management problem.

The big dog is called Schultes, after the legendary ethnobotanist Richard Evans Schultes. The little dog is called Cachorrita, which means 'Little Puppy', and she bites democratically, without distinction or favour between victims.

There are six cats: Ibrahim, Lola, Luna, Princesa and two who seem to be nameless. They are at once DeCoux's familiars and, it appears, his tormentors. He sits down heavily at a table. One cat immediately leaps up to perch on his right shoulder, another curls round his neck, and a third tries to eat his lunch.

'Fuck off, cat!' shouts DeCoux, swiping at the lunch thief.

All around us, we can see the forest extending in ridges and valleys. Mist hangs in scarves. The forest froths with sound: cicadas, birds, frogs, all singing and calling and signalling in a vast semiotic broth.

DeCoux seems to have stepped straight from the pages of a late Graham Greene novel. He is North American by birth and youth, but swilled around the Caribbean and South America for decades. He ran a bar in the Dominican Republic in the 1980s. He has a background in what he calls 'left-wing American radicalism'. He toggles from drawly Spanish to drawly English as fast as a railcar switches tracks. He pronounces my name *Raa-burt*. He hawks, harrumphs, snorts, spits. And he hazes *everyone*. Like Cachorrita, before he can be nice to someone, it seems he must first aggress them. Hazing is DeCoux's love-language. I will get used to this, and become content to weather the rudeness to get through to the occasional moments of kindness or vulnerability, and to the stories he has to tell. But at first it is challenging.

'Well, sit down then – what the hell are you waiting for? An invitation?'

DeCoux's cats wind around him again, growing like wraiths from his shoulders, arms and ankles, or waiting stock-still and with patient attention at the side of his plate, like small deities.

Cups of tea are poured. The rain is very heavy now, running from the rim of the roof around the hexagon like the thick plastic strips in a butcher's-shop doorway.

How will we be able to function in the high forest, I wonder, *if this intensity of rain persists?*

Deafening hoots suddenly fill the air around us. The sound vibrates in the lungs like a drum-and-bass beat in a club. Cosmo's eyes widen in excitement.

'Howlers,' says DeCoux. 'Loudest animal on the planet. Louder than a jet plane taking off. They're just talking, though. If they were roaring, well, you'd know about it. It's loud from five kilometres away.'

An open-air library runs along two sides of the hexagon. I can see familiar spines: Ursula K. Le Guin, Richard Powers's *The Overstory*, novels by John le Carré and lots of regional field guides.

I wander over and pull a couple of titles from the shelves. The spines are soft and damp under my fingers. The pages are mottled with mould: invisible life, drifting on the air, settling in the text. I think of the all-consuming spore-forests in Hayao Miyazaki's film *Nausicaä of the Valley of the Wind*.

'Books don't last long up here, Robert,' says DeCoux.

'I've brought you two gifts, Josef. Something for your table and something for your library.'

I take out a litre-bottle of Tanqueray gin and a copy of *The Epic of Gilgamesh*.

'There's a relevance to the book, which I'll explain at some point.'

'Thanks for these.' DeCoux looks wistfully at the gin. 'I wish I could still drink like I used to,' he says. 'I used to be a proper drinker, you know. Highly, highly enthusiastic. Now it just makes me feel sick.' DeCoux had been diagnosed with cancer and underwent chemotherapy during the pandemic. It must have been brutally hard recovering from that up here in the forest, alone.

We sip tea and DeCoux tells us an abridged version of his forty years or so in the forest. Though he's dismissive of his own role, it is unmistakably an extraordinary story – of limpet-like resistance to outside forces, of a gnarly, heroic dedication to the forest's protection, of a cussed, anchoritic existence.

Listening to him talk, I begin to think of him less as a bear and more as a castaway, his clothes ragged from sun and rain, self-marooned up here in this little hilltop clearing, islanded in an immensity of forest.

After leaving the Dominican Republic (escorted off the country's premises at the end of a gun, he implies, for reasons he doesn't disclose), DeCoux washed up in Quito, and from there somehow found his way up to Los Cedros. He pitched his tent – and has barely left the forest since, fighting running battles to keep the forest safe from mining and logging, and to help the local communities who live on its fringes. His commitment to the Cedar Forest has come at significant personal cost: his partner and children peeling away from his life; illness, loneliness, danger.

I remember something I'd been told in Quito by a leading figure in the Ecuadorian Rights of Nature movement, a tireless and inspiring person called Nati Greene. Now in her early forties, in 2008 Nati was a young feminist academic-activist working to improve the lives of women, especially Indigenous women, in Ecuador. She quickly became a key figure in the process of constitutional redrafting that first brought the idea of nature's rights to the world's attention. She has also been closely involved with the defence of Los Cedros.

I keep expecting to hear that Josef has been murdered, she'd said to me. *It would be easy to arrange. If the forest has a guardian, that's Josef, and he lives there by himself. There are people who want that forest for money, who are angry at his protection of the forest, at the Rights of Nature ruling. It would be simple to say he was drunk, he fell over . . . He is* definitely *at risk – and we have to protect him.*

'I spent my first three years here living down by the Río Los Cedros,' says DeCoux, 'in a shack that I built myself to replace my tent. It's collapsed now. You'll see it when you go down to the river. People sometimes call it "The Ruin". I prefer to think of it as a carefully curated relic.'

'Why did you dedicate your life to this place?'

He scowls at me. 'Well, there was a lot of forest around here.'

'But what is it about *this* forest that kept you here, made you fight for it?'

Cachorrita snarls and nips at Giuliana's calf. Giuliana bends down and with surprising speed catches hold of the dog, then whispers something terrible in her ear. Released, Cachorrita bolts into a corner and hides there. She is no further trouble.

'I'd been a Boy Scout in the forest where I grew up in the US. I *like* forest, Robert. I'd lived in Colombia; I knew how benign forests could be at this altitude. Horseflies, sure, but no leeches, no real disease.'

To me this seems an oddly passive motive, given the hardship the forest has imposed upon his life for so long. He notices my puzzlement.

'What more can I say, Robert? I've liked forests all my life, and I've been involved with radical politics most of my life. We're trying to save the planet, or at least something like that – isn't that right? So I've got to play a part. In the Dominican Republic, it was harder to get a licence for a chainsaw than a licence for a pistol! The military controlled the forests, and it worked there. I was told Ecuador was an oasis of peace and calm, not like Colombia, not like Peru.' He snorts his derision at this. 'So – I came here, and, well, I've been here ever since. The moral of this cautionary tale is: if you want to do something, you'd better watch out, because you might just end up doing it for the rest of your life!'

When DeCoux laughs, he really laughs. Great, phlegmy gusts of laughter, which end in a coughing fit.

'I've been in shit-fights with so many bunches of powerful people over the years. One lot, back in the 2000s, had such influence in the ministries that they just . . . *disappeared* all the ownership paperwork to the forest. Made it vanish. Then they proved inside their internal courts that the existing property deeds to Los Cedros were null and void. But we managed to turn it into a *Bosque Protector*, a Protected Forest – and that put a stick in their wheels. There's always a new fight round the corner. This last one with the mining companies has been a big one, though.'

DeCoux chuckles tiredly. He looks and sounds like a bare-knuckle boxer in the closing rounds of a long fight, at the end of a long career.

'Hell, though, the Constitutional Court ruling! That was a good moment! And now the two of you are here in the forest at last!' he says to Agustín and Ramiro, with the closest to warmth I've heard from him yet.

Agustín looks down at his hands, embarrassed by the attention. Ramiro thumps the table and lets loose a whoop of triumph.

'How's the weather been here recently?' I ask.

DeCoux looks at me as if I'm an idiot, which may well be the case.

'Rain. More rain. This is a cloud-forest, after all – what the fuck do you expect? And that was the dry season coming to an end. We're on the threshold of the wet season now. I hope you've got your water-proofs with you. They say this was the only place where rain continued to fall during the ice ages. So – go figure.'

It's the first occasion in my life that I've been given a deep-time weather forecast. I find it curiously reassuring. If it *does* rain on us throughout our time in the cloud-forest, well, it really isn't our bad luck.

Cachorrita has hopped up onto Schultes's back and begun kneading her old dog-flesh with little feet.

'Ah yeah – the little dog likes to ride on Schultes's back, and the cats like to suckle on Schultes's tits,' says DeCoux.

'Interspecies suckling is an amazing phenomenon,' says Cosmo, approvingly.

72

Giuliana brings out copies of her two field guides to the fungi of Chile.

'I brought these as a gift for you, Josef.'

He grunts his negligible thanks.

'Have you had a species named after you yet?' she asks.

'Yeah, an orchid, but it's fucking tiny, you can't even see it without a magnifying glass. But I did tell my daughter she didn't need to name her first child after me – I'm already immortal!'

He laughs again, then breaks off into another percussive coughing fit, his head jerking forwards with each cough like an assault rifle hacking out its bullets.

~

That first night in the forest, stories are told.

Word of our visit has spread in the area. A few people have made the long journey to meet us in this distant place. They want to speak with us about Los Cedros, about what it means to have fought for these rivers and this cloud-forest, and about the wider history of resistance to *mega-minería* (mega-mining) in the Intag region. They want Agustín and Ramiro to understand what they've saved with their Rights of Nature ruling. And, in consultation with the judges and César, they want to find ways of securing the lives of the rivers and forest for the future.

As the day closes, figures appear from the path, stepping out of the shadows. There is José Cueva, a coffee farmer who's been involved in anti-mining activism since he was a teenager and is now one of the main organizers of resistance in the valley. He wears a black T-shirt printed with the words *Guardián del Bosque* – 'Forest Guardian'. His grey-streaked hair is held back in a ponytail. He has working hands, a clear mind and a ready smile, and strikes me as a person who knows *kairos* when he sees it.

With him is Monse Vásquez; a younger protestor-resister, and

Cueva's partner. Monse is quiet – a listener. But I notice Cueva casting his eyes to her when he speaks, as if checking his account with a higher authority. Monse identifies as *mestiza* (of mixed Spanish and Indigenous ancestry) and is a significant figure in OMASNE, the anti-extractivist organization which formed after the mass granting of mining concessions in 2017.

Monse brings news of an atrocious event from Ecuador's north. Only two days earlier a 24-year-old water defender and anti-mining activist, Alba Bermeo Puin, was murdered in the canton of Cuenca. She was five months pregnant. She was shot in the chest. Bermeo Puin was part of a community on the banks of the Río Blanco which in 2018 had succeeded in forcing a Chinese-Ecuadorian gold-mining joint venture to suspend their operations and cease contaminating the river. Since that victory, however, illegal mining activities in the area had proliferated. With them had come a steep escalation in violence: beatings, burnings – and now a killing.

There's a broader sense among the people gathered here that Ecuador – which has for decades enjoyed a stability unknown to many of its neighbours – is slipping swiftly into violence and lawlessness. Bermeo Puin's murder is the third attack on female land and water defenders in recent months in just one province. An unholy alliance of wildcat mining and drug cartels is brewing terrible violence in the north-west, with cartel *sicarios* running enforcement on behalf of the miners.

'We are seeing, you could say, the Colombianization of Ecuador,' says César, gravely. The kidnappings, the bombings, the murders and mutilations: he remembers them all too well.

'What can we do?' Monse asks, calm but afraid.

'It is crucial that the eyes of the world stay upon what is happening here,' says César. 'If it's thought no one is watching, then the disappearances and the killings, well, they simply . . . happen, and don't even exist as a statistic in a Human Rights Watch report. With that comes both a sense of impunity for the killers – and actual impunity itself. You must forge relations with international allies, get other voices to amplify yours. Visibility isn't a guarantee of safety – but it's far better than not being seen or heard.'

At 8 p.m., everyone gathers in the hexagon. The night is pitch-black but blazing with insect sound.

Two bright bare bulbs illuminate the space, and scores of moths beat about the bulbs like rags, leave smudges of wing-dust when they bump us. The artificial light and the oily dark of the forest give the scene a Caravaggio-like intensity of chiaroscuro. The many lines on DeCoux's face are etched in black, as if soot has run down them. Cueva sits on the back of one of the benches, his feet on its seat, so that he's raised slightly above the rest of us. Monse sits opposite him, watching.

'My friends,' Cueva begins, 'friends of this forest. We have thought' – he glances to Monse for confirmation – 'that we would like to tell you something of the history of resistance in the Intag Valley.' His voice is deep and measured. A moth lands on his face, and he lifts it away with a finger.

So begins an extraordinary narrative, which runs for over an hour. Cueva speaks mostly in Spanish; Giuliana whispers a simultaneous translation to me. Monse contributes now and then: subtilizing, emphasizing. Together they tell an oral epic of sustained, intergenerational resistance in this valley, in the face of plausibly deniable violence deployed by multinational mining corporations and illegal miners, often tolerated or supported by the state; of a shadowy, powerful instrument of international law known innocuously as Investor–State Dispute Settlement, which gives private parties – typically foreign companies – the right to sue a sovereign nation in a forum other than that of the nation's domestic courts, if they feel the state has failed to guarantee the terms of the investment; of poor communities and families being torn apart by the arrival of mining companies; and of sustained injustice to the humans, rivers and forests of the Intag Valley.

Cueva is a gripping speaker. I half expect him to produce a guitar and sing the *corridos* of this long, slow battle against what Monse calls *extractivismo de muerte*: 'death-extractivism'. There are raids, arson attacks and kidnappings. There is the 'Battle of Junín': villagers in wellies armed with sticks, facing men in bulletproof vests toting pepper spray and pump-action shotguns. A five-year-old child is tear-gassed, then a one-year-old. Cueva describes an area of cloud-forest where a mining company overcame local opposition and prospected for copper for four years, drilling test boreholes from more than a hundred plat-forms. There is now a clearing in the forest, he says, where two waterfalls cascade down a cliff. The left-hand waterfall flows from a watershed in which no drilling has occurred: its waters run silver and clear. The right-hand waterfall flows from a watershed containing numerous drilling platforms: its waters run orange with poisons, ore and silt.

'The thing is: bread today means hunger tomorrow,' says Cueva. 'The timescales are that over one to ten years, maybe, mining pays. But what happens after that, when the mine is exhausted, when the company goes? What is left behind? *Nothing. No life.* This *cannot* happen in Los Cedros.' He chops the edge of one hand into the palm of the other in emphasis.

I have a strong sense of embattlement: of siege having been method-ically laid to this cloud-forest over many years – and of enemies still circling, out there in the darkness.

Listening to Cueva and Monse speak, I'm pierced again by hope and futility: the two streams of the waterfall. Hope at the tirelessness of these people, resisting across generations. Futility at this living for-est's vulnerability in the face of the force that comes from the barrel of a gun or the corporate profit motive. Could such power *ever* be brought to recognize the river and forest as complexly alive?

Luna the cat traps a big moth whose wings are as patterned and plush as flock wallpaper. She idly pins its thorax to the wooden floorboards with one paw and shreds its wings with the claws of the other, leaving the moth tattered and dying.

~

That night, Giuliana, César, Cosmo and I sit up late on the deck of one of the timber buildings.

We turn off all lights and let the darkness ink us.

'I think perhaps the grip of death is loosening a little on me here,' says Giuliana from within the shadow.

The forest stretches away in the night's black felt. Only the ridge-lines and canopy edge have detail. I can sense the mountain rearing huge to our north: where we will go to seek the fungi, almost a vertical kilometre and at least a day's hard journey above us in the forest. In my mind I trace out the course of the Río Los Cedros, running time and its current backwards in my imagination so that as it rises it thins and its tributaries diminish in number, until right beneath the peak's summit it is a single stream, a first flow.

'It'll take time to find the fungi, if I can find them at all,' Giuliana says. 'I've got trail locations from Bryn for the first findings, places deep in the forest – but these locations are more than a decade old, and of course fungi *move*, can travel as fast and far as the wind can carry their spores to the right substrate. There's no reason to think that they'll still be present where Bryn found them – or that I'll still be able to hear them if they are.'

Giuliana smokes a roll-up cigarette. Its orange tip flares as she draws on it, dims as she exhales.

'I don't think I've ever listened to such a pristine soundscape,' says Cosmo. 'If what Josef tells us is right, this forest has been speaking more or less like this for tens of thousands of years or more – way back into the Ice Age. Listening to it is like trying to learn a hundred differ-ent new languages at once. I'm struck by how much more . . . spacious the relationship between the forest's speakers is here than in England, for instance. Each voice has its own rhythmic room and frequency. It's a hell of a place to be an ear-witness.'

Fireflies wander the middle distance. The night is glass-clear. Sheet lightning snaps blue-white across the sky to the south.

I see a shooting star, and then two more. Three scratches on the world's tin.

~

The next morning we walk into the forest and it swallows us whole.

Green on green on green, a roiling green and the floor a frothing brown of sumptuous rot and rich decay. Trees steeple above us, shutting out light and sight.

This is a world of mimics, cryptids and scale-shifts: of tree ferns thirty feet high and ten feet across at the canopy, of fifty-foot-long lianas hanging down like wiring cables in a derelict building.

An arrow-shower of emerald parrots fleets off from us, their calls pinging clear as glockenspiel notes.

In the distance, amid the seethe, I can hear the beginnings – right at the very edge of my ears – of the song of the Río Los Cedros.

You'll meet the river today, DeCoux had said as we left the Scientific Station that morning. *It would have got screwed up by the miners, totally fucked.*

'I'm crossing fingers and toes that we see a white-capped dipper,' I say. 'Dippers are very good indicators of clean water, of a super-healthy river.'

'You're sounding like a birder again,' says Giuliana, suspiciously.

'No, definitely not. I talk a good bird game, that's all.'

'I'm not strictly anti-birder,' Giuliana says. 'Some of my good friends are birders. I just prefer fungi to birds. A *lot*.'

A half-foot-long millipede crosses the path ahead of us in a pool of sun, its segmented armour gleaming and supple as it moves, unhurried and steampunk. There's a powerful, dissonant sense of rot and growth; of an ancient process which decomposes distinctions between death and life.

It's Agustín's birthday. He smiles shyly when it's announced. I feel moved to be present when this gentle person, who helped save this place from ungentle forces, meets the forest and its rivers for the first time.

Hoo-hoo, hoo-hoo – the rocking, overlapping calls of the toucan barbets murmur through the canopy again. 'They're calling in near-perfect syncopation,' says Cosmo happily.

The path descends, and we help each other down thick-rooted steps slick with mud. Yesterday's heavy rain has cleared to leave blue sky. Rafters of sun angle from canopy to forest floor: huge gold beams, so timber-seeming that I reach out to touch one, only to see my hand dissolve in it.

The song of the river grows and grows; the path rises, crooks round a corner – and there is my first glimpse of the Río Los Cedros.

It is wide, shallow, leaping and silver.

Sunlight lies in ingots on its bed.

Quartz crystals glint in the sand between the stones.

It is instantly . . . charismatic, I think: as lively as any river I could imagine.

Hello, river. I've come a very long way to meet you.

The river says nothing back.

For several hours we walk the Río Los Cedros and its valley: following slender paths deeper into the forest, criss-crossing both main channel and tributaries, stepping and hopping from boulder to boulder, between stone and stone, much as the river does.

'Look!' Giuliana calls out suddenly at a shadowed turn in the path. 'Myxomycetes! These are slime moulds. The protists. People think they're fungi but they're *not*; in fact, they often feed on fungi. No, these belong to another kindom *entirely*! We have animals, plants, fungi – and then the protists. Slime moulds mapped the Tokyo subway, you know.'

'"Kindom"?' I ask.

'Yes – I prefer to speak of "kindom", not of "kingdom". Why say "kingdom"? Why not "queendom"? Better still, why not neither? Who wants monarchy when we're speaking of *life*?! So I say "kindom" – a forest, a river, as a gathering of kin!'

I know that Giuliana will already have been looking hard for the fungi we've come to find. Right now, it seems impossible to me that she will locate them. The forest is just too large, too concealing.

Then I recall a story Cosmo once told me: about how late one night he and his brother Merlin were driving down a forest road in Chile with Giuliana, at the end of a day collecting fungi and making core samples in search of underground mycelial networks. Suddenly, without word or warning, Giuliana pulled over, got out of the car and disappeared into the dark forest. A minute or so later, Cosmo and Merlin heard the tell-tale *woo-hoo!* They found Giuliana fifty yards into the forest, flat on the ground, her head-torch beam focused on a colony of *Avatar*-blue mushrooms: *Stephanopus azureus*.

I have literally no idea how she knew they were there, Cosmo said. *They're only above ground for a couple of days. It was dark. They were deep in the forest, totally invisible from the road. How the fuck did she find them?*

'I didn't see the mushrooms, exactly,' says Giuliana when I ask her about it. 'I heard them. If you know how to listen, fungi just . . . tell you where they are.' She shrugs. 'I'll get this feeling that there's a fungus around. I feel, no, I *know*, that there's something – no, somebody – who wants to see me. You get a call-out from them.'

She pauses. 'The fuzz in the matrix. That's still the best way I can describe it. I can say very definitely that it's a communication – a two-way interaction. The fungi know I'm there, as well as the reverse. Fungi have a different vibration to plants and animals. The colours move differently, I find. And fungi have a . . . *shine* that's different to the shine of plants. It's more . . . *opaque*. And they have a very different energy than plants – much more of a watery or liquid feel.'

~

We do not knowingly enter the cloud. It moves up from below us or gathers from around us; I cannot tell which. But we are in it, it is on us.

Fog numbs sound; mist sparkles on skin and cloth.

It is peaceful to be in that cloud of unknowing. I feel ignorant in the forest, and at ease with my ignorance. Any questing after fact and reason is overwhelmed by profusion and difference.

The path thins towards nothing. We begin to criss-cross the Río Los Cedros more often, working slowly uphill, following the water's path back into the higher forest. A white noise becomes audible at the edge of things, then fills the gaps between them, rising slowly to a roar. We turn a corner. Silver surges through green.

A wide, white veil of waterfall is above and ahead of us – thirty feet or more high and twenty feet or so across – crashing into the wide pool it has hollowed from the bedrock over thousands of years. This is the biggest waterfall on the Río Los Cedros. Spray-mist floats and dances, rainbowed where the sun finds it.

The invitation is not to be refused. I strip to my shorts and wade in, boulders slippery underfoot, my arms out for balance like a funambulist's, feeling steel manacles of cold slide up my legs from ankles to knees to thighs – and then I just launch myself, huffing with the shock, and strike out across the pool towards the waterfall.

Others follow me in: first Giuliana and César, then Ramiro, who yells so loudly he sets the forest echoing and startles birds from the trees. Then Agustín, who peers moleishly without his spectacles and is tentative on the greasy rocks.

I swim back across the pool and wade out to help Agustín. He reaches out both hands for support. I take them and guide him in: him stepping forwards and me backwards. We move like eighteenth-century dance partners hesitantly working out a quadrille.

'This is the river you helped save, in the forest you helped save,' I shout to him over the sound of the waterfall.

'I was only one among very many,' says Agustín. 'And the forest . . . spoke for itself, spoke to us all.'

We embrace. I am touched. When we reach the deeper water, Agustín releases my hands and leans forwards into the river, feels it take his weight, support him, then he swims in neat breaststroke across to the base of the waterfall.

I watch in surprise as Agustín first stands up, then backs into the white veil of water so that it's pummelling his head and his shoulders. He lifts his head back, closes his eyes, flings his arms out wide and stands there, cruciform, with an expression on his face partway between joy and agony.

'Happy birthday, Agustín!' I shout, but he can't hear me.

Then I realize that the water pouring over the lip of the waterfall is running rust-red, stained by silt and cyanide from the forest's felling, from the mountain's mining, from the river's poisoning – and that red is pouring over Agustín's head and shoulders and is filling the pool itself with old blood . . . and then I blink and the mining has not yet happened and may never happen, and the forest is still unfelled, the mountain whole and the river clear.

A few minutes later I swim over to the waterfall. As Agustín had done, I find my footing on the bed of the pool, then lean back into the shifting, turbulent veil of water. A thousand little fists punch my shoulders, a thousand cold wasps sting my skin.

I close my eyes, feel skin and scalp and spirit ringing and singing. It elates me. *This river has an aura into which we have passed*, I think, *and which is changing our being, enlivening us. Would a dying river do this?*

It seems clear to me then, in that strange, bright water, that to say a river is alive is not an anthropomorphic claim. A river is not a human person, nor vice versa. Each withholds from the other in different ways. To call a river alive is not to personify a river, but instead further to deepen and widen the category of 'life', and in so doing – how had George Eliot put it? – 'enlarge the imagined range for self to move in'.

But then I'm counterstruck by the sheer, incorrigible *weirdness* of this white water, by the profoundly alien presence of the river – and all that I've just thought feels too easy, too pat. Is this thing I'm in really *alive?* By whose standards? By what proof? As for speaking to or for a river, or comprehending what a river wants – well, where would you even start with that process? Surely all our attempts to bend the law round so that it recognizes the rights of rivers or forests will only end up with human proxies, jockeying for their own positions and speaking in incorrigibly human voices – ventriloquizing 'river' and 'forest' in a kind of cos-play animism.

We could call it the 'Solaris Problem' – the question of how on earth to open a plausible line of communication with a river – after Stanisław Lem's 1961 SF novel *Solaris*, about a planet whose ocean behaves in ways that perplex the usual mechanistic reductions of water to matter. In ways, in fact, which seem to human observers to be intentional, sentient . . . *alive*. Entire institutes become dedicated to the study of 'solaristics': theoretical attempts to comprehend the ocean's properties and ontology, and practical attempts to establish contact with it. All methodologies, however, prove futile.

Standing there with the water clattering my skull – as I clumsily, hopelessly probe the River of the Cedars for legibility, for utterance – a line from Lem's novel bounces into my brain: *How can you hope to communicate with the ocean if you can't even understand one another?*

I notice Giuliana has swum to a corner of the pool and is floating there quietly, looking downstream, facing away from the rest of us.

I think that it's unlike her not to be whooping, not to be at the centre of the party.

I wonder if she is dreaming or remembering.

Then I see that she is crying, adding her tears to the river's flow.

~

An hour's walk on from the waterfall, we find one of the cedars which give the forest its name. It is a vast tree, centuries old, with buttresses that stand out like fins on a rocket. The tree's wood is a pinkish red, which glows through its brown, almost feathery bark. There are only a few hundred cedars left in the cloud-forest now: the others have been felled and dragged out in chains for their soft-grained, sweet-smelling wood.

I step into the curved gap between two of the buttresses. The tree cups me like a cave. I look up. Above me, the crown of the cedar is invisible, obscured by the whirl of branches, the density of moss, by lichen and epiphytes, by bright-red bromeliads with their red-spiked flowers flared like open penknives.

Below me, the roots of the cedar are invisible, questing down and outwards into the earth beneath my feet, connected by hundreds of thousands of pale fungal hyphae to the thousands of trees and plants that surround it.

This is unmistakably a World Tree, an Yggdrasil of the tropics, spanning the realms.

'There will be so much soil and humus held up in those branches,' says Giuliana. 'A whole other ground suspended up there, with its own ecology.'

Cosmo is already sitting cross-legged at the base of the trunk, head-phones on, pushing contact microphones deep into the root-world of the cedar. 'Wow, there's a *lot* going on down there!' he says, tapping his headphones.

Across the Andes, thousands of the 1.5 million trees felled each day in the Brazilian Amazon crash to earth or go up in flames.

In Toronto a Canadian mining company finalizes paperwork to build the largest open-pit gold mine in Brazil, on the banks of the Xingu River.

Coo-coo-ta-coo, *coo-coo-ta-coo*, cries a quetzal somewhere near us, scarlet and green and unseen.

It happens on the way back to the Scientific Station from the World Tree. We are tired from a day on the trails and in the river. Our little group has become stretched out.

'*Wooooo-hoooo!*'

A cry, longer than any we've heard that day from Giuliana – and loud: howler-monkey loud. I turn and jog back up the path. *Can it be . . . ?*

When I reach her, Giuliana is already belly-down on the ground.

The mushroom isn't much to look at: a single tiny brown witch's hat atop a slender cream-coloured stalk, perhaps three centimetres tall, and a few feet off the trail. It's nowhere near the location of the first collection, made more than a decade earlier.

She issues a series of rapid-fire orders. 'Rob, can you please make a note of the GPS coordinates of the find-site? Cosmo, could you pass me my backpack? Does anybody have a little box? And could some big-hearted person please make sure nothing large and dangerous crawls onto me while I'm down here on the ground making the collection?'

She rolls onto her side, a wide smile on her face, and opens her backpack. Out comes a small foil reflector, which she places around the mushroom to light it as she photographs it: from below, up into the gills, from both sides, from above. She makes a record of the substrate upon which it's growing. Then she digs the mushroom out, taking care not to break the base of the stipe where it meets the earth, and puts it into a little metal cigarette box that Cosmo has been carrying.

Once the mushroom is safely collected, Cosmo plunges his contact mics into the earth, right at the point where the fungus emerged, and starts recording. He hears ticks and clicks and crepitations. He hears knocks and thuds and tremors: a busy, encrypted earth-traffic of signs and sounds. Up on the surface, hummingbird alarm-calls needle the air. A butterfly creaks its wings open in a pool of light.

'Well, I'm pretty confident this is the second collection of one of our as-yet-unnamed species,' Giuliana says, sitting back on her haunches now. 'It's at a much lower altitude than I expected. Look, you can see already that it's changing colour. *Psilocybe*s bruise blue.'

'Like us,' I say.

She pauses, considering this comparison. 'Yes. That's true. Like us. Or we bruise blue like them.'

'Are there any more?' asks Cosmo hopefully. I know what he's thinking.

'There's only one, I'm afraid. We're very lucky. It's relatively dry at the moment here in the forest. They rarely show themselves when it's this dry. But here's one, erumpent!'

'"Erumpent"?'

'Erumpent is one of my favourite words. To be erumpent is to be part in and part out of the soil. Some fungi are fabulously erumpent!'

'But by that definition, aren't almost all plants erumpent too?' I ask. Giuliana's eyes harden a little.

'The dictionary decisively allocates the word to fungi,' she says.

~

Back at the Scientific Station that night, DeCoux seems relaxed, almost friendly. I summon my courage and sit down next to him at his table in the hexagon. *The Epic of Gilgamesh* is still lying next to the bottle of Tanqueray gin. Monse and Cueva are with us.

'Thanks for this,' says DeCoux, tapping the copy of *Gilgamesh*. 'It comes at a good time. I've nothing to read. I've just finished with Le Guin's *The Dispossessed*.'

'Do you know Le Guin's *The Word for World is Forest*? I can't stop thinking about that one here. The colonial extractors landing on the forest planet to establish a logging colony, enslaving the Athsheans, teaching them violence.'

'Yeah, I know it,' says DeCoux. 'That's a good one. The word for world is forest, for sure. She got that right.'

He gestures outwards, at the immense green sea upon which the little wooden ark of the Scientific Station floats.

How had Le Guin described her world-forest? *No way was clear, no light unbroken, in the forest. The ground was not dry and solid but damp and rather springy, product of the collaboration of living things with the long, elaborate death of leaves and trees; and from that rich graveyard grew ninety-foot trees, and tiny mushrooms that sprouted in circles half an inch across . . .*

'You said you'd explain why you brought me *Gilgamesh*,' says DeCoux.

'Yes. Well, it's hard to know where to start. The echoes and parallels are so many, so strong. *Gilgamesh* is the oldest written story we know of in the world: four thousand, four hundred years or so in the earliest, Sumerian version. And right at the heart of the *Epic*, right at the beginning of world literature – is a Cedar Forest.'

'No kidding?' I've got DeCoux's interest now.

'No kidding. A sacred Cedar Forest – and it's threatened with destruction by forces who want to extract stuff from it.'

'Same cedars as here?'

'Different. *Gilgamesh*'s cedars were cedars of Lebanon: *Cedrus libani*. Beautiful trees – big trunks, long branches, dark-green islands of needles. They look like they've come from a Studio Ghibli animation.'

'Ours are mountain cedars,' says DeCoux. 'Different genus. *Cedrela montana*.'

'Two forests. One mythical, one real. One then, one now. Both cedar forests, both sacred in their ways. Both alive. Both under threat.'

'How did the story survive?' asks Cueva, who has been following closely. 'It was written on the walls of a . . . building? A structure?'

'No, it was inscribed on tablets made of river clay, in a script called cuneiform which was pressed into the clay using the end of a green river reed as the writing tool. Those clay tablets were the first books.'

'Well, hurry up and tell us the goddamn story,' growls DeCoux. 'What happens to the forest?'

'You don't mind spoilers?'

'Spoilers are fine.'

So I tell them.

I tell them how, thousands of years ago, a god-king called Gilgamesh rules the city-state of Uruk, which flourishes on the banks of the Euphrates in the land now known as Mesopotamia: the 'realm between two rivers'.

One day – determined to prove his might and to bring back plunder for his greater glory – Gilgamesh sets off for the great Cedar Forest which lies at the outer brink of his empire. He's accompanied by his friend Enkidu, a wild man who was raised by wolves and antelopes.

This Cedar Forest has grown undisturbed since before the start of human history. There the moss lies five feet deep; trees are bearded with lichens and ferns, and the call-and-answer of birdsong embroiders the air. A river runs through the forest's heart, too – the young Euphrates.

This is a forest, the *Epic* specifies, who is *alive*. Who speaks and sings, who is aware, who has a *mind*. And protecting the Cedar Forest is a giant spirit called Humbaba. Humbaba is the manifestation of the Cedar Forest's life. He's a shape-shifting being with seven magical auras that give him the power to repel those who come to harm the forest.

After a seven-day journey across the desert, Enkidu and Gilgamesh reach the edge of the Cedar Forest. And there they pause, awed by what lies before them. Resting their great swords and axes upon the ground, they marvel at the splendour of the cedars, as well as the sheer extent of the forest, which laps over ridge and valley for as far as they can see.

Gilgamesh and Enkidu's hesitation on the edge of the Cedar Forest is the moment when human history trembles on the brink of a new, destructive relationship with the living world. They might still turn back. They might leave the forest and the river intact and alive.

They do not. They cross the threshold of the Cedar Wood and set about its destruction. First, they strip Humbaba of his protective auras, flaying them from him one by one. Humbaba begs for mercy, offering an annual tithe of lumber in return for his life. Enkidu and Gilgamesh ignore his pleas and lift their weapons. They slit Humbaba's throat, then they tear the tusks from his jaws, then they slice out his lungs and hold them aloft. Lastly, they hack off his head – and Humbaba's blood runs into the Euphrates River.

Once Humbaba lies dead, the two raiders are free to turn their axes upon the forest. Gilgamesh cuts down the trees right to the banks of the Euphrates, while Enkidu locates the best timber. Together they fell the tallest of the cedars and plank it into lumber; it will make a fine temple door for Uruk. They lash the trunks of the smaller trees into a raft, load it with their plunder and the severed head of Humbaba, and push themselves out onto the currents of the Euphrates, who will bear them back to Uruk.

They turn what had once been a living river-forest into a poisoned wasteland. Anima, slaughtered. Life, reduced to resource.

I don't know what 'human nature' is. Maybe leaving descriptions of what we wipe out is part of human nature.

When I've finished speaking, Cueva shakes his head and whistles at the eerie clarity of the echoes.

'I think that by extrapolation,' I say, 'this makes you the Humbaba of Los Cedros, Josef.'

DeCoux laughs. 'I'll take that. Not many auras left now, though.' He gestures at his collapsed face, his threadbare clothes.

'How old did you say this story is?' asks Cueva.

'Four thousand years or a bit more. But here in this Cedar Forest, you've written a different ending to it.'

'Robert,' rasps DeCoux, 'I can't say that we've seen the end of this Gilgamesh story, nor will our descendants see the end of it, nor theirs. We're heading for outer space and the deep seabed now – and we're gonna do the same thing there.'

~

Days pass in the Cedar Forest.

We learn the paths. We follow the river. The promised rain does not fall.

We find a twenty-foot-long pool into which the river cascades off a stacked ruckle of boulders. Here the river has opened the canopy wide enough that sun falls directly upon the pool, gilding its depths. The white noise of the cascade, with its repeating elements, is a Philip Glass composition. We swim. The water is cold in the shadow, and where the light falls upon us our skin shows bronze as carp. Below the cascade, the current places its hands on our shoulders. Afterwards, we lie on warm stones to dry. A grey hawk lands on a high branch, shivers its wings and gazes down from its perch at the long-limbed figures sprawled on the rocks. To my joy, a white-capped dipper appears to bob and fish the rapids.

At night, fireflies score the dark like slow tracer bullets. Glow-worms throb in the understorey. In the outer dark of the forest, the great creaturely orchestra plays on.

The forest listens. The river sings. We do not find the second mushroom.

One evening I peg a bedsheet to a line strung between two cedars, and shine a moth light onto it. Half an hour later, I return to find that wonder has fluttered from the night to shiver on the sheet: moths birthed by dark to flock together on cloth, thickening air to froth.

I have names for none of these hundreds of species of moths. Each is unique. One's wings are of Sherwood green, as if snipped from jerkin or tunic. Another's are fine lace; another's seem made of bark; another's are patterned like a William Morris print. And all this moth-life here, before me, I know to be just a fraction of the unknowable sum of moth-being which flourishes in the cloud-forest.

More moths come, and more. They perch on my hat like a fisher-man's flies, on my shoulder like leaves, on my cheek like touch after gentle touch. I am in a dream. I have foliage, not skin, shifting and alive.

A single huge moth ebbs out of the darkness towards me. It lands on my raised hand and its abdomen throbs softly, ticking up and down. I lift it towards my face, and as I do so its upper wings click suddenly open to show two dark-red circles with black pupils in their centres – a pair of wide eyes, gazing back into me.

~

Sometime around 1500, Hieronymus Bosch picked up his pen and, using oak-gall ink and bistre, he sketched a little-known work he called *The Wood Has Ears, the Field Eyes*.

At first glance, Bosch's drawing is a conventional landscape study. An old oak tree stands in open ground, with an owl perched in its hollow heart and three sharp-winged birds in its branches.

But then you notice the ears. Hidden in the stand of trees behind the oak are two ears, humanly shaped but not humanly sized. Then you notice the eyes. Embedded in the meadow that fills the foreground and encircles the trees are seven eyes: four above and three below.

Suddenly you, the viewer, are no longer the looker; you are being looked at and listened to. The natural world is watching and hearing: not just the owl, but the trees and the vegetation too. I find Bosch's image both unsettling and comforting. It reminds me that we are companioned in the world.

The anthropologist Deborah Bird Rose wrote of the 'double death' of the Anthropocene; she was referring to the way that the rapid extinction of life in the present leads also to the foreclosure of its future possibilities. Life's tendency is to flourish, and to flourish diversely. Epigenetics and endosymbiosis now show us that this flourishing is happening within individual lifespans and between species in ways that far exceed the Darwinian account of evolution by orderly generational descent. But when human action depletes life's existing diversity, its potential for flourishing to come – for future 'shimmer', in Bird Rose's word – is also depleted. The result, wrote Bird Rose, is an unravelling of 'the work of generation upon generation of living beings; cascades of death that curtail the future and unmake the living presence of the past'.

Of the names given to the Earth epoch we are currently shaping – the Anthropocene, the Capitalocene, the Great Acceleration – among the most disturbing is that suggested by the biologist E. O. Wilson, who spoke of the Eremocene. Wilson coined the word from the Ancient Greek καινός/*kainós*, meaning 'new', and ἔρημος/*erēmos*, meaning 'an isolated place', which is also the root of the familiar word 'hermit': one who dwells alone and apart.

The Eremocene is the Age of Loneliness.

The loneliness Wilson had in mind is not that of a human deprived of the company of other humans, miserable though that can be. It's the solitude of one species which is left, as a consequence of its own actions, isolated on the Earth. It is the silence of a mute planet on which the speech, song and stories of other beings have become inaudible because extinguished.

~

The next morning, we are woken by howler monkeys, hooting and hollering. Their calls swoop up, then plummet like fireworks. They boom like a shaken metal thunder-sheet.

The air is clear at dawn, but by the time we have packed, cloud has risen up to engulf us in silence and whiteness. Heat builds heavy. The air is so humid it feels as if I could grip coils of it in my hands and wring them out.

Cosmo, Giuliana, César and I are leaving for days in the high forest. We have a second fungus to find – and the source of a river to reach.

Only one path picks a clever, balancing route up from the Scientific Station towards the summit of the central mountain of Los Cedros, joining ridgeline to ridgeline as it climbs for many hours. But in the three or four years since anyone last took that path, the forest has reclaimed it. Deadfall timber criss-crosses it. Vines have reached out their tendrils from either side, clasped together and pulled the forest shut.

The name given to this path is 'Sendero de los Osos', the Path of the Bears. Andean spectacled bears, the only southern-hemisphere bears, live in this forest – and it is their path before it is ours.

Preparation takes time. The route is impossible for a mule, so we must carry everything. At last, by mid-morning, we're ready to depart. We wear tall rucksacks, bulky and unstable on our backs, heavy with tents and pans. Coming with us is Martín Obando, who lives in the nearby village of García Moreno and knows the high forest superbly well. Martín is about my age, but unlike me he is made of steel and stone. His muscles have muscles on them. He has a wide, generous smile and a quick, generous laugh. He is a part-time guide, a part-time coffee farmer and an exceptional field naturalist. Years of close experience have given him the power of near-instantaneous identification of anything in Los Cedros, from just the flicker of a wing or the whisper of a sound.

DeCoux lumbers out to bid us farewell.

'Gonna be real hard yards for you today,' he says, encouragingly. 'Six hours, eight, maybe ten. And even if you make it, there's nothing up there. You know that, right? Just a tiny clearing not much bigger than three tents side by side. That's all. Nothing else.'

'There's the forest and the river, Josef,' I say. 'That's why we're here, after all.'

He softens. 'I wish I could get up there with you. Don't think I'm going to be doing that again in this lifetime. Did you enjoy your moths last night, Robert?'

'They were unforgettable.'

'The world divides into moth people and butterfly people,' says DeCoux.

'I think I'm a moth person.'

'Yeah, well, the world splits along those lines. The Germans are all moth nuts. The French are all for butterflies. There was once a rude French lepidopterist here, and when I asked him if he wanted to use a moth light, he looked like I'd asked him to shit on the floor.'

'Who can count up all the moths in a forest?' says Cosmo. 'A mothematician!'

'I think it's time to go,' I say.

DeCoux shambles back into the shadows of the Station.

Walking away into the green, we hear a parting volley of yells and curses.

'Hey! The cat ate my breakfast! Luna! That was you! Bad cat! Bad beast!'

That day is tough. Progress on the Path of the Bears is measured in hours, not miles. In many places what passes for a path is so steep that we can only proceed by using roots and trunks as ropes and handholds to haul on. This is a dangerous game. Red fire-ants mill like embers in the leaf-litter. Putting a hand down to steady myself, I am bitten by one on the fingertip and I cry out instantly: it feels as if a soldering iron has burned into my skin. The pain takes five or six minutes to dull.

Our packs pull us back with each step. I mutter thanks for the unseasonal dryness of the past few days; in slick mud and falling rain this would be a terrain of slips and falls, perhaps even impassable.

Once we are given a glimpse through a gap in the canopy to the distant pyramid of the summit peak far above us. It is white-cliffed – and a single cloud is tethered to its top.

Two hours into the climb, we find the first evidence of bear: a steaming pile of fresh scat, green-brown and filled with shiny ovoid seeds. A few yards on from the scat, we find a paw-print, padded and clawed, pressed cookie-cutter crisp into a patch of mud.

The higher we go, the smaller the trees, but the greater the density of epiphytes upon them. It becomes hard to see between the plush trunks. The forest here is gluttonous in its excess, glutinous in its relations. Only the fall lines show that we are following a ridge. Otherwise, the sense of a world beyond diminishes as the sense of remoteness grows.

Lushness beyond imagination. Greenness beyond measure. *Viriditas.*

Four hours in, we break for a rest. We slump on our packs on a slope: filthy and fly-bitten. Even Giuliana has stopped searching for fungi.

'The last hour is flat,' says Martín, encouragingly.

It is not flat. In fact, it is very unflat. And it is not an hour. In fact, it is more like three.

Martín and I pull ahead of the others. At last, along the thin eyeline of a scant trail, I see something like a clearing. There are the traces of an old fire-site.

'We've made it!' I call. 'We're here!'

From back along the path come echoing whoops of relief and celebration.

There are two small clearings, not one. They're joined by a narrow path that unzips the green. Martín examines both carefully. He deems the first and bigger one to be unsafe for the tents due to the risk of tree-fall. We'll eat and rest in the bigger clearing, he decides, but sleep in the smaller one.

It's a vulture's perch of a site. Pale doves tumble and call. Ground falls away to our west into a river gorge. I can hear a white, rushing noise and my heart leaps: it must be the young Río Los Cedros, down in the ravine.

There's barely room for our tents side by side in the second clearing. We rig a big plastic sheet over the space as a rain-tarp, running a central ridgeline of nylon cord taut from tree to tree, then tying off the corners of the sheet and pitching camp beneath its simple shelter.

Cloud is boiling up in the valleys below us, the ridgelines dark green and stark between. We move fast to pitch the tents before the rain comes. As we work, hundreds of horseflies descend. They're twice as big as any I've seen before, with glinting compound eyes and mandibles that look big enough to tackle a steak.

The rain never arrives, but hummingbirds do. They move around and between us with ear-vibrating thrums, shifting so quickly they seem to beat time. They are so gifted and interdimensional that I long to become one. These are the real ores of the forest, I think, its rare earths: the coppers, silvers and golds, all lapped metal and whirring clockwork.

I'm resting on a log in the first clearing when two hummingbirds rocket together towards my face, split at my nose – one going left and the other right – and then reseal into position afterwards. The sound of their wings vibrates my throat as they go by. It's all done in fractions of a second. I feel traversed, shivered, as if a compound ghost has passed right through me.

Suddenly my body tenses. I feel a prickle between my shoulder blades and the absolute knowledge that I'm being watched by a big creature or creatures. It's a lancing fear of a feeling, so strong that I jump up and crash back to the second clearing with its reassurance of company.

Late that afternoon, round the fire, we write a song together. It happens fast and surprisingly: lyrics jotted into a muddy notebook, Cosmo quickly hearing rhythm and melody, recording samples into his phone, then mixing and editing verses and chorus together – and laying down beneath them an undersong of the cloud-forest's own voices that he's gathered with his microphones: cicada creaks, dove coos, the clicky patter of a bat's echolocating sonar bursts, the wind stirring heavy, leathery leaves. Giuliana murmurs a current of river phrases in Spanish: *corre río, fluye río, baja río, corre río* – river run, river flow, river fall, river run.

We call it 'Song of the Cedars' because we know we couldn't have written that song anywhere other than in that place, at that time. The river and the forest have made it possible. It is clear to us that Los Cedros has been our active collaborator, the song's co-creator.

That evening, I look back at my notes on the anthropologist Eduardo Kohn's book *How Forests Think*, based on four years of field-work with the Runa people and the rainforest of Ecuador's Upper Amazon region. Kohn's engagement with the Runa expands to become an account of the life of thought itself – and of thought's aliveness. The forest is experienced as a densely populated realm of seeing and signing forms, who together constitute a complex and always interacting 'ecology of selves'. By reimagining a semiotically constituted basis of relations, Kohn seeks to develop a model of what he calls 'sylvan thinking', whereby thought is dislodged from the entities that appear to produce it, and is instead understood as a 'becoming', always occurring between rather than within bodies.

~

Does a forest have a mind?

Across the Amazonian regions of the nation states known as Ecuador and Peru, a resistance movement called Kawsak Sacha – a Kichwa phrase which may be translated as 'The Living Forest' in English, and 'Selva Viva' or 'Selva Viviente' in Spanish – is spreading. Facing extractivist projects so vast as to be world-ending for the places and people upon which they are imposed, communities have rallied around the recognition that every part of the rainforest, 'from the smallest to the largest, forms one living being with its own consciousness'.

The Living Forest movement originated with the Sarayaku people, whose land lies on the banks of the Bobonaza River in the Ecuadorian Amazon. Growing up there, recalls the Sarayaku elder José Gualinga Montalvo, it was simply a given that the forest and the river were 'alive', and that together the water, trees, humans and creatures of the forest formed a 'living, thinking being'. It would be inaccurate to speak of the 'living forest' as a 'belief' of the Sarayaku people, even less so as an 'Indigenous belief' or an 'animism' – for to designate the forest's aliveness in this way would be to locate it inside historical formations (religious faith, indigeneity, anthropology) with which it is incompatible.

Since the early 1990s the Sarayaku have suffered the repeated incursions into their territory of often violent extractivist forces. Miners, loggers, oil drillers and bio-pirates have all come to Sarayaku territory to plunder: the latest iterations of a long line of invader-exploiters dating back to the first Spanish conquest. In 2002 an Argentinian oil and gas producer called CGC, supported by Ecuador's military, arrived at the Bobonaza River to begin building facilities and digging wells. As with Los Cedros, concessions for oil exploration on Sarayaku land were issued by the Ecuadorian government without sufficient consultation or consent. The Bobonaza had for thousands of years been the highway, pantry, pharmacy and companion of the Sarayaku, but after CGC's arrival, it was rapidly regulated and militarized. Checkpoints were set up, and camps of armed men, equipment and explosives were established. Four hundred and sixty-seven wells were dug or drilled, and 1.43 tonnes of a military-grade high explosive called pentolite were buried in the forest floor for purposes of seismic prospecting.

Confronted by CGC's numerous intrusions, the Sarayaku people realized that what was self-evident to them – that the forest was aware and alive – was invisible, even inconceivable, to others. Discussions with oil company representatives and politicians became charades of mutual incomprehension: the *agon* of incommensurable discourses which simply had no overlap, nor even any borders, with one another. The Sarayaku people decided that they must re-explain the fact of the forest's aliveness in ways that might be communicable beyond the banks of the Bobonaza. So it was that in 2012, after several years' preparation, they published a declaration entitled 'Kawsak Sacha – The Living Forest. A Living and Conscious Being: The Subject of Rights'.

It is a brief, formidable document, which recognizes the multigenerational struggle by the Sarayaku people 'for freedom' and 'against external aggression, invasion, and colonization', and which invokes Ecuador's constitutional commitment to upholding the Rights of Nature (while identifying this aspect of the constitution as merely a legal formalization of a far older set of customary practices). The 'intrinsic and binding rights' of the forest to flourish, and the river to be 'clean' and 'abundant in fish', the declaration says, have been 'recognized since time immemorial' by the 'ancestral nation' of the

Sarayaku. 'We do not want the forest to be classified within protected areas or protective forest areas,' they state, 'or within the legal structures that already exist, such as natural parks. No, we do not want to fit into the categories that are already in use. We explicitly want the territories to be declared living forest territories, a sacred territory.'

The Living Forest movement asks what an environmental politics would look like which takes seriously the idea that a river-forest is, as Gualinga Montalvo puts it, 'a living, intelligent and conscious being'. So far, the Ecuadorian government has declined to entertain this thought-experiment. It remains unimaginable to the political mind of even this enlightened nation state.

~

Near dusk at the high camp, we gather in the bigger clearing. Martín builds a fire with moss and leaves for tinder. Nothing is ever quite dry here; the fire starts reluctantly, smokily.

The day burns itself down. Dusk furs the forest.

'I want to be taken to the forest when I die,' says Giuliana. 'Or take myself, if I can – like cats take themselves off to a quiet place to die. I want to be in the forest, and I want to be absorbed.' She thinks for a while. 'I feel I need to make this more explicit in the paperwork,' she concludes.

Flicker of bats, distant thunder, owl cry.

I sleep only fitfully that night, dreaming in vivid bursts. I dream of a line of leaf-cutter ants, marching purposefully past, holding aloft fragments of something that is not leaf but is grey and brittle. They are carrying it off to their nest. They are grief-cutter ants, disassembling sadness, growing new life from it.

At one point I'm startled awake by what I think is a storm breaking over us. But no: it is César and Martín both snoring sonorously and in perfect syncopation, so that no second is left undisturbed. They are the toucan barbets of the high forest.

99

When I wake at five and creep from my tent, there isn't a cloud in the blue-black sky that shows through the canopy.

The last few stars are still visible, but they fade out quickly.

~

I am not present when the second mushroom miracle occurs, a mile or so from the high camp.

I have gone on ahead of the others, enjoying the temporary solitude. At a turn in the path on a thin fin of ridge, a sight-line unexpectedly opens up to my south and I am jaw-dropped. Hanging there in the sky is a shining, glaciated peak – surely a dream mountain, immensely distant across several forested ridgelines. Vast snowfields gleam like porcelain. Mist hides the peak's lower slopes so that it appears suspended above the Earth's curvature. It is Cotopaxi – and it seems impossible that it can share a planet with the sauna of green in which I am contained.

It was on Ecuador's ice-clad volcanoes – Cotopaxi, Chimborazo and others – 220 years earlier that the explorer-naturalist Alexander von Humboldt developed his understanding of the natural world as an interconnected web of life, in which nothing existed in isolation and humanity was not the central actor, merely a node among many in an immense, rhizomatic network. Humboldt's perception was only 'new' to Western science, of course; it reprised Indigenous cosmo-visions which had been thousands of years in the making.

Everything is connected to everything else, I think, *relation is life*.

Watching Cotopaxi's glinting ice, I remember the funeral held for Iceland's Okjoküll Glacier in the summer of 2019, after it suffered what even glaciologists call 'death': receding to such an extent that it ceased to move, becoming merely a diminishing frozen puddle. More than a hundred mourners attended, including Iceland's prime minister and the former UN High Commissioner for Human Rights Mary Robinson. A memorial plaque was fixed to a rock at the site; it bore a

'Letter to the Future': 'This monument is to acknowledge that we know what is happening and what needs to be done,' the plaque reads. 'Only you know if we did it.' Around the world, people are fumbling for forms of ceremony and language with which to express the speed and severity of loss – creating new-old rites of nature.

We are living in mythological times. Truly, we have never been modern.

Then I hear voices, calls: tone and tempo audible before words can be made out, the excitement unmistakable. I stride back towards the sounds.

'She's done it again!' Cosmo calls out as he sees me. César and Martín are both shaking their heads in amazement. Giuliana is carrying Cosmo's small metal box.

'It was *incredible*, Rob,' says César. 'Giuliana suddenly said, out of nowhere, "I think they are close now . . . "'

Cosmo picks up the story: 'And then she walked on, perhaps fifteen yards and round a corner, further than her eye could possibly have seen, and . . .'

'Then *woooo-hoooo*!' shouts Giuliana, ecstatic. 'I *woo-hoo*-ed like crazy, because there it was! Just one mushroom, again, but different to the first, certainly. Rotting wood as its substrate. I'm pretty confident it's the second of the *Psilocybes*. Definitely a new collection.'

'But *how* did you know it would be there?' I ask. 'It's miles from the location Bryn gave you for the first collection. One tiny brown mushroom, round a corner in the path.'

'I don't know, really. It's that . . . *fuzz* again. I can only describe it as being like a force declaring itself within matter, giving different vibrations and tone: these are what told me I was very close.'

She pauses. 'We think of fungi or mushrooms as still, as fixed, but they're not, they're fast-moving and brief in their appearances. Each meeting with a fungus is an encounter; we've crossed their paths, as well as them crossing ours.'

She pops open the box. A small brown mushroom with a neat bonnet and a long, slender stem lies inside.

'*Hola!*' I say to the mushroom. 'Nice to meet you!'

'You're learning fungal manners, Rob. I approve,' says Giuliana.

That evening there's a kingfisher sunset of orange and blue. White-rumped martins hawk the first moths at dusk.

~

An hour after dawn, we go to find the young river.

Our aim is to descend the ravine to the west of our camp and reach the Río Los Cedros, far below us. There is no real path. It will be a matter of sliding and scrambling and improvising until we get to the water. I am determined to reach this river, as near as we can get to where it is born from the clouds, the forest and the mountain.

The descent to the river is at times almost an abseil. We lower ourselves using vines and branches, kicking heel-holds on slick ground so steep it seems gravity claws even at sunlight.

The ravine is an intensely dynamic space, constantly reshaped by water action and the fall of trees on its shallowly earthed sides. Martín labours to break a trail. We learn to move under and over the trunks of the deadfalls, weaving ourselves through these obstacles like shuttles on a loom.

'Who would dare say that this is a dead tree?' says Giuliana, as we crawl under a trunk that is glossy with rot. 'No, it's a fungal city! When the tree falls is when the glory begins. This is when the tree is brought back to the soil!'

The river's song begins to rise in volume as we move to meet it.

A thinning in the tree cover discloses the cirque that rises around us. The watershed of this first vein of the Río Los Cedros stands stark against the sky: a jagged ridgeline that curves around to form a rough amphitheatre, plucked to the peak at its centre.

A final, awkward ten-foot downclimb on slippery rock takes us one by one into a canyon channel – and there is the river, leaping and avid, throwing up a fine, drifting spray. It has changed its character so often as we have moved upstream, against its flow: at once a creature of mists and condensation, of slow, reflective pools, of shining turbulence – and all of its temperaments and songs are tangled with those of the forest.

I crouch, cup my hand, dip and drink; feel the cold burn down throat and into belly; feel silver fill me. I pour handfuls of water over my head in a rough and functional baptism, rinsing off the sweat and dirt.

This deep in the gorge, there is only shadow. The sun has been lent to another planet.

We follow the river's course downhill. Movement is slow here in the vertex of the ravine; the narrow channel is choked with trunks and chock-stones. The water descends in jumps, gathers in deceptively deep pots. César is leading when he suddenly disappears up to his waist in a pool no bigger than a puddle.

After fifteen minutes we emerge into a clearing created by a recent landslide, which has taken trees down with it and opened a hole in the canopy. Butterflies with art deco wings bask on the sandy slope where the light falls.

In a wide tub of rock, the river plunges and boils. It is shaped like a natural font. Giuliana dips, bathes. Then we all lie in the sun of the clearing to warm ourselves, while hummingbirds flit around us.

We are soaked in life in a sacred cedar forest, a few hundred yards from where a river begins. I think of the springs at Nine Wells near my home: the weakness of their flow and the faintness of their pulse during the drought just ended.

'The mining would kill this river stone-dead,' says Giuliana. 'If you take away the forest, you take away the rain and the mist – and so the river dies. Where they destroyed the forests to the north of here, the rivers don't even run year-round now.'

It's an anti-*trophic cascade,* I think. *You raze the forest, you lose the cloud and the rain. You lose the rain and cloud, you kill the river. You kill the river – and all life leaves.*

'You know, there are in fact three rivers flowing here, now, around us,' says Giuliana. 'There's the one at our feet, the Río Los Cedros, the one we can all see and hear. Then there's the one *beneath* our feet. That's a fungal river. One of the things that ectomycorrhizal fungi do – and there will be thousands of miles of them in the soil beneath us – is to extend the area of water absorption for a tree or plant, connecting and creating a micro river system of water and nutrients that flows between trees, through the earth. And the volume of flow through these ecto-networks, because of the sheer extent of the mycelia, can be *huge*.'

'And the third?' asks César.

'Oh, the third is the sky-river above us. The flying river! By this I don't mean only that the atmosphere is a water-bearing medium, though of course it is, but that there are specific currents and flows within it, and that some of these flows move *uphill*, against gravity, transporting immense quantities of water back from sea to mountain summit, in order to fall again. So, here we all sit *between* and *among* rivers: the sky-river above us, the Río Los Cedros before us, and below us the mycelial streams and the groundwater – moving from the aerial arteries of the planet right down through the veins of the forest and into the capillaries of the earth itself.'

There's one more river, I think, a fourth, above us now, higher even than the sky-river: Eridanus, the constellation named after the mythical river who runs through Hades. Eridanus meanders across almost the entirety of the southern celestial hemisphere, from up near Orion's Belt, through supervoids and nebulae, down to Achernar, the blue-white-hued star at its southern tip, whose name means 'the river's end'.

But *this* river, I wonder, the river dashing and crashing at our feet – is this really a 'legal person'? In the flaring brightness of the ongoing moment, it seems bizarre to think in these terms. I can't help but feel a fundamental incommensurability between the stiff discourse of 'rights' and 'standing' and this quicksilver being running three yards away from me.

'You know,' says César after a while, 'I work on lost causes. Things that seem to be hopeless. Many of the cases I take on concern ecosystems that are extremely deteriorated, where peaceful people have been pushed violently out of the land. The situations I work in can be *truly* dire. So to be here is, for me, to remember what land was once like, what land can be like again. The forest, the river: they're telling me that there is a lot left to fight for, in ways I haven't felt for a long time. To recognize the river's personhood is, I think, the beginnings of a basis for reciprocity. I want to bring my students here, show them how to imagine otherwise.'

I feel a flash of optimism. This place, saved both by law *and* by imagination, is part of a geography of hope. Maybe there's still a way out of this mess, if people like César and Giuliana are on the side of the rivers and the forests?

~

At dusk we light another fire in the clearing. I lie on my belly, blowing into the kindling and tinder, watching flames lick and curl with each dragonish breath.

'It's two months to the day since my father died,' says Giuliana. 'Presently, I'm keeping his ashes in my bedroom in a bag that says "HOLY SHROOM" on it. I'm going to get everyone who's present at the scattering of the ashes to write their name upon a rock and then throw it into the Pacific, which is also where his ashes will end up.'

Cosmo sings Johnny Flynn's song 'The Water':

All that I have is the river,
The river is always my home . . .
The water sustains me without even trying
The water can't drown me, I'm done with my dying.

Giuliana cries quietly in the shadows. Cosmo and César hug her.

'It's so odd,' she says after a while. 'I spend my life as a mycologist praising the necessity of decomposition. Dammit, I spent the whole of last year making a film in praise of rot!'

It is time to lose the fear of death; we must let things die, we must let things rot.

'And then – the irony – I spent a month *fighting* decomposition, trying to keep my father's body from decaying while I waited to get him out of Brazil and home to Chile.'

Through observing our teachers, the fungi, we can learn to accept cycles, the end of cycles, the beginning of others.

'What is the word in English?' says Giuliana. '*Be . . . wilderment?* Yes. The forest and the river have *be-wildered* my soul again. I had taken on a heavy task and I needed lightening.' Her eyes are wet.

'After twenty-five years of finding fungi, of knowing how to find and meet their life,' she says, 'to go through what I went through for seven weeks: my father's death, trying to bring him home . . .'

She trails off. Musters herself.

'I was cracked and scared when I landed in Quito. I thought I'd lost the power, that death had drawn it from me. I felt *heavy* with lifelessness. But then meeting the forest, the river, you all – these things filled me up with life again, and I felt my power return, and I was ready to greet the *Psilocybes* when they were ready to greet me!'

This is the night at high camp when the forest comes alive and alight: when the bioluminescence of the mycelium sets the rotten stump glowing; when the kinkajou watches us with red eyes.

After the others have turned in, I sit up for a while by the fire. The trees are ancient shadow-forms above me. Stars crack and pop in the canopy gaps. A lemon-slice moon rocks on its back.

Corre río, fluye río, baja río, corre río.

River run, river flow, river fall, river run.

I imagine the sky-river flowing invisibly above, the surface river tumbling its way through the gorge, the star-river filling the heavens, and the fungal river flowing in the earth.

Where does mind stop and world begin? Not at skull and skin, that's for sure.

I wonder how on earth to write about the anima of this place; what language might meet its aboundingly relational being, could convey this emerald pluriverse where life forms and forms of life become metamorphically indistinguishable from one another . . . Robin Wall Kimmerer calls for a 'grammar of animacy' – but surely, as with fungi, each such grammar must be specific to its substrate. What would a cloud-forest's animate grammar be? Here, life is in constant hyperdrive, splicing and splitting, folding and tangling symbiotically, epiphytically. Its orchids and quetzals, its horseflies and viruses, the invisible, inconceivable underland of its fungal presence, its rivers and trees: these are all elements of its teeming, points in its web. An animist grammar of this place would need a syntax of hypotaxis, not parataxis: one of maximum correlation, proliferating connections quaquaversally; a branching, foliate, fractal, super-furcating language structure. Or maybe this would best be attempted not in grammar but in form: in patterns embedded deep in a text, made of echo and image that begin to reach and radiate towards one another, creating gossamer-thin webs and meshes, moving mycelially or fluvially as the veins of the forest move, as the rivers and the trees spread . . .

I've never more strongly than here – in the seethe and ooze of the forest, in the flow of the river – perceived the error of understanding life as contained within a skin-sealed singleton. Life, here, stands clear as process, not possession. *Life is as much undergone as done. We are constitutionally in the midst.* This forest, this river – they enliven. Hell, they've brought Giuliana back from within death's shadow. There's no arguing with that.

River stacked on river. The running earth below, the running sky above.

Sparks, spores; a shooting star, then another.

The next morning two troops of howler monkeys begin an echoing duet of roars and cries.

We cannot place where they are in the forest. They are moving relative to one another and to us; this is all we know.

The Río Los Cedros sings on.

The Springs

(Winter)

December, England. High pressure, no wind. We wake each day to find the land baked hard in a kiln of cold.

Everything is winter-struck. The puddles have frozen lids which can be lifted out or shattered. In the hedgerows, scarlet haw-berries wear jackets of ice. One evening there is freezing fog at dusk; the next dawn everything exceeds itself with a trim of hoar frost.

At night, above the wheelie bins and defunct TV aerials of the sub-urbs, the moon creates shifting haloes of colour as its soft light refracts in ice crystals at the outer edge of the atmosphere.

Redwings have arrived from Iceland, Norway, Sweden. They move over fields in rippling flocks, the russet flash of fox-orange showing beneath their wings, calling quietly to one another to keep in touch as they move.

I can't get the Cedar Forest out of my dreams or its fever out of my bones. For weeks after returning from Ecuador I'm sick: aches, dizziness, burning up. Everything in me is jangling and off-kilter. Giuliana is similarly affected – we have dengue fever, she thinks – and, worse, a spider-bite she received on her inner arm while we were in the high forest will not heal, 'has not been at peace', she writes to tell me.

I hold on to the memory of the River of the Cedars, and of Lula's victory in the Brazilian election: how we danced and drank and sang high in the cloud-forest when the news reached us; how Lula turned immediately to the rivers and the forests in his victory speech. *Brazil and the planet need a living Amazon! A river of clear water is worth more than gold extracted at the expense of mercury that kills fauna and risks human life.*

There is other good news. The second mushroom, the one Giuliana heard on the path near high camp: it turns out to be not a *Psilocybe* but a *Protostropharia*: 'The first of its genus that has psilocybin and grows on wood,' she tells us. 'It's a missing link in evolutionary terms and extremely exciting.' Its discovery will help to fortify the case for protecting Los Cedros under the Rights of Nature articles.

I go to the Cumbrian mountains to climb with my older son, Tom. High on a ridge, with bright sun to our east and cold mist to our west, I encounter my Brocken spectre: a rare optical phenomenon created when sunlight projects the silhouette of an object upon ice-mist, haloing it in concentric rings of rainbow light. That day, a breeze stirs the mist, causing the rings of colour around my spectre to ripple, as if the sky were my river and I a pebble cast into it. For days afterwards I am haunted by my meeting with this uncanny other, this chimerical twin, peering through into my realm as I peered back into its.

When I return from the Lake District, I walk on my own up to Nine Wells Wood, where the springs rise at the foot of the chalk hill.

Low-slung winter sunlight. The whole landscape hammered into glittering stillness by the frost. The city has crept another few yards closer to the wood over the autumn. Men in hi-vis jackets sight off theodolites on the meadow where the skylarks nest.

The air burns my ears. I can feel the shape of my lungs in my chest as I breathe in the cold.

A sparrowhawk drifts over on blunt wings, towing a scarf of alarm-calls as small birds scatter. The hedges are bare-branched. There are fewer places to hide.

Two rivers in Cornwall run white for miles after tons of kaolin clay are illegally dumped into them. The water looks like linen. If you didn't know otherwise, you might think it was a misconceived work of land art.

The newspaper says: *Every single river and lake in England is polluted beyond legal limits.*

I cross the footbridge into the wood. The branches of the beech trees stand stark against the sky and double themselves in the water's mirror. I startle a wood pigeon and it flaps away like dropped crockery. There is the distant cry of a buzzard. The bark of the beeches is cool as marble to the touch.

In the hollow where the springs rise, I stop, surprised – the water, warmed by its time in the earth, is steaming in the cold air.

The level is low. There still hasn't been enough rain for the aquifer to recharge after the long months of severe drought. But unlike in the summer, when Will asked if the water had died, there are signs of life. In two places at the edge of the pool, the surface throbs with the pulse of water.

Red strips of cloth have been tied to the branches of the hawthorn and the privet that border the springs – six or eight of them. I've never seen this here before, but I know what it means. People have been making a clootie tree: 'clootie', from the Scots word for rag. In Scotland and Ireland, clootie wells are sacred springs, healing wells. The tying of rags is a curative ritual. You dip the cloth in the water, speak words of greeting and supplication, then tie the rag to a hawthorn if there is one, or, failing that, to an ash.

Through the trees I can see the outlines of Addenbrookes: a hospital-city. It makes sense that this should be happening here, I think. Tens of thousands of the sick and dying pass through the hospital each year; hundreds of thousands of their friends and relatives come to visit, to console, to murmur by bedsides. Some of those people have walked the five hundred yards or so to the wood of the springs – and a few of those have tied red rags to the branches above the water, in the hope of helping to heal themselves or others.

I remember something my Gaelic-speaking friend Finlay MacLeod – a historian of holy wells and springs, whom I had brought to the wood once – had written: *Springs are special places and people viewed them as living locations, alive with their own particular spirit. Water was a live and powerful element, and people were drawn to it.*

Frost crystals show white on the red rags. Bird-shadows cross the pool.

A week later, once the thaw has come, I walk back up to the springs and tie a red ribbon onto the hawthorn that overhangs the second spring pool. I murmur improvised words, feeling self-conscious – but also oddly sure I should be doing it.

PART II

Ghosts, Monsters and Angels

(India)

The river had to be killed for the city to live.

Yuvan Aves (2023)

Before landscapes die, they first vanish in the imagination.

Bhavani Raman (2017)

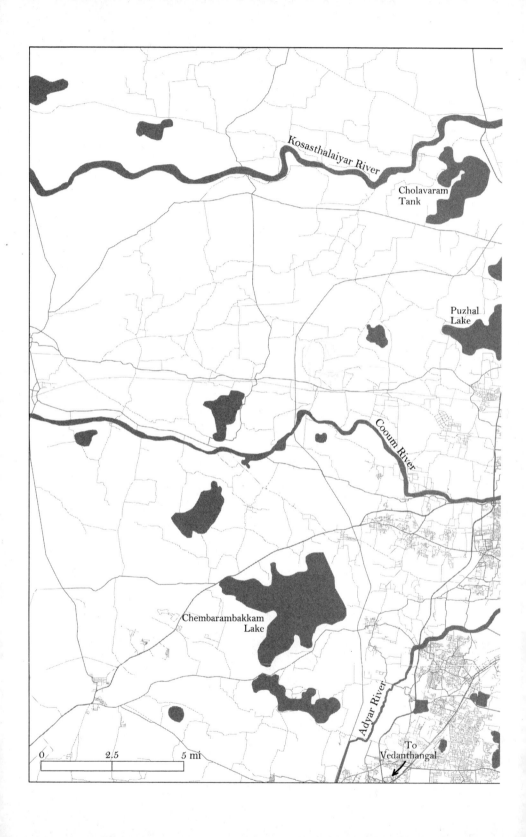

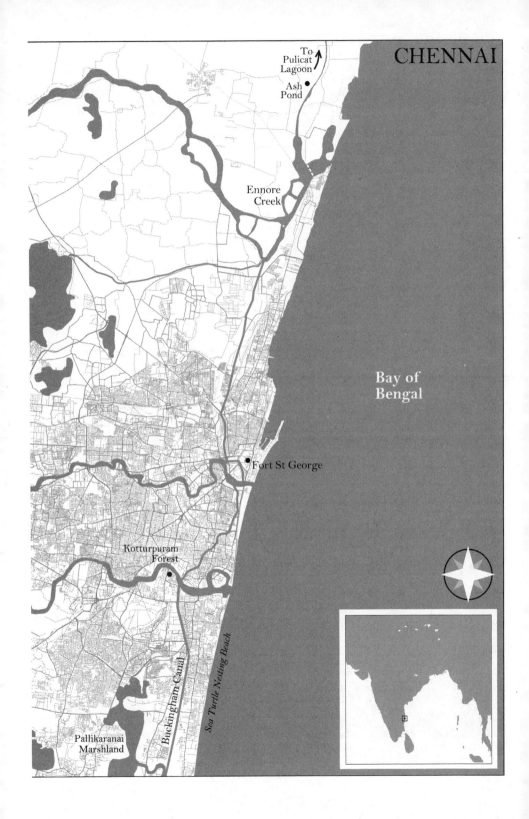

The setting sun lays a copper path eastwards across the mouth of the Adyar River and out over the Indian Ocean, where waves wait their turn to break.

Four green bee-eaters perch along a telephone wire, bright as beads on a child's abacus.

Red ghost crabs are starting their nightly clean-up work on the Chennai beach, flowing up and out of their burrows before scuttling sideways then forwards, like knights on a chessboard, one outsized claw held across their faces like dying heroines, their eyes out on the ends of stalks like Tom when he spots Jerry. The crabs are so alien I can only see them in similes.

'What is your dæmon,' I ask Yuvan as we trudge over the sand towards the Broken Bridge, 'the creature with which you feel most affinity?'

He considers my question in silence for several paces, then replies.

'I would choose three, not one. First, the millipede. The millipede is a recaster of meaning and matter, you know. It turns the shit of life into something valuable; takes it in, absorbs its harm, transforms it. Turns death into life, waste into compost, endings into beginnings. It's a detritivore: part of an under-appreciated group of species who do this vital, ethical work. Red ghost crabs are detritivores also. Likewise, cockroaches, maggots, dung beetles, all of this much-despised class of cleaner-uppers. So – I use the millipede patronus when there's suffering or adversity which must be converted into something positive.'

I know that Yuvan has suffered terribly, has gone through

unimaginably more adversity in his twenty-seven years than I in my forty-six: violent abuse at the hands of his stepfather; the recent, sudden death of his younger sister. That he has somehow become a young man dedicated to healing both rivers and people from harm is living proof of his 'detritivore' ethic in practice.

A single crimson rose butterfly passes overhead, struggling southwards along the shoreline towards Sri Lanka: a scrap of silk on a 500-mile migration.

'And your second?'

'Oh, my second is the mongoose! Here in Chennai, and across India's cities, the mongoose is thriving in the cracks of human life. Like your red fox, it's a space invader. It finds ways to adapt: it'll cross a busy road safely, it'll have its pups in the sewers. It's my dæmon of reimagination, you could say. It helps me think about how to move within, and even disrupt, existing systems of power, although they are so large. The mongoose also helps us visibilize what we cannot see – helps us hear the stories that don't get heard.'

The air jitters with tiny clicking sounds, as if it is being snipped into a million strips. I realize it's the noise of countless ghost and fiddler crabs snapping their claws.

'The mongoose is also a deft survivor, right?' I reply. 'An exploiter of weakness in the face of hostility? All those lunges and nips that it makes in its dance with the cobra, which are eventually deadly to the snake?'

'Exactly!' says Yuvan. 'Also, if you've seen it, you know it's a spring-loaded creature. It never walks, it bounces. And its fur is ever in hackles: it's alert to each living moment.'

A group of girls and women – some of them holding hands in pairs and threes; a grandmother with a stick; a granddaughter in a sparkling sari – is wandering the beach ahead of us. They laugh and smile. One films the sunset on her phone.

In Chennai's reservoirs, giant invasive catfish rise and sup between the water-hyacinth leaves, their whiskers spiking half a foot out of the water as they roll and re-submerge.

Over Chennai's suburbs, black-winged stilts fly in perfectly lateral flight-lines, their wire-thin legs trailing their wide wader-feet behind them, as if each were towing a little dinghy.

The newspaper says: *It's official: Chennai's rivers are dead. All major waterbodies running across the city are dead for all practical purposes, a new water analysis report shows.*

There's a large, domed object on the tideline fifty yards ahead of us. As we near it, I see it is the corpse of a sea turtle, her shell fractured by trawler strike. Her eyes have been eaten from their sockets by the ghost crabs. It's the fifth turtle corpse we've met that day. The geometry of her shell-scales is beautiful even in death. She stares sightless from blue-white eyeholes.

We walk on. The Adyar estuary widens to our west. A jackal-like cry pierces the air: a pied kingfisher swoops steeply up, hovers like a conductor's baton raised for the off, then plunges into the chromium-poisoned water of the estuary.

'And the third of your dæmons, Yuvan?'

'Oh, my third is the banyan tree. Not long after my sister passed away, and I had scattered her ashes in the ocean just south of here, I went and sat with the great banyan tree at the Theosophical Society for almost two hours.'

Yuvan points inland, to where the silhouette of a forest interrupts the city's skyline, curving down towards the edge of the estuary.

'My mum was wholly shattered and all my energy was going into supporting her. As a result, I didn't get a chance myself to grieve the loss of my sister, and it was messing me up inside. So I went to the banyan, one of the biggest and oldest in India. Its main trunk is at least ten embraces wide. Krishnamurti would give talks within its shade. The banyan, to me, is a figure who can see far – a deeply rooted mother of millions. It has an anarchist canopy that preaches sedition to all symmetry. When you have existential questions of the meaning and purpose of life, well, the banyan can help you think.'

'Because it delves both up and down, with those aerial roots that banyans have?'

'Something like this. It has to me a deep-mind-likeness, as well as a long-livedness. They say the far vision contains the near, and the banyan helps me to see both distances.'

'But how do these ideas sit with the fact that the banyan takes life,' I ask Yuvan, 'that as a strangler fig it first grows on a living tree, then demolishes the life within it, eventually leaving only the void of the tree that once existed there – and in so doing creates itself?'

Yuvan pauses. He weaves his head in a gentle figure-of-eight pattern: a sign that he is considering my words. 'I'm not sure how to look at the violence of that initial phase.' He pauses again. 'It is a small violence, perhaps.'

He thinks again. 'Actually, what I mean is that I appreciate the banyan's ambivalence as a being. I like that it exists between notions of "good" or "evil", making a nonsense of both. And I like *anything* that undoes binaries!'

He grins, then laughs, a wheezing chortle-chuckle that makes me smile too.

'Your laugh is a very fine thing,' I say.

'Thank you, but it's not mine. I borrowed it from a bird called the rufous treepie!'

~

I have come to Chennai in search of ghosts, monsters and angels.

The ghosts are those of the rivers who had to be killed for this city to live.

The monsters are the terrible forms those river ghosts take every few years, when they are resurrected by cyclone or monsoon.

The angels are those who watch over the lives of the rivers where they survive, and who seek to revive those who are dying, and Yuvan Aves – teacher, naturalist, writer, water activist – is one of these angels.

'Cities grow along riversides,' writes Yuvan, 'then slowly forget their ecological, hydrological genesis. Later they slowly collapse under their own weight – unless perhaps there is a powerful re-invocation of what birthed a city in the first place: a river.'

~

Humans have lived and died by the rivers of south-east India for 1.5 million years.

On 30 May 1863 an English officer of the Geological Survey of India called Robert Bruce Foote was excavating a ballast pit at a site called Pallavaram, close to what is now Chennai airport, where low hills rise from the southern banks of the Adyar River.

Foote was only twenty-five at the time, and a rising star in the Survey. Trained as a geologist, his primary expertise was in reading the deep-time histories of rocks. But he was also fascinated by the ancient human stories which the landscape held and told, and so from the start of his work in Tamil Nadu he folded archaeological investigation into his geological surveying.

Foote was inspired by the ferment of archaeological discoveries that had occurred in Europe and the Middle East over the previous decade – among them Hormuzd Rassam and Henry Layard's spectacular excavation of Ashurbanipal's palace and library at Nineveh in the early 1850s, and Joseph Prestwich's confirmation to the Royal Society in 1859 of the authenticity of humanly crafted stone hand-tools found together with the extremely old fossil bones of wild cattle and elephants in gravel drifts in northern France. The absurdity of Archbishop Ussher's durable dating of the Earth's creation to 4004 BCE was at last plain for all but the most dogmatically faithful to see – and the study of human prehistory was fast emerging as a field in its own right.

'The news of the remarkable revelation of chipped flint implements

[as] the earliest human artifacts then known,' Foote wrote of Prest-wich's paper, 'had turned my thoughts to the necessity of looking out for possible similar traces of early human art in South India where my work then lay.' On that May day in Pallavaram, Foote made his first find in the ballast pit: a slender, pointed cleaver, bifacially worked to produce its edge and point, and fashioned from a stone not local to the area. Foote felt immediately that it was a Palaeolithic implement – and he was right, spectacularly so. Subsequent research by Indian archae-ologists has dated the cleaver to around 1.5 million years old; the presumption is that *Homo erectus* was the toolmaker. Four months after his discovery at the ballast pit, while excavating a dried riverbed near a village called Attirampakkam – which lies to the north of present-day Chennai, near a tributary of the Kosasthalaiyar River – Foote found another axe and several flake tools. These have since been dated to around half a million years old.

Foote's work was crucial in establishing the antiquity of early human presence in south-east India. It also illuminated the chronic, intricate relationship between the lives of water and the lives of humans in that landscape.

~

Today, the region's rivers are dying.

Chennai is a city of three rivers. Moving from north to south along the coast, they are the Kosasthalaiyar, the Cooum and the Adyar. These rivers all have their sources in the Eastern Ghats hills, all flow roughly west to east, and all empty into the Indian Ocean. The three rivers are joined near the sea by a single long canal – the Buckingham Canal, running north to south – which was built under British orders during the desperate years of the Great Famine (1877–8) as 'famine relief work', whereby starving men, women and children were given meagre wages of food in return for each day's heavy labour.

A 2023 report by Tamil Nadu's Pollution Control Body found that across forty-one sample sites on the Adyar and the Cooum, the water was 'unfit for any kind of life form as there is no dissolved oxygen'. It also recorded disastrously high levels of heavy-metal concentrations, faecal matter and coliform bacteria. The results came as little surprise, given the rivers' treatment as open sewers. Chennai's population growth has been steep. In 1901, 500,000 people lived in the city. Today there are around 6.5 million, and the city's population density is one of the highest in India: Chennai is around 25 per cent the area of Mumbai but has around 40 per cent of its population. An estimated 55 million litres of effluents and sewage are discharged directly into the city's waterways every day.

Chennai's rivers have been poisoned. A longitudinal study of fish species in the Cooum detected forty-nine species present in 1949, twenty-one in 1979 and zero in 2000. Mass fish die-offs in 2014 and 2017 left tens of thousands of sardines and mullets littering the beach around the Adyar estuary; they had been killed by chromium levels thirty times higher than the maximum permissible limit. The dead fish were too toxic to be eaten by humans, so they were dried, powdered and sold to the poultry-feed industry. As fish and other aquatic life have disappeared, so too have the livelihoods and health of the artisanal fisherfolk who for centuries have hand-fished Chennai's inland and coastal waters.

This systematic abuse of water is a relatively recent development in the region. Water was at the sacred heart of the Dravidian empires which rose and fell in southern India from the third century BCE onwards. In his book *Neer Ezhuthu*, the great Tamil scholar Nakkeeran describes the history of water in Tamil Nadu – and notes water's role as the central sacred element of Dravidian culture, compared to the fire-worship which characterized the northern kingdoms. While northern Indian kings would build a *Jayasthambam*, or rock pillar, to mark a victory in war, Tamil kings would by contrast create 'lakes or water monuments called *Jalasthambam* for the same reason'. Ancient Tamil documents record curses specific to the sin of defiling water ('May they perish for the sin of polluting a waterbody!'), and the Tamil language is rich with watery proverbs, including the absorbing observation that 'Water cannot be displaced by water.'

For thousands of years, Tamil Nadu was of necessity a profoundly water-literate area. Water-husbandry and water-reverence ran deep in the region – and this hydroculture has left its marks on the landscape. If you unroll a large-scale map of the greater Chennai region, you will first see the routes of the three great rivers, winding their blue arterial paths towards the city from the west, then through the city and out into the vastness of the Indian Ocean. You will also see the marsh-lands, shaded green, which dwindle in area as the city thickens. Then your eye will be caught by hundreds of what look like blue horseshoe-marks or hoof-prints, made in the floodplains of the rivers. All these marks have a rounded edge, usually on their eastern or south-eastern sides, and always perpendicular to the gradient of the land. Lastly, you will notice the web of fine blue capillary lines that joins these hoof-prints to one another.

The hoof-prints are humanly made water-tanks known most commonly in Tamil as *eris*. Some of these *eris* are as wide as half a mile; the smallest are little more than ponds. The rounded edge is the berm – the dam wall. The fine blue lines are the channels and slender culverts which allow the water to cascade between catchments during times of flood, or when redistribution is needed. Together, the *eris* – also known as *kammai* in the south of Tamil Nadu – along with other water-storage structures (the names of which vary according to their nature, location and function: *ilangi, kooval, kulam, kundam, kundu, kuttai, kuttam, ooruni, poigai, sengai, thangal*) constitute a vernacular form of hydro-logical architecture and landscape design.

The *eri* system came into being as a response to Tamil Nadu's cli-mate, which causes water levels to wax and wane seasonally between extremes: the immense inundation of the monsoon season on the one hand, and on the other the dusty drought-months of spring and summer, when rain scarcely falls. The *eris* gather and store the monsoon water for the villages that have sprung up around their banks. This standing water is used for washing, drinking and irrigation, and also slowly recharges the groundwater and aquifers. Meanwhile, the marshes – those which are left, at least – perform natural versions of the same vital functions: absorbing, storing, releasing. 'Once upon a time,' Yuvan has written, 'people understood that the only way to live successfully in this landscape was to create space for water to be stored, and to allow it to flow . . .'

Now, though, the terms for this venerable hydroculture are falling into disuse, and the waterbodies they invoke are fast vanishing from both mind and land: drained, filled in and built over. The historian Venkatesh Ramakrishnan dates the start of the decline of Chennai's water literacy to the early nineteenth century, when the population of what was then called Madras was under British colonial rule: 'When the rivers were tapped for drinking water in the 1800s,' he writes, 'they began to die.'

Each October the monsoon rains cross the Deccan Plateau and sweep down onto Chennai, filling the rivers, the *eris* and the marshes. Over the course of the rest of the year, the visible water of the landscape slowly dwindles. Wetlands become grasslands; marshes become grazing grounds. Indeed, if you were to come for the first time to Chennai in June or July, you might think it a city built on bedrock or desert and not on marsh. An urban planner who does not understand the seasonal rhythms of the landscape's swelling and shrivelling might mark off what look temporarily like grasslands as *patta*; that is, land which can be zoned for development. The huge Pallikaranai Marsh, originally covering around ninety square miles, was drained to around twenty square miles by the 1970s. Now only around five square miles remain as open marsh within the city's bounds – and the streams who used to connect it to other areas of wetland are choked with garbage and blocked by buildings and roads.

One consequence of these throttled waterways and spectral marshlands is that when the monsoon arrives with unusual intensity, or when a cyclone hits the region, water spates through the constrained river channels – and bursts destructively out into the city.

Chennai is now locked into a brutal cycle of flood and drought, which unerringly brings most harm to the city's poorest communities. Each year between April and July, the mains water is periodically switched off in parts of the city by the authorities. Citizens must conserve water in baths, tubs and pots for periods of each day. For weeks at a time, deprived neighbourhoods are served only by standpipes or water trucks. In 2019 the whole of Chennai ran out of water, and neighbouring states had to send water in convoys to relieve the stricken city.

In the winter third of the year, by contrast, water becomes monstrous in its excess. Chennai was flooded by monsoons and cyclones in 1903, 1918, 1943, 1976, 1985, 1999, 2005 and most severely in 2015, when the city was officially declared a disaster zone: hundreds of people drowned, patients on ventilators in hospitals died after power was cut to 60 per cent of the city, and the dwellings of millions of people were flooded.

In *Rivers Remember*, her book about the 2015 floods, Krupa Ge describes the systematic injuring and forgetting of Chennai's rivers over centuries. 'We displaced them,' she writes:

> disallowed them from entering their own turf. And then we built on top of their homes. They had been around . . . for as long as time can be. And yet we said there was no place for them in the city. All we saw of them was their struggle for survival . . . when we passed by them, we covered our noses and looked away.

But Chennai's rivers, Ge continues, are beings with long memories – memories which reawaken in times of flood. 'We didn't think they'd remember,' she writes ruefully, 'but they did':

> They remembered their many homes, every single one they had breathed in before, thrived in. It was as if nothing had changed. As if

someone had turned the clock back. Their ancient homes looked different now, but once they started to make their way in, they claimed them as their own again.

~

When Yuvan and I meet on my first day in Chennai, we embrace tightly, as old friends do who have been apart from one another for too long. In fact, we have never before met in person, though we've been corresponding and collaborating for almost five years. He puts a green-gold silk scarf of welcome around my neck, and we fall straight into conversation about the days that lie ahead of us.

The intention for our time together is to trace Chennai's rivers and waterbodies from inland to coast. We will meet them where they still flow clear and strong, braiding into complex channels as they re-sculpt gravel floodplains after each monsoon; to track them through the *eris* and inland lakes who are recharged by the winter rain, and provide home and life to astonishing populations of birds; to find them again in the city itself; and finally to end at the immense interzone of the coast. Our journeys will be defined by gradient: following the rivers' songlines as they run from their higher reaches down through floodplain, wetland and marsh, to coastal creek, lagoon and estuary – and out at last into the vastness of the Indian Ocean.

Rivers run through Yuvan too. Water is what he both thinks about and thinks with: it is the substance that defines both his landscapes and his ductile, fast-flowing mind. Faced with the slow violence visited upon the rivers of his city, Yuvan reimagines how water might be. Faced with conditions in which the life-giving powers of rivers have been forgotten or erased, he works to reanimate new-old ways of seeing and listening to them. 'All stories from Chennai must contain the rivers and the sea and their many forms of agency,' he has written, 'and if they do not, there is surely something missing.'

On 11 September 2011, Yuvan ran away from home. He was sixteen years old – and his name was not then Yuvan Aves.

He ran because for years he had been physically abused by his step-father, whose violence towards Yuvan was regular, methodical and committed. He used his hands, and whatever was to hand, to injure Yuvan. Fists, ashtrays, sticks, chairs: anything hard would do. He once slammed Yuvan's head in a gate as punishment for refusing to kill a snake. When Yuvan was bitten on the forearm by a wolf snake, his stepfather wouldn't allow him to go to hospital, even when the wounds became infected and Yuvan's arm swelled up such that he couldn't fit it into the sleeve of his shirt. Sometimes the beatings were so severe that Yuvan was left unable to walk until he had healed.

Yuvan's stepfather claimed to be an astrologist. He couldn't bear that his bright stepson might gain knowledge of the world that far exceeded his own hucksterism. He once asked Yuvan what his favourite subject at school was. Yuvan made the mistake of telling him the truth. *Biology*, he said, *the study of life*. So his stepfather found Yuvan's biology textbook and forced him to burn it in front of him, page by page.

On that September morning in 2011, Yuvan's stepfather was dis-satisfied with the way Yuvan had swept the kitchen floor. So he beat him badly, and then said he would stop Yuvan from attending school any longer. School was Yuvan's only escape. Without it, he would be locked into a house of torment. So he grabbed a few rupees from the table – and ran.

Yuvan had no plan. He knew only that he needed to escape, and that he couldn't return home. His first thought was to walk inland until he reached an area of forest or mountains, where he might live like a wan-dering pilgrim or mendicant. Instead, he walked to school and told the principal, a man he trusted, what had happened. The principal made a series of telephone calls, including one to Yuvan's mother, then he gave Yuvan directions to a residential school called Pathashaala, around fifty miles from Chennai. *They will be expecting you there*, he told Yuvan.

The chrysalis phase of butterflies is still poorly understood by entomologists. This is partly due to the Schrödinger's Cat nature of the chrysalis: if it's opened in order to study its contents, it dies and the process halts. It is known that during chrysalism, the cells of the caterpillar become a kind of 'soup' within the hard case of the chrysalis, swirling around and somehow re-forming into the entirely other creature that is the butterfly. The caterpillar creates its cloak – a dull sarcophagus of skin to contain its soft and gaudy flesh – and within that chamber occurs a metamorphosis of which Ovid would be proud. It is surely one of the commonest and most wondrous miracles of life.

Pathashaala was Yuvan's chrysalis. There, in a school surrounded by *eris*, set within the floodplain of the nearby Palar River, he underwent his transformation. Over the course of the four years he lived at Pathashaala, a traumatized and injured teenager was somehow reassembled as a young man committed to healing others, from humans to snakes to rivers. There, he became a self-taught naturalist. There, he changed his name, from M. Yuvan to Yuvan Aves – 'Aves' meaning 'avian' – in order to honour the importance of birds in this second phase of his life.

Yuvan's years at Pathashaala were an education in and by the wild. His interest in the more-than-human world was deeply democratic and stretched across the five kingdoms of life. He became fascinated by all of existence and in love with most of it. He learned that patience was perception's ally; that he must retune his own sense of time in order to watch life's network thrumming and trembling around him. 'Waiting is the act of witnessing life unfold beyond the constraints of one's will,' he wrote in one of the journals he kept.

The pedagogical spirit at Pathashaala was inspired by the Indian philosopher, speaker and spiritualist Jiddu Krishnamurti (1895–1986), for whom closeness to nature was an ethos rather than a posture. 'He always had this strange lack of distance between himself and the trees, rivers, mountains,' wrote Krishnamurti, looking back in the third person upon his younger self. 'Have you ever sat very quietly without any movement?' he asked in *Think on These Things*:

> You try it – sit really still, with your back straight, and observe what your mind is doing . . . Watch it as from the banks of a river you watch the water flow by. In the flowing river there are so many things – fishes, leaves, dead animals – but it is always living, moving, and your mind is like that.

Waiting, watching and witnessing, sitting *really* still: these became Yuvan's method. He deduced from patient observation that nymphalid butterflies have their olfactory organs on their forelegs; that they approach a potential host plant and then drum on its leaves with their knees like a tabla player in order to identify it from its scent. A butterfly who smells with its knees!

He noted that the fastidious bush-cricket so disliked proximity to its own excreta that it would synchronize the release of a dropping with a perfectly timed and powerful back-heel kick, flinging its faecal matter a distance of several feet. What a shit-kicker!

He discovered that hundreds of toads would sleep cuddled together in the cracks between the boulders that marked the edges of paths in the school – and decided to study their scat in order to understand their diet. Dissecting toad faeces one night, Yuvan discovered not only the remains of worm-snakes and scorpions, but also rubber bands and staple pins. Truly an omnivore!

Snakes played a conspicuous role in the life of Pathashaala, slipping in and out of drains, classrooms and playgrounds, and often ending up where humans did not want them. Yuvan generally took the side of the snakes, on the grounds that it was in fact humans who had ended up where snakes did not want them.

Of necessity, he quickly learned how to identify and handle non-venomous snakes, as well as how to recognize the four great killers of southern India: the spectacled cobra, the Russell's viper, the saw-scaled viper and the common krait, who between them cause the deaths of an estimated sixty thousand people in the country each year – a shocking number. He taught himself how to spot a bronzeback snake high in a palmyra tree, or discern the emerald body of a green vine snake amid the foliage where it waited for bird or bat. Once, after cleaning out a drain which had become blocked by a family of aestivating ornate narrow-mouthed frogs, Yuvan made the mistake of handling a banded kukri snake without washing his hands first. The snake, detecting prey by scent, quite reasonably mistook Yuvan's hand for a frog – and promptly attempted to swallow it.

Another evening, Yuvan and a friend were up late playing chess in their dormitory when they heard a hesitant knocking at the door. The knocking stopped, then restarted: blunt little nudges of noise. The door handle rattled. Yuvan's friend stood up from their game, crossed the room, opened the door – and a seven-foot rat snake fell upon him. The record does not show whether the snake or Yuvan's friend was more surprised by this event. Yuvan leaped up, knocking over the chessboard as he did so (fortuitously, as he had been losing the game), rushed across the room and seized the rat snake by its neck. He carried it away and released it into the scrub around the school. The snake had been scaling the door of the dormitory, Yuvan later deduced, to reach a plump gecko who had taken up residence by the light above the entrance, to the bulb of which the moths were drawn each night, creating a kind of late-night fast-food servery for the gecko. Moths to light, gecko to moths, snake to gecko.

As word of his snake-handling abilities spread, Yuvan became the go-to snake-guy for the school. He was especially busy in the aftermath of the 2015 floods, when the rising water forced many snakes to seek refuge in the school's buildings. Once, he was called in to deal with a furious wolf snake which had become enraged after being poked with crowbars by the workers who had discovered it. When Yuvan arrived, the snake was so angry that it was growling in the lupine manner which gives it its name. Yuvan advanced, using a dustbin lid as a shield to block the snake's strikes. When he was close enough, he took the snake's neck gently in one hand, supported its body weight with the other, and then stroked its belly with his little finger. Slowly, the snake became calm, and wrapped itself around both his wrists, tying his hands together, he remembered later, 'like a thick, gentle rope'. In this way, he could carry the snake safely to the paddy field beside the school, and watch it glissade away into the grass.

When he wasn't snake-wrangling, Yuvan was reading. He became a library omnivore, gulping down books with the appetite of a cormorant. He signed up for distance-learning programmes: first A levels, then degrees. Moving between field and library, he learned from his assembled tutorial team of snake, toad, butterfly, thrush and text: from what he came to think of as 'the entire abounding community of life around'. Over time, he was taken on to the staff of Pathashaala as a teacher.

It cannot always have been easy to be Yuvan's colleague at Pathashaala. Each year he would delay the start of spring-cleaning until he had been able to gather up all the spiders from every vertex and corner. He would then, he recorded in his journal, release a number of these spiders 'into the long hall of the staff residence . . . to acquaint myself better with these arachnids'.

Safe from his stepfather's persecution, Yuvan's body healed fast. His mind took longer, but the transformation was even greater. From a childhood marked by atrocious violence and vindictive egotism, Yuvan found himself developing a different understanding of community: one where, as he put it, 'relating and relationship, synergy and symbiosis and being there for one another, are regarded above everything else'.

'How does a moth know that it can fly when for so long it was a caterpillar?' Yuvan wondered aloud to his journal; 'how can it know what its wings can do, when it suddenly acquires them?' Within the mysterious shroud of the cocoon, 'how does such a total transformation of body and consciousness take place? What does it really mean to burn all our old bridges, to shed away all our previous ways of living, to emerge from a cocoon, to be reborn, to see all the world in an entirely new light?'

What indeed. If anyone knows the answers to these questions, it is probably Yuvan.

At the age of twenty he made his way back to Chennai, where he lived in a series of hostels. One day he learned that his stepfather had assaulted his mother again, this time seriously. So he walked to the house he'd run away from four years earlier – and confronted his stepfather. The broken teenager was now a strong, confident young man, with a highly magnetized moral compass and, at last, a firm footing upon the Earth. 'If this happens again,' Yuvan told his stepfather calmly, 'you know how it will be.'

Yuvan's plain words had the performative power of a banishing spell. Cowed and speechless, his stepfather realized that a single sentence had dethroned him as the tyrant of the household. He could not bear the sudden, total loss of his power. Within days, he had moved out from the apartment he shared with Yuvan's mother, Margaret. He lived apart from Margaret, Yuvan and his sister, and did not harm any of them again before his death in 2021.

Somehow, Yuvan now bears no ill will towards the man who abused him for so long. Rather, he sees him as a victim. 'My stepfather was himself the casualty of intergenerational and unprocessed trauma,' he told me. 'His father and grandfather were even more violent than he was. At Pathashaala, I came to understand that it was up to me to break this inheritance – that my only chance was to convert what I had suffered into something positive.'

Hurt people often hurt people. It takes great courage and clarity of mind to metabolize pain into goodness. It was Yuvan who led the funeral rites for his stepfather. It was Yuvan who gathered up the ashes of his cremated body and poured them into a clay urn, Yuvan who carried them across the wide sand beach in central Chennai, south of the mouth of the River Adyar, and Yuvan who scattered them – just as he had done for his sister's ashes, only two years earlier – into the warm waters of the Indian Ocean, where the breakers rolled in and sluiced them away into the vastness, grey into blue.

In 2021, Yuvan founded a trust called Palluyir, dedicated to advancing ecological knowledge and practice in Tamil Nadu and beyond – and to fighting for justice for humans and more-than-humans together. Palluyir's motif is a circle containing diverse images of life from four kingdoms: from child to fungus, dolphin to greenbottle fly, earthworm to beech tree.

The word *palluyir* itself is Tamil and may be translated as 'all of life'.

~

We begin our river-journeys inland – leaving on Yuvan's moped an hour before dawn, weaving through Chennai's sleepless streets.

Cool air, barking dogs. A half-moon with a fuzzy dust-haze halo. A house crow strutting around the sand of a school playing field, glossy and bossy in the halogen arc-light.

Then westwards in a bus as the land wakes up. Mist lies thick as crop in the paddy fields. Two palmyra trees curve towards one another like a pair of brackets. Hunting egrets stand stock-still in ditches, hinged as anglepoise lamps.

Bedrock starts to show through the earth, then lifts into roadside crags. 'All this is marked as "stony waste" on government topo-maps, meaning it can be re-zoned for development at *any* time,' says Yuvan, pointing at the crags. 'But I know that eagle owls live in those outcrops.'

Our bus is banana yellow with a long, stout snout: a school bus.
With us are thirty or so of Yuvan's pupils from the Abacus Montessori
School, aged between ten and twelve. Their excited chatter fills the
cabin. They pelt Yuvan with the big questions of the day. 'Sir, sir, do
turtles dream?' 'Sir, if birds could talk, what would they say?'

Three ibises fly overhead, holding a perfect triangle formation,
their feathers gleaming like oil. Temples stand footless in the mist.
Every bush and verge wears a multicoloured coat of garbage shreds.
Drongos perch on the power lines, their long, forked tails silhouetted
against the blueing sky.

'The drongo is a mimic and a ruthless raptor-bully!' says Yuvan.
'Golden orioles will sometimes nest close to them in order to get protection from their enemies.'

'I like the sound of them,' I say. 'I'd like a couple of drongo friends.'

A scatter of houses. Another temple. 'The name of this village in
Tamil means "the village of the pale termite mounds",' says Yuvan.
'The area is honeycombed by termites, but the villagers give rice to the
termites each morning, so that the termites don't eat their buildings.
And it works! I am very interested in this idea of so-called "pest species"
being better understood as "tax collectors" for the more-than-human
world.'

We're en route to a vast lake called Vedanthangal, fifty miles west
and inland from Chennai. It is an *eri*, thirty hectares or so in area, who
is fed and filled each year by the monsoon rains, and by the rivers
who roll down from the hills.

'I can't wait for you to see Vedanthangal. It is the oldest waterbird
sanctuary in India,' says Yuvan. 'The hydrological invention of the *eri*
has here created an ecological haven, where farmers, villagers and
birds share kinships that are literally centuries old. It is good that we
are beginning here, where the relations of water and humans are recip-
rocal and life-making.'

Records show that as early as the eighteenth century, villagers local
to Vedanthangal understood that the abundance of bird life in the lakes

and tanks of the region was to their benefit: the water they drew from the lakes and used to irrigate their crops was unusually fertile because of the amount of nitrate-rich guano in it. What was good for the birds was good for the people.

We're getting close now. The bus slows to a trundle as it crosses the wide bed of the Palar River. Here, the water runs clear in dozens of braided channels, weaving their ways between shingle banks. It is plainly beautiful.

'I'm glad you've seen the living Palar, Rob, still flowing from the monsoon recharge. The water of Vedanthangal runs into it a few miles downstream of here. *Development, development, development*: this is the mantra of our Hindutva government. But I think a river is a fantastic form of development. It's been developing for millennia.'

Yuvan unrolls a map of the greater Chennai region, and we spread it across our knees. He guides me around the terrain like a general surveying his campaigns, pointing with his little finger. '*Here* we have a fight ongoing against an illegal limestone quarry. *Here* is Ennore Creek, where we will go soon, to see what a dying river looks like. And *here* – within the exclusion zone of the Vedanthangal sanctuary itself, is the Sun Pharma factory. These bastards' – he says the word with relish but quietly, conscious of the example he must set to his young pupils – 'have been discharging toxins into the sanctuary: toluene, mostly; it stinks like nail polish, poisons local people, ruins crops, kills birds. That's one reason we've come here today: to continue a fight with Sun Pharma which is already under way.'

A thin brown cow chews cud in a patch of roadside shade. Each nub of its spine stands out like a thumb, and its skin is stretched tight over its bones, like tent canvas pulled taut by guy ropes.

A few minutes later, the smell of nail polish fills the bus. We pull up in a stand of young eucalypts. Two hundred yards away, shielded by mature trees, looms the bulk of a factory with a galvanized grey smokestack chimney poking skywards. There's heavy security on the single access road.

'That's Sun Pharma,' says Yuvan, 'as you can smell.'

The air around us is suddenly shimmering. But it isn't pollution. It's dragonflies — hundreds of them. They're like no dragonflies I've seen before. They seem to have borrowed their wings from butterflies; they are colourful, like stained glass or tapestry. Yuvan tells me their common names, which have a poetry to them: 'wandering gliders' and 'picture wings'.

'Those dragonflies — odonates — are extraordinary migrants. They migrate along the intertropical convergence zones, using navigation systems we're only now beginning to guess at, letting the wind carry them. At times there are so many that they form a river of life and flight. We are just too small to see this river's flow. In fact, the rivers and river basins of south India themselves form the crucial flyways for those butterflies who migrate from hills to plains and back, driven by the two monsoons.'

Yuvan's phone rings: it's a journalist. He rattles out directions to Sun Pharma, explains the nature and evidence of the violations. He's turning up the heat on the factory hidden behind the trees.

Overhead, higher than the dragonfly-river, a steady stream of birds is flowing eastwards: hundreds of them, storks and egrets and pelicans and herons. The egrets are magnesium white, almost too bright for the eye to see.

'They're off on their morning commute,' says Yuvan. 'Don't worry, there'll be plenty of birds left for us!'

We follow the stream of birds against its flow — and it leads us to Vedanthangal. We park, and spill out of the bus. The children mill excitedly around a big banyan, from whose branches issues a familiar-unfamiliar rocking call. Yuvan cocks his head to listen, and raises a finger, in a stance I'll come to recognize.

'Coppersmith barbet! So named because its call is like the beat of hammer on copper or bronze,' he says with a broad smile. I am back in the cloud-forest, with the toucan barbets calling in counterpoint.

Suddenly, Yuvan stops a passing pupil. 'Wait, what fresh hell is this?!' he exclaims. 'Your T-shirt is mixing Marvel and DC characters? That's heresy!'

Her black T-shirt has a grid of nine superhero heads on it, each set in its own tile, like a busy Zoom screen. She looks puzzled.

'Sir, what are you talking about?'

'That's Superman on there. What on earth is he doing alongside Iron Man, Wolverine and Captain America?'

'Sir, that's not Superman, that's Dr Strange!'

'Oh.' Yuvan falls silent.

'The shame of it, Yuvan!' I say. 'You can identify three hundred different birds from the glimpse of the tip of a feather, but you can't ID a superhero correctly when he's printed on a T-shirt in front of you!'

He face-palms.

As we walk up the slope of the berm, before we see the water, a cacophonous sound fills the air and my ears. It is the tutting of ten thousand tongues, ten thousand clacking drumsticks, ten thousand clicking castanets – and a compound creaking, like an old ship's timbers might make in a storm. I reach the top of the berm and am halted by what I see.

It is a floating city of birds – an avian Venice.

Deep water spreads away from the edge of the bund as far as the eye can see, and out of the water emerge rounded islands of . . . yes, *trees*: hundreds of tree-islands, with channels of clear water between them.

The water, the air and the tree-islands are teeming with tens of thousands of birds. Glossy ibises, spoonbills, grebes, cormorants, egrets, night herons, terns, garganey ducks, pintails, teals, grey herons, open-billed storks . . . The trees quake with them.

Pelicans make stately traverses of the air. Painted storks carry nesting materials back to breeding sites in the trees, their wings creaking as they fly. A snakebird seems to Möbius-strip its neck as it dips and fishes.

In the shallows, where algae baizes the water, green frogs surface slyly, inflate their throats as if blowing bubblegum, then sink slowly back under the water.

The first stork chicks have already hatched, and young birds are flapping their wings by way of strengthening exercises. The clacking, the castanets: this is the noise made by courting and mating storks, as they knock their beaks together. I guess if you have a two-foot-long beak for a mouth, the art of kissing is hard to master. *Clickety-clack, snicker-snack!*

We have stepped back in time, into a prehistoric world of avian abundance.

'Place fidelity is intense here,' says Yuvan. 'It's a pattern built over centuries on these trees. Pelicans, egrets, open-billed storks: they'll all try intergenerationally to come back here and nest on the *exact* same spot as their parents and grandparents.'

The children are in awe and so am I. Here is water's miraculous power of life-making spectacularly at work, creating this cauldron of noise and activity.

'This is nothing, Rob! There's been a rapid decline recently – what you see is maybe thirty thousand birds fewer today than a year back. Less water, more poison. Blame Sun Pharma. Blame climate change and pollution working together. The year after the 2015 floods, there were so many birds here, perhaps seventy or eighty thousand, that we *literally* could not hear each other talk over their noise; we had to lean close and shout. It was *fantastic*!'

We walk to the edge of the *eri*. The children are fizzing.

'Yuvan, sir, have you ever seen a nightjar?'

'Blue roller, sir! There! I love the roller! Such a beautiful bird!'

We sit looking into this wild, wet world. It is the best show imaginable.

The sun presses down upon us like a shield. It is 35°C in the shade, in February. Yuvan organizes the children. They will each keep a species list. He explains to them about Sun Pharma – about the decline in bird numbers at Vedanthangal. He encourages them to use crowd-sourcing apps and websites to record their sightings. He teaches them how to estimate numbers of a species in a bird-dense place such as this. Data-driven citizen science is a core part of Yuvan's water activism and, as I will discover, it can lead very fast to powerful change.

'What have you noticed?' he keeps asking the children.

'When we were observing the little owlet in the tree,' answers one girl, 'it was observing us back.'

'Yes!' cries Yuvan, air-punching.

'Children are born as animists and then they lose that power, Rob,' he says to me later. 'Or rather it is taken from them. I'm not really a history person, but – what on earth *happened* to the world? What's happened to a world where animism is a rarity, or is seen as "weird"? What is "weird" about seeing the extent and vitality of the life that surrounds us, the lives with which each of our own little lives is entangled?'

That afternoon, before we leave for Chennai, the children arrange a deputation to request my company at the back of the bus on the return journey. I'm delighted to comply. They organize a rota system for sitting next to me, each for about twenty minutes. Their conversation is bright, effervescent. We range across such perennial subjects as the relative merits of Manchester United or Manchester City, how to start writing a good detective story – and why my nose is so big.

I ask one of them, Som, if he thinks a river is alive. Som is an excellent naturalist, one of Yuvan's stars in the field. He considers my question thoughtfully for twenty seconds or so. Then he nods and says calmly, 'Yes, a river is alive.' He gives no reasons and I do not ask him for any. It is simply his conclusion.

A boy called Surya takes his turn next to me. He is constitutionally mischievous, with a waggish grin and curly hair. He reminds me of a young Cosmo. I want to smile simply on seeing him. We discuss, in considerable detail, the state of the English Premier League. Then I ask him the same question I have asked Som.

'This is a very good question,' Surya replies. 'I would say a river is alive. When I sit with my legs in the river up to my knees, I can feel the currents in the water pushing me, both holding and pulling my legs. This is when a river is most alive to me – and I like it!'

~

Can you murder a river?

In late March 2017 a man called Brij Khandelwal rang the police station in the city of Agra. He had a crime to report, he said: a violent assault, an attempted poisoning. But the victim wasn't human; it was the Yamuna, the river who loops and meanders through Agra. The intent wasn't homicide but rivercide. And the perpetrators Khandelwal named were the government officials who had allowed the terrible wounding of the Yamuna to occur.

Khandelwal's phone call was provoked by a groundbreaking judgment issued four days earlier by two judges in the Uttarakhand High Court, who had decreed that the Ganges and the Yamuna – two of Hinduism's most sacred rivers – should be recognized as 'living entities' with attendant rights. It was a first: no precedent existed in Indian law for the recognition of the legal standing or rights-bearing capacity of a river, mountain or forest. As the judges openly acknowledged, they had been inspired by the passing only ten days earlier of the Whanganui River Claims Settlement Act in Aotearoa New Zealand.

The Uttarakhand judgment was short, passionate and forceful. It ordered the immediate cessation of mining in the riverbed and floodplain of the upper Ganges, and the establishment of a body of guardians to ensure the upkeep and protection of both rivers as legal persons and as 'breathing, living' presences, 'sustaining the communities from the mountains to the sea'.

Both the Ganges and the Yamuna have their sources in the glaciers of the Himalayas: the Ganges at the Gaumukh, or snout of the Gangotri Glacier; the Yamuna further west at the Yamunotri Glacier. The

Yamuna flows south to Delhi, before bending eastwards through Agra and past the Taj Mahal, to unite with the Ganges – and, supposedly, the mystical underground Saraswati river – in the city of Prayagraj (formerly Allahabad). Until it reaches Delhi the Yamuna is a life-bringing river, who carries in its cold blue waters the memory of its glacial birth. In Delhi, it becomes one of the most polluted waterways in the world. Oxygen content collapses to near zero. About the only life is extremophile bacteria – and the thousands of pilgrims who bathe in the waters of the river each year, believing it will spare them from hell in the afterlife. Many of these water-worshippers emerge from their baptism covered in toxic river-sludge. Further downstream, where the Yamuna flows past the mintcake-white, hyperbolic love-token of the Taj Mahal, its waters are oily-black and rancid. For the Yamuna, as elsewhere in India, holiness does not equal cleanliness.

The police officers laughed at Khandelwal when they realized he was reporting the attempted murder of a river – but his point was a logical one. Theologically speaking, the Ganges and Yamuna are deities. Legally speaking, at least according to the Uttarakhand High Court judgment, they were both juristic subjects and living beings. So if the river is dying or dead, Khandelwal reasoned, then someone can be held guilty for 'attempting to kill the river by slow poison'. He urged the police to open a case file on the crime. They declined to do so.

The Uttarakhand judgment represented a first attempt to shift Indian law away from anthropocentrism and towards something like ecological jurisprudence, underpinned by social justice. Since 2017 more Rights of Nature cases have been brought in India, and more judgments have followed. Among them, issued less than a year before I arrived in Chennai, was a high-court judgment recognizing the Rights of Nature across Chennai and the whole watery state of Tamil Nadu. 'The natural environment is part of basic human rights of "right to life itself",' Justice S. Srimathy declared, but 'the few remaining original forests – our biodiversity treasury – are being destroyed to make way for huge mines or dams or lucrative real estate projects.

[This] is not sustainable development, it is sustainable destruction.'
She proceeded to skewer existing environmental legal doctrines as
demonstrably inadequate to the scale of the challenges in hand, and
encouraged instead the establishment of a 'Nature's Rights Commission' in India, which might recognize in law the rights of 'rivers,
streams, rivulets, lakes . . . wetlands . . . springs and waterfalls'.

Reading these judgments, I wonder heretically if so many people
are drawn to the notion of nature's rights because they are longing for
something like transcendence from the law; beckoned by an over-
enchanted dream in which judicial language acts with a moral lucidity
as clear as the waters of the Río Los Cedros. Perhaps, though, there is
no good reason to believe that this new framing will get us out of our
old conflicts, or slough off the confusion, bad faith and apathy that
bedevil any attempt at betterment.

When I contacted Khandelwal, six years on from his call to the Agra
police station, he sounded defeated. *Rivers are dying a slow death with
no clear policy for their conservation . . . my complaint was neither here nor
there. The authorities did not take it seriously. Pity. In my own humble
way, I continue to do what I can do. Write, campaign, send letters . . . But
nothing happens.*

~

Yuvan's apartment is a dangerous place to be.

'It's best if you don't go onto the balcony, Rob.'

'Oh. Why's that?'

'Well, there are paper wasps nesting there on the ixora plant, you
see, and they can become somewhat prickly if disturbed. They've been
living with us for three years now.'

'Ah, I understand.' I don't really understand.

'The paper wasps used to nest inside the vacuum-cleaner cover on
the balcony, but very interestingly, after Cyclone Mandous in December, the majority of them moved to the ixora. I don't know why.'

'How many are there now?'

'Oh, I think around forty wasps. I recently had to apologize to two people who visited to do some work in the apartment. Though I had clearly warned them about the ixora, they nevertheless disturbed the nest and one of them was stung rather badly on the hand. It was necessary to explain to them that they must not blame the wasps.'

'How did that go?'

'Better than you might imagine. There are not only paper wasps living with us here, but also sweat bees and blue-banded bees. Last week, by the way, I picked up my towel to reveal two paper wasps resting there. Understandably they both stung me, and I was grateful to them for this because their stings caused me to realize that I wanted to write my next book on insects.'

'Of course they did.'

'Come and look here.' Yuvan points to a small hole in the wall above the melamine desk at which he works. On the desk directly below the hole is a tiny spill-heap of brick dust.

'I drilled this hole to hang a photo frame, and now as you can see it has been taken over by a mud-dauber wasp, *Chalybion bengalense*. She cleans out the brick dust you may witness below the hole. Then she captures and kills a spider, brings it back and stuffs its body into the hole, lays her egg in the burrow by the spider carcass, then seals the end of the hole with wet chalk, which I believe she scrapes off nearby walls. She is an amazing navigator, this wasp, and knows her way around my apartment, no problem – the doors and windows, all the ins and outs.'

Yuvan continues his tour of the small apartment where he and his mother live, introducing me to more of their flatmates.

'There is a total of four mud-daubers nesting with us now, I think. One of them uses the hole in an electric socket. Also, in the mirror cupboard in the bathroom there are three mud chambers built by a black-and-yellow mud-dauber.'

He opens a small floor-level cupboard. 'Oh – and see down here, Rob!'

I stoop, then rear back. There's a rucksack in the cupboard. It is fused to the side and ceiling of the cupboard by a chambered, ash-grey wasps' nest. A menacing humming emanates from it.

'Got it. You can close that now, Yuvan,' I say.

We return to the balcony door. The view is across dry, scrubby ground, to buildings and a railway line. There are pockets of green reeds, indicating remnant areas of marsh.

'All this was once wetland,' says Yuvan.

Ten months later, Yuvan will send me a photograph of this same view after another cyclone hits Chennai, bringing devastating floods. In the photograph, what was land has become river. Yuvan's building stands door-deep in water. Catfish cruise over the scrubby ground. Crocodiles march down the roads of north Chennai. Yuvan and his mother are trapped in their apartment for days.

Rivers remember. They remember their many homes, every single one they had breathed in before, thrived in . . .

Yuvan beckons me a step or two forwards, raises a finger to his lips and points towards the centre of the ixora bush, which stands in a pot on the far right of the balcony. I can see and hear the wasps' nest on the plant now: hexagonal cells, a seething, fizzing noise, the impression of molten bronze being spun and whirled.

'So much life lives here with you, Yuvan!' I say.

Death too. The biggest room in the small apartment is dedicated to the memory of Yuvan's sister. Its door stands open.

Yuvan's mother, Margaret, has joined us now.

'Please, come in with me,' says Margaret, gesturing into the memorial room. In the far corner from the door is an altar to her daughter, Yuvan's sister, Yazhini. Yazhini died of heart failure, following kidney failure in November 2019, aged only sixteen. She was prescribed incorrect drugs to treat a persistent stomach-ache. Instead of curing the stomach-ache, the drugs clogged her kidneys and killed her.

A framed photograph of Yazhini, perhaps three feet high and two feet wide, is mounted on the wall. Its frame is wreathed with yellow, orange and white chrysanthemum chains. Yazhini looks peaceful in the photograph. She has a beautiful smile.

In front of the photograph, a small desk holds offerings to the gods and to Yazhini: a burning candle, more flowers, more photographs, an apple, a packet of biscuits, two bronze pots. Every morning Yuvan's mother comes in not long after waking to leave new flowers for her daughter, and every evening she does the same.

Margaret and I walk over to the shrine. We stand and look at Yazhini's photograph in silence. Then Margaret produces a long silk scarf of delicate oranges and pinks, and reaches up to place it around my neck. We embrace briefly, awkwardly, and I find my eyes are damp from the awful sadness of it all.

I know that in the garage downstairs, mounted on the dashboard of Margaret's car, is a small clear plastic cube. A laser has 3D-etched an image of Yazhini's head and shoulders into its interior. Since Yazhini's death, Yuvan's mother travels everywhere with this little floating ghost on the dashboard, so that she is never far from her daughter.

'I am thankful for the unknowable field,' wrote Yuvan. 'It lets me see my paper wasps with wonder every day. It also lets me see my sister and uncle in some place together in the hereafter, unknowable from here. It grips me with fright sometimes when its field shows me the abysses, the thresholds of the knowable. Death among them – as though life and death were a binary! Then the unknowable field queers that binary, showing so many unknowables as deep as death, in life itself.'

When Margaret and I emerge from Yazhini's room, I see that Yuvan is closely inspecting a wasp that has landed on a wall. I join him, and we peer at the insect.

The wasp seems to be washing itself, wiping its forelegs together, running them over its antennae and skull as it rotates its head side to side, much as a dog or cat might clean themselves, but more methodical, more digital. Its chitin glints. It flickers its elytra, and when it does so its whole being shivers like a glitching hologram.

'Do you know Thomas Berry's work, Rob?' Yuvan asks.

I do. Berry was an American ecologist, historian, scholar of religion and one of the philosophical fathers of the modern Rights of Nature movement. He did not like being referred to as a 'theologian'; his deep-time perspective meant that he preferred to think of himself as a 'geologian', a distinction I like. His world view was both urgent and optimistic: he believed that humanity, after centuries spent despoiling the planet, was close to recognizing its new, true role as part of a far larger, interdependent Earth community of beings.

For Berry, we stand at a crossroads. If humans can reimagine themselves along these lines, we will enter what he called the Ecozoic Era, in which we re-comprehend and re-organize ourselves as part of a web of entangled life. If we fail to do so, we will intensify what he called the Technozoic Era, in which we continue to degrade both justice and life on Earth, leaving a deep-time future signature of destruction and extinction.

Berry wasn't naive about the difficulty of reaching the Ecozoic. 'The Great Work' was what he called the gigantic effort required to reimagine everything from subject-object relations through human governance systems to the role of capital; an echo of Le Guin's 'great reach outward of the mind and imagination'. 'We are talking only to ourselves,' Berry wrote, 'we are not talking to the rivers, we are not listening to the wind and stars. We have broken the great conversation.'

Crucial to Berry's 'Great Work' was the recognition of Earth as home to what he called 'a communion of subjects, not a collection of objects'. He is credited with coining the phrase 'Earth Jurisprudence' to refer to a philosophy of law and governance which was founded upon recognizing and upholding that communion. At the heart of his Earth Jurisprudence is the recognition that fundamental 'Earth rights' have always obtained to the planet's many subjects. 'Trees have tree rights,' wrote Berry, 'insects have insect rights, rivers have river rights, and mountains have mountain rights.'

'Rivers have river rights, so insects have insect rights,' I say to Yuvan, who nods and smiles in recognition. 'And — wasps have wasp rights, right?!'

Yuvan laughs. 'Yes! And Berry coined the word "inscendence", as you are surely aware, meaning "to enter deep within",' he says. 'Where "transcendence" is the impulse to rise above the world and its cares — the weight of the body, say, or the burden of mortality — "inscendence" is the impulse to climb *into* it, to fathom its depths and delve towards its core.'

We consider the wasp as it completes its ablutions, lifts off with a sound like rustled paper — and then makes for the balcony and the open air beyond, thorax hanging low.

'For me,' says Yuvan, 'Berry's verb "inscend" lives close to the word "insect". Insects *call me in*. Indeed, they are almost always boring or tunnelling or entering something or somewhere — and in turn, I find, they invite the same movement if you watch them very carefully.'

That dusk we go birding at a pocket handkerchief of marshland, crammed between three housing projects. Its sewage stink is a punch in the nose.

'You're sleeping on former marsh while you're here, Rob,' says Yuvan. 'Me too, as you saw: our apartment block is built over marsh. This whole city was once marsh, is now almost all real estate. I sometimes ask my students what the commonest marshland species is. They say the mosquito, or the pond heron, or the painted stork, of course. I say: *No! It's the IT professional!* Four hundred and eighty IT companies or so on the Old Mahabalipuram Road alone — and all built on marsh and wetland!'

The sunset has slaughter in it, and spills scarlet onto the vast clouds massing inland. Swallows sit like musical notes on the staves of telephone wires. Twenty-foot-high columns of midges warp and fold above the marsh. Scores of bee-eaters loop-the-loop through the midges — glittering rainbows, scoffing their fill at this glorious, all-you-can-eat buffet. Among the reeds a swamp hen walks with the exaggeratedly slow gait of the mime artist, its iridescent-purple neck glinting in the sun like mithril, its feet leaving sharp prints in the mud.

'"Barrenness is almost always a state of mind, only rarely a state of land,"' says Yuvan, almost to himself.

Within thousands of chrysalises under the leaves of the city's trees and bushes, cells merge and swirl as life reformats itself. Spring is coming.

Before sleep, I watch hundreds of fruit bats in flight to their roosts, moving with slow pterodactyl wingbeats, silhouetted against the blood-red sky.

That night, in the brackish waters between sleep and waking, I dream briefly but distinctly that my body has grown marshy. I look down to find fingers and toes become reeds, my belly a pool of slow water.

~

On the banks of the blighted Adyar River in central Chennai, I witness Yuvan's inclusive vision of life in practice.

I have seen the clear-running rivers far to the west of Chennai. I've seen the immense, threatened life of the vast Vedanthangal *eri*, with its tens of thousands of birds. I've followed the eastwards flow of the water as it enters the city, to where it pools in nearly murdered marshes.

Now we're deep in Chennai — and here the rivers are desperately stricken.

The Adyar is thirty yards to our north. It reeks. It scarcely flows. Humpbacks of sewage show themselves; the waterside bushes wear skirts of garbage. The Adyar, here, is as close to death as any river I have seen in my life.

'Oh, but this is *nothing*!' says Yuvan. 'Now, the River Cooum . . .' He whistles. 'Well, the word "Cooum" is used as a synonym for filth here in Chennai. If you swear a lot, your mouth is "Cooum". If rubbish rots in an alleyway, it's "Cooum". If you call someone "Cooum", it's an insult. Compared to the Cooum, the Adyar is in *fine* health. The thing is, even the Cooum runs clear before it enters the city.'

We are in a thin slice of woodland, perhaps three acres in area, wedged between the river and a road. It is called the Kotturpuram Urban Forest, it is open to the citizens of Chennai, and twenty years ago it did not exist. It does not seem so at first glance, but this riverside forest fragment is part of the geography of hope.

'When I was a sixth-grader, Rob, there was no forest here on the banks of the Adyar,' Yuvan explains to me. 'This land was a dump-yard, and the soil was contaminated. So we, the people, *organized*. Over six hundred trees were planted here by volunteers and students from across Chennai. I would come here after school, and hand-pump buckets of water, then carry them to water the young trees. Now it is here for the general welfare of Chennai.'

I think of the eleven-year-old Yuvan, helping to grow this river-land back into life, even as his own emergence was being contaminated by violence at home. I think of both land and boy finding ways to transform themselves, to cleanse themselves of poisons that have set-tled deep down, over a long period of time.

But memories of Los Cedros are still vivid in my mind, and I am struggling to categorize both these places under the sign of 'forest'. Compared to the old-growth cloud-forest, Kotturpuram feels com-promised and degraded. Then I recall Yuvan's gently warning words: *Barrenness is almost always a state of mind, rarely a state of land.*

With us in Kotturpuram are two of Yuvan's young apprentice nat-uralists: Sridevi, a student and excellent birder, and a ten-year-old boy called Mithul. Mithul darts from tree to tree, keen to show and share his findings with us, to seek and to name. He is eager for Yuvan's approval. Yuvan is very patient with him.

'This is one of my favourite places!' Mithul says.

'Why do you like it so much?'

'I like being with the trees,' he says simply. 'And there are so many pollinators here. I like being with the bees and the wasps and the flies.'

From beyond the trees comes a medley of horn beeps and honks. Moped, truck, taxi, rickshaw. Brassy light. A mash-up melee of sounds. Someone somewhere is playing 'Mull of Kintyre' on a recorder. The mega-city is dense here. It hums and cries around us. Everywhere is busyness. Everything is either being pulled down or thrown up. It reminds me of the life-on-life-on-life intensity of Los Cedros, but here that life is humanly improvised and constituted: metropolis as cloud-forest.

We walk Kotturpuram together. Seen through Yuvan, Sridevi and Mithul's eyes, I begin to realize, this little slice of woodland, sandwiched between a roaring road and a dying river, bustles with life. A Burmese lynx spider waits in its hunting pose: a lethal assassin, legs bristled as blackthorn boughs. A leaf-cutter bee snips an intricate doily out of a banana frond. A lacewing nymph has created a collaged carapace out of the bodies of beheaded ants and snippets of snail shells, before gluing its folk-horror assemblage to the bark of a tree and retiring inside it to consider its options.

'Come! Look!' exclaims Yuvan, 'A flying fox, there in the tree! Our largest fruit bat. A new colony must be starting here, I think. This is very exciting. Fruit bats are highly site-specific. We have three or four large colonies, and they need quiet spaces. The forest gives them this.'

I spot more of the bats, hanging upside down in the crown of a tall tree like pendulous fruits, leathery wings wrapped tight around themselves. A few yards away, the Adyar festers in the heat.

'Ah, see, a palm-fly butterfly!' says Yuvan, as a shred of winged velvet flutters past us. 'A satyrine – it migrates here from the Western Ghats.'

Yuvan seems to hold in his mind the migratory paths of scores, perhaps hundreds, of species across the various kingdoms, all indexed to the seasonal and weather conditions which shape these incredible journeys: a vast map of moving, traced with scores of criss-crossing lines. I remember a phrase from the scholar-poet Siddharth Pandey: *Everything is alive and everything is speaking.* In Yuvan's company, this becomes true.

We reach a tall grey-green bush, with downy stems and waxy white-purple flowers beginning to show.

'Aha! I have been wanting to introduce you to this plant for some time, Rob,' says Yuvan. 'Mithul – tell him what it is.'

'It is the giant milkweed,' says Mithul, proudly.

'*Calotropis gigantea*,' adds Yuvan, respectfully.

Recalling the interspecies manners that Giuliana taught me in the forest, I incline my head to the bush in greeting.

The milkweed plant is remarkable for the number and diversity of invertebrate species who partner with it. It thrives on supposedly waste ground and roadside verges, in cracks in pavements. Through its veins runs poison of a kind: its sap is so alkaline that it can kill grazing cattle, or burn human skin like lye. Its hardiness, defences and adaptability make it one of the commonest of Indian urban plants – so much so that it is rarely honoured with close attention.

'*Calotropis* is less a plant, more a planet,' says Yuvan. 'There was a milkweed plant right outside my apartment when I was growing up, Rob. I called it my "faraway tree", because it was something into which I could escape from the violence of daily life. The milkweed was a place for dreaming for me back then – and its everyday alchemy still amazes me.'

Yuvan shows me and Mithul some of the insects that partner with the milkweed. They comprise a magnificent bestiary – a parade of weird wonders from the Insects' Ball. There is the masked crab spider – an eight-legged *bandito* – and the carpenter bee, *Xylocopa fenestrata*, with its iridescent blue-and-yellow wings. There is the plain tiger caterpillar, so spectacular a striped and dotted colourful being that it seems to have fallen straight out of Yayoi Kusama's imagination; so flamboyant it makes me wonder what on earth the 'unplain tiger caterpillar' might look like. There is the Indian aak weevil – fusty and dusty and purposeful – and the painted grasshopper, a gleaming miracle of chitin and design, a harlequined Grayson Perry ceramic. There are beasts who only have scientific names – and for these Yuvan has invented new names in English and Tamil, seeking to make the creatures memorable to the children and educators with whom he works. Among them is the so-called 'Darth Maul bug' which looks, well, exactly like Darth Maul.

Then Yuvan brings me back to earth.

'But there are thousands of milkweed bushes right along the banks of the Cooum which have almost zero life on them, Rob,' he says.

When a river is dying, life in its aura dies too.

~

The ghosts of rivers lie all about us.

Among the most exquisite maps I know are the so-called 'Fisk Maps' of the Lower Mississippi. In the early 1940s Harold Fisk, a geologist and cartographer working for the US Army Corps of Engineers, found a way to deep-map the histories of the Lower Mississippi River as its course moved around over time within its meander belt.

For the Mississippi, like any unhindered river occupying a wide floodplain over time, was restless. It *wandered*, in great hooping loops – and those loops left their traces in the land.

Fisk spent three years hunting river ghosts from southern Illinois to southern Louisiana. He cross-checked sediment archives with geological and geomorphological historical maps. He studied inhabitation patterns in the meander belt, he surveyed extensively on the ground, he consulted historical maps and above all he drew on aerial photographs of the region. Combining these data, he was able to plot reliable routes for the Mississippi at different moments in its past.

So he began to draw his maps. To each phase or 'stage' of the river's former lives, Fisk assigned a different colour or tone. Its present course was white, and that line was continuous on the maps. Below the present river curved its self-haunting predecessors: the Mississippi's course in 1880 shown in mint green; 1820, a chalky lipstick pink; 1765, a duck-egg blue – and so on across twenty-eight different stages. Fisk's maps reached back so far into prehistory that the most ancient three stages were older than the Mississippi River Belt itself. These stages Fisk coloured an appropriately spectral grey. He had found a means of representing in a single image the many past lives of this huge and wilful river. He had mapped the Mississippi's memories.

Fisk's fifteen plates, tracking the meander plain contiguously from north to south, are works of art. In them, the Mississippi comes to life: twisting like mating snakes, writhing with river ghosts. Seen in Fisk's cartographic imagination, plotted colourfully across both time and space, the Mississippi becomes an itinerant, wandering being. 'Looking at them,' as the American designer Jason Kottke puts it, 'you are invited to imagine the Mississippi as it was during the European exploration of the Americas in the 1500s, during the Cahokia civilization in the 1200s, when the first humans came upon the river more than twelve thousand years ago, and even back to before humans, when mammoths, camels, dire wolves and giant beavers roamed the land and gazed upon the river.'

Since Fisk, advances in remote-sensing technologies and computer imaging have permitted the deep-mapping of any given river, delta or floodplain. Topographic and bathymetric LiDAR measurements now use lasers to map with extreme precision both land and seafloor contours, and riverbed elevations. These techniques can also make visible geomorphic features of a river's past, including abandoned channels, scroll bars and oxbow lakes. Using colour grading – lighter for higher elevations, darker for lower elevations – intricate and luminous histories of waterbodies become legible. Visually estranged in this way, rivers assume new kinships. Deltas are tangled wildwoods. Estuaries are single, stag-headed oaks. Meander plains are serpentine swirls. Tributaries are wisps of smoke curling from the furnace of the main channel. Flowing water organizes itself within land much as blood does within body.

Leonardo da Vinci knew this six centuries before the advent of LiDAR. He understood that we carry waterways within ourselves. One of his sketches shows the outstretched left arm of a man, with veins and capillaries drawn on the surface of the skin: flowing down either side of the bicep to converge near the inner elbow, branching dendritically beneath the flexor muscles of the forearm, forming a delta at the hand and fingers. Leonardo had learned these carnal patterns the bloody way, by performing post-mortem dissections on more than thirty cadavers. In a watercolour painting, Leonardo envisions a section of the Arno River near Florence as seen from a bird's-eye view, with the river's channels – present and former – picked out in blue and grey. The accuracy of this image arose from Leonardo's intense hydrological literacy: he had studied the dynamics of currents, using seeds and dyes to make flow patterns visible, and he had long been fascinated by the Arno, within whose watershed he was born. The family resemblance between the flow patterns in Leonardo's sketch of the human arm and his painting of the Arno is uncanny. He has enrivered the body and embodied the river. 'The idea appeals to me that the earth is . . . much like the system of our own bodies,' he wrote:

> in which there are both veins (vessels for blood) and arteries (vessels for air). In the earth there are some routes through which water runs, some through which air passes. And nature fashions these routes so like the human body that our ancestors call them 'veins of water'.

Recently, a LiDAR-based image was made of a section of the Cambridgeshire Fens. In that landscape, the life of water went from one of absolute freedom to near-total control in less than a century. But even in the reclaimed land where fields replaced marsh, the old routes of rivers and stream-channels are still traceable, if seen from above in certain lights or at certain times of year: a meandering line of wheat or barley which grows slightly differently from the rest of the field; the patterns of colour in earth which show up like bones in an X-ray when long droughts come. These are the routes of old watercourses ghosting into visibility.

The LiDAR image I have in mind is coloured yellow and red. The yellow represents the soil of the fields. Cutting across it in dead-straight dark lines are the dykes and lodes which were dug as part of the drainage infrastructure: their rectilinearity speaks of their task. But perceptible within and beneath both yellow earth and dark dyke is an intricate network of living groundwater, shown as red in the image, which spreads and seeps in the same branching, veinous forms. Looking at this image, I have to remind myself that what I am seeing is water not blood, field not flesh.

~

Question: how do you make a river disappear overnight?

On the orange earth of a dusty park in north Chennai, a young man called Raju unrolls a map and tells a story by way of an answer.

The map is riverless — and the story seems to have been scripted by Kafka.

The map is around three feet long and one-and-a-half feet wide, and it is titled 'Coastal Zone Management Plan of Tamil Nadu'. It is a mundane name for a magical document — for this is a map so powerful that it caused a river to vanish.

Yuvan and Raju — a young fellow activist with a quick, bright smile — refer to it as 'The Fraud Map'. It may be thought of as the bureaucratic equivalent of a magician's trick, such as one of Jasper Maskelyne's wartime hoaxes or David Copperfield's grandstanding illusions, which turned a column of tanks into thin air or made the Statue of Liberty evaporate.

Except that this trick is not in the service of morale raising or entertainment; it's in the service of river death. And the magician is a government official who waved a pen over a complex area of human and more-than-human water-land — and simply . . . *disappeared* its river.

The Fraud Map was produced by the Tamil Nadu government in 1997, Raju explains, in response to a national directive to coastal states compelling them to zone and management-plan their coastlines. In Tamil Nadu, this caused a problem. For the government realized that one of the areas it had been instructed to map was an area north of Chennai called Ennore Creek – in effect, the shallow backwaters of the Kosasthalaiyar River, who flows down to Chennai from the highlands of western Tamil Nadu. Ennore Creek was also the region where the state had been locating its heaviest industries, known as Red Category industries, including petrochemical 'parks', coal-fired power stations and chemical factories.

The presence of Ennore Creek provided an outlet for the discharge of waste heat from toxic by-products from the Red Category industries, and was therefore useful. But the new national directive meant that the existence of the river and its associated ecological features – sand dunes, mangrove forests, salt pans – would place restrictions on which industries could be situated near it.

This was highly inconvenient. So the state authorities came up with a boldly simple solution. They would erase the creek's existence.

When they issued the 1997 Coastal Zone Management Plan map, it looked very unlike the land it represented. Salt pans: vanished. Mangrove forests and sand dunes: deleted. And a long stretch of Ennore Creek: expunged.

People sent photographs to the Environment Ministry, showing themselves standing up to their necks in the water of Ennore Creek, and waving at the camera. *Hey, there's a river here!* they said. *Change the map back!*

No dice. Because no river, no problem: develop away.

The consequences of this cartographic sleight-of-hand have been disastrous for the area. For a quarter of a century, slow-moving Ennore Creek has been infilled, built over, constrained and desperately poisoned. Without existence on the map, it has no legislative protection – for how can you protect a river who doesn't exist? And without protection the creek has become a sump for all the Red Category industries' waste products.

The thousands of traditional fisherfolk in Ennore – among the most economically marginal residents of Chennai, and those with the least political voice – have suffered terrible harm. The oyster reefs, fish and shrimp they used to hand-fish have declined drastically. Their skin has been blistered from wading in toxic water, and burned from wading in water heated at times to scorch-point by thermal power stations. Their villages have become hemmed in by factories, and their children now play in pools of toxic fly-ash.

Hydrologically speaking, the creek's ancient role as a retention zone for water during monsoons and cyclones has also been drastically reduced. Today, a principal reason for the flooding of north Chennai is the degradation of Ennore Creek, which had previously protected around a million people from inundation. Today, when cyclones and monsoons hit hard, the ghost of the Kosasthalaiyar returns as a vengeful monster.

Raju finishes his story and releases the map, which flick-rolls back up into a cylinder with a puff of orange dust.

The ambitions of Raju, Yuvan, and the group of young activists of which they are part, are immense. They want to reverse the bad-magic trick of 1997: to put Ennore Creek back on the map, to restore its health, and to see justice done for all the inhabitants of the creek, from the fisherfolk to the oysters and ospreys.

It's a heck of a dream. They want to reimagine and transform a major stretch of river. They want Ennore Creek – flayed, wounded Ennore Creek – to be recognized as a complex, vulnerable wetland ecology, rather than an invisible dumping ground. They want to defeat the pollutocrats. They want what they call 'multi-species justice'.

Right now, that looks to me like a Herculean labour. Standing there, aware they are awaiting a response from me to this bleak story, I feel another wave of hopelessness wash over me. What chance do these courageous young people have to change any of *this*?

The dusty orange park is in a poor, northern district of Chennai that still bears the dismal colonial name of 'Blacktown'. It was into Blacktown and Ennore that the British pushed aspects of Chennai they felt compromised their Victorian fantasy of an Indian Venice: a languorous water-city of clear-running rivers and canals. Deprivation, pollution and lower castes were all driven northwards by colonial zoning practices.

That infrastructural racism has left a long legacy. Today, the roads through Ennore have names like 'Ash Pipeline Road'. Today, the pollution plumes streaming from the factories are so thick that they show up on satellite images, visible from space like malign volcanoes. Ennore Creek has become a 'sacrifice zone': one of those places which lie outside the limit of power's self-interest, largely outside the reach of observability, monitoring and justice, forfeited in order to enable thriving elsewhere.

A young girl, maybe ten years old, is doing timed sprints in the park, kicking up the orange dust with each pace. The air is so acrid that it is uncomfortable to breathe. The girl's father is crouched at the start line he's drawn in the dust with a stick. He's holding a stopwatch, calling out proud encouragements. He catches my eye, smiles proudly. *Isn't she amazing?* I smile back, try to beam a *yes* to him.

Two huge new tenement blocks loom over the park. Rising in the gap between them are the chimneys of two coal-fired power stations. The air is violent with pollution. A puppy with a white blaze of fur on its forehead worries a flip-flop in the dirt.

We drive further north towards Ennore Creek itself, and stop on a massive road bridge which crosses the point where the Kosasthalaiyar meets the backwaters of the creek, and they both turn towards the sea.

A barrage of lorries shudders the bridge. The air crackles. Ahead of us is the North Chennai Thermal Power Plant, with a vast cumulus cloud, four or five thousand feet high, stacked above its cooling tower. *It's creating both weather and climate, this power station,* I think.

Around and beyond the power station are at least a dozen more chimneys and flues from other factories. All but two are billowing smoke, steam or fumes. Pylons stride across the landscape, arms out, power lines held in their steel hands. I realize the crackling is the sound of voltage being shed by the miles of power line which criss-cross the air here.

Not far north, sight is lost in a toxic haze. The air is now so polluted we must all wear face masks to stop it biting our throats. My skin prickles. My eyeballs sting.

Ennore is a slow Bhopal. Here, where the poorest of Chennai have been systematically shunted, numerous oil spills, gas leaks and other forms of industrial violence occur. Monitoring is scant, regulation scarcely functional, punishment absent. Less than a year after I am in Ennore, an ammonia leak from a fertilizer factory will hospitalize sixty people and affect thousands more.

This is a sensitive area. The last time the group was here, police arrived to prevent them from taking photographs and to move them on. So we post a watchman: a young man called Lokesh, who keeps an eye out for incoming trouble.

'In Tamil there's a saying, "When the dragonflies are low, a storm is coming,"' Yuvan says. 'It's an old way of forecasting using insects. When there's a lot of atmospheric pressure gathering, the wandering gliders – those migratory dragonflies I told you about, Rob – get pushed lower in the air column, sometimes very close to the ground. If you see them that low, you know rain is coming. But a villager from Ennore told me a different proverb. He said, "*Thattaan keezha parandha moochu adaikkum*": "When dragonflies fly low, breath gets blocked." On cloudy days, or days of high atmospheric pressure, the mixing height of the chemicals from the smokestack descends. The same pressure pushes the dragonflies lower in the air column. So, when people *here* see the wandering gliders gathering near the ground, they know that in a few hours the air quality is going to become *even* worse, that it will be *even* harder to breathe.'

Under our feet, below the bridge, is the convergence of the main Kosasthalaiyar River and Ennore Creek. It's a wide tidal channel of mixed salt and fresh, perhaps a third of a mile across.

The water flowing in from Ennore Creek is grey-green and sluggish. But the water from the Kosasthalaiyar is worse. It's so slick with effluents, sewage and other pollutants that it's almost black. At the mixing line, the colours lick tongues.

Where water comes together with other water . . .

A ragged line of white egrets crosses the creek in flight. They meet and mingle with a scatter of black crows in a brief moment of bird chess. Two glossy ibis pass high overhead, glinting like electricity wires.

'Here, look through these at the shoreline across from us,' says Yuvan, handing me his binoculars. I lift them. The far shore pops into focus. I see a bare line of mangroves, standing on the brink of the muddy water, with what look like brown bony knees sticking up between the roots.

'Pulicat, the vast lagoon to our north, is the anglicization of a Tamil place-name, Pazhaverkadu, meaning "Old Jungle of Roots",' says Yuvan. 'Mangroves are hugely powerful shore-protectors – the best buffers you could want on an eroding coastline. Highly salt-tolerant, and wonderful habitat for countless creatures. They even filter pollutants. Truly a miracle tree! Mangrove used to forest this whole area of Ennore Creek. Now there's hardly any left: they've been poisoned or cut down.'

The history of extraction on this coast stretches back almost four hundred years – and contains atrocity. For two centuries, Pulicat was the hub of the Dutch East India Company's trading activities in the region. Through Pulicat they exported diamonds, nutmeg, cloves – and slaves. The numbers of humans being sold at the height of the trade are staggering. Archives examined by a Dutch scholar, Wil O. Dijk, show that between 1662 and 1665, 26,885 enslaved women, men and children were processed through Pulicat, of whom 1,379 died. Brokers at what is now Chennai were employed to undertake the 'slave catching', organizing the raiding of coastal villages in Bengal and elsewhere. Enslaved people were clad in coarse cotton dungarees, traded at Pulicat for rates of between four and forty guilders each, then shipped out. Many details of what is known as the 'Coromandel Slave Trade' are only now coming to light – for the Dutch have been more efficient than even the British at disguising the barbarisms of their empire.

The sun beats hard as steel upon us. It's the hottest day yet.

On the far shore of the channel, nearest to the factories, we walk down to a mudflat in the shade of the bridge. As we approach, the entire surface of the mudflat lifts up, flickers like a wave, shifts sideways – and then vanishes.

'Fiddler crabs!' says Yuvan with delight. Thousands of them, each with one outsize claw, have risen up from their position on the mud, scuttled sideways and disappeared into their burrows, with a mass synchronicity that a North Korean military parade would envy.

'It looks like territoriality, that movement – and in part it is,' says Yuvan. 'But it's also eusociality at work. Recent research shows how these movements are coordinated across a large area of fiddler communities, to create a crab version of the Mexican wave! It's thought to be a way of warning off predators. Of whom we, to them, are one.'

Then Yuvan calls out excitedly, grips my shoulder and points. 'Oh! There! Look! A mudskipper! Such a beauty! She has blue spots that shine when she's angry.'

'I'd like a set of those,' I say.

Further into the industrial zone, right on the eastern bank of Ennore Creek, we stop on the roadside, still keeping watch for police. Ahead and around, I can see only damage. The devastated river. Barbed-wire fences enclosing factories. Networks of rusting iron pipes, in stacks of three or four, moving satanic substances around.

Away to the north is what seems to be a big grey lake, the area of several football fields. It's an ash pond. Fly-ash from the chimneys of the power stations has been dumped here over years into a part-set slurry. Fly-ash has also been baked into supposedly 'green bricks' and sold or given to the villagers who still live in this zone, so they can build rudimentary houses with them. But fly-ash – even that produced by conventional power stations – is radioactive. The state knows this. The power-station administrators know this. Still, though, the villagers are building their houses from radioactive bricks.

'In the village next to the ash pond,' says Raju, 'they call the pond the "floating world". That's where the children play; it's all they have to play with.'

Because the ash sets into a jelly-like colloid, its surface is the closest thing the children have to a trampoline. They bounce together on it, as it ripples radioactively beneath their feet, and as they laugh they breathe in loose fly-ash.

'We've created a map called "The Lost Wetlands",' says Yuvan. 'We want to use that map to help tell hopeful stories about how the river can be conserved and protected by those who really know it. Through this initiative, two thousand acres of wetland should be preserved on which the inland fisherfolk can continue to thrive. And Nityanand Jayaraman, the activist-writer who is a mentor to many of us, forced a thousand acres of fly-ash in Ennore to be cleaned up and restored to wetland.'

Their victories amaze me. They come so quickly and often. Their work is a kind of counter-mapping, I realize. They want to counter-map life back into this landscape; to re-render the presence of *palluyir* – the web of being. They're practising an anti-desecration cartography, one which re-inscribes complexity and de-zones conformity.

But I can't share Yuvan's optimism, though it's not my right to doubt it. I've never seen rivers as close to death as Ennore Creek and the Kosasthalaiyar. I've never seen water so chemically polluted that it blisters human skin, or radioactive trampolines for children.

A green bee-eater turns two emerald loops, then lands by an ash pile.

'What would a "good" Ennore Creek look like?' I ask. 'What future do you want for this landscape, this place and its life?'

There's silence for a while. Then Raju answers, this time in Tamil. He speaks slowly, with seriousness. His smile is absent. Yuvan translates.

'To change a landscape for the better,' he says, 'you must first have the ability to dream – to dream a good dream.'

He pauses. A golden plover cries like rain.

'But here in Ennore Creek, people have been deprived of the ability to dream. At one meeting we held, when I asked what they would want for the future here in the Ennore Creek, a villager replied, "We're all getting cancer. It would be nice if we just got asthma." *That* was her dream. Asthma rather than cancer. Another time we asked a group of fishermen to speak of their dreams for the Ennore Creek, but they said it was too difficult here to dream.'

A blue-faced malkoha cackles past, its eye-ring lustrous as deep water in the light.

'Before the people of Ennore Creek can shape a good future for this place, they need to be helped to dream again. When we speak with them, we ask them about their ghosts and their monsters. They know these terms. These terms help them to speak of loss and fear and hope. The ghosts are the things they have lost, which they would want alive again, like the river. One of their ghosts is clean water. Thirty years ago, they could drink from Ennore Creek. When we ask the children here what they want, they say, "I wish to bathe in the river." That's *their* dream. A simple dream. But they have been almost entirely deprived of the ability to dream, from childhood onwards. Those are the ghosts. And as for the monsters . . .'

Raju shrugs. He does not need to say more. There are many monsters and they are very powerful and we can see them all around us.

~

'Bodies need water, but water also needs a body,' writes Astrida Neimanis. We are all bodies of water, receiving, circulating, giving onwards; all participants in the hydrosphere, with the flow of the wet world running through us. But what do we *do*, Neimanis asks, with the recognition that one's 'body is marshland, estuary, ecosystem'? How does an ethics arise from it, let alone a politics?

In Chennai, I keep returning to Neimanis's good, hard questions, and I begin to think that Yuvan is answering them as well as anyone might. For over a decade he has dedicated himself to pursuing to its logical ends the realization of his body's porosity to water. 'My kidneys are marshes,' he wrote while in hospital once, thumb-jotting a prose-poem on his phone after his own kidneys had briefly failed, 'my blood flushes through reedbeds and rushes . . . connecting body to cloud, lake and ocean . . . I am primarily hydrosphere.' Through intense observation and reflection, Yuvan has come to see his self – and all selves – as an ecotone or intertidal zone, in constant exchange with the world around.

Inner and outer merge, and one simultaneously walks on all shores . . .

~

Dusk falling fast on the coast. A night wind rising. Chennai flashes and blinks behind us.

Huge surf breaks and withdraws, breaks and withdraws, filling the air with its roar. Somewhere a dog-pack howls.

In the black ink of the ocean, night travellers are approaching shore, drawn and directed by instincts etched deep into their brains by evolution's needle.

Sea-mist shows grainy where arc-light falls. Salt in the nose, stinging lips. A barn owl is hunched on the skeleton of an abandoned building. Its feathers glow faintly white: a phantom in the girders.

Yuvan and I have at last, in our slow descent of the rivers of Chennai, reached the sea. We have arrived at the long shore where the

Adyar, the Cooum and the Kosasthalaiyar meet the Indian Ocean: Chennai's celebrated beach, a vast intertidal zone, a meeting of worlds which stretches for miles along the coast.

Tonight we will not sleep. Tonight we will walk the beach, watching and waiting for female Olive Ridley sea turtles – those night travellers – to haul themselves ashore, dig their nests and lay their eggs.

The fossil record shows that sea turtles have been voyaging the oceans of Earth for at least 120 million years: that is to say, some 70 million years before the Indian Plate crashed into the Eurasian Plate to create the Himalayas and fuse what is now India to what is now Asia.

Sea turtles have survived much upon this Earth in their long tenure, but it is possible they will not survive us. Human predation, exploitation and habitat destruction are proving severe challenges for these gentle, deep-sea voyagers. For centuries now, sea turtles have been caught and killed for meat, eggs, bait, leather and oil. Turtle meat was a fuel that powered the engine of colonialism: the British would stack the storage decks of their ships with living sea turtles in order to provide a durable source of fresh meat for long voyages. Now far fewer turtles are killed for their meat, but many more die after being struck by the hulls or propellors of ships, snagged in trawl-lines or tangled fatally in the thousands of abandoned 'ghost nets' which haunt the world's oceans.

Between January and April each year, hundreds of female Olive Ridley turtles come ashore in the darkness to nest on the Chennai coast. And for thirty years, during nesting season, a group of volunteers has been walking the beaches every single night, in order to guard the mothers from harm and ensure the safety of their eggs. They call themselves the 'Turtle Patrol'.

Yuvan has walked with this group many times. The leader is a man called Arun Venkatraman. Few people know more about sea turtles' lives and deaths in southern India than he does. Arun is fifty or so. He is tall, tired and articulate.

'It is a bad year for the turtles so far,' he says to me. 'We have had around a hundred nests and a hundred dead turtles. We walk the beach each night to the smell of rotting flesh. Those are the ones killed off-shore, who then wash up here. All the nice dreams about leaving the turtles to their nesting have gone up in smoke. The beaches have become very unsafe. Tractors will collapse the egg pits, feral dogs will dig the eggs out.'

When turtle hatchlings do emerge from their eggs, and excavate themselves from the sand, they are evolutionarily attuned to move towards the dazzle-path of moonlight on the sea or the biolumines-cence of breaking waves. But now Chennai's bright lights confuse them. Street lamps and building lights lure many hatchlings inland, where they die on dry land, eaten by dogs or crushed by the wheels of vehicles.

This is why the Turtle Patrol walks the beach carrying soft cloth bags. When a new turtle nest is found, they dig it out by hand, then carefully lift the eggs out and bag them, counting them as they surface. The eggs are then carried to a hatchery: a safe, fenced area on the beach. There they are reburied in the sand, in new nest-holes hand-dug to the same depth and dimensions as the true nest from which they have been taken. Records are kept of each nest: time, location and date of both finding and reburial; size of nest; number of eggs.

Around forty days later, the sand above the new nest will begin to quake – and out will struggle scores of hatchlings, whom the Patrol oversee as they make for the ocean, turning back any that head inland.

Arun estimates that the Turtle Patrol releases twenty thousand hatchlings in a good year. But many more nests and eggs are lost to dogs, and the burn rate of those hatchlings who do emerge from the hatchery's eggs is very high, even under the care of the Patrol. Only around one in a thousand will survive to reach sexual maturity as an adult turtle.

Of all the threats sea turtles face, perhaps the greatest is climate change. Fascinatingly, the sex of a sea turtle hatchling is determined by the temperature at which the eggs gestate. The flip-point for sea turtle sexing in India is 31.5°C. Below that, the majority of eggs become male. Above that, the majority become female. Today, due to global warming, the sand on Chennai beach is reliably in the thirties, even as early in the year as February. The result is that future breeding ratios are heavily skewed.

Yuvan, Arun and I wait together on the night beach for the rest of the Patrol to gather. We eat slices of hard mango sprinkled with salt and chilli powder, which set our lips tingling. Men sit alone in the dark on sand, silently watching the ocean. Couples hold hands. Boys in trainers laugh as they play chicken with the waves. Yuvan and I face the ocean and read aloud a praise-poem to the sea turtles – a ghazal – called 'Night-Swimmer' that we have written together over the past few months:

What stories, what wishes, what warnings do you bring, night-swimmer? What wonders, what perils – the whale pods, the ghost nets – have you seen as you explore, Sea Turtle . . . ?

Hauled up along the beach are sharp-prowed wooden fishing boats, painted yellows and blues and reds, with powerful outboards lying flat on their sterns. These are the workhorses of the fisherfolk. They are fleet, elegant craft, designed to ride out through the big surf and then to work the waters within half a mile of the shore, rocking on the rollers.

Far out at sea the mast lights of the trawlers can now be seen: seven or eight ships at least, harvesting perhaps six miles offshore, their long nets and lines slung behind them. This is the gauntlet the mother turtles must run to reach the shore safely: hulls, propellors, flipper-snagging nets and hooks.

Other people drift out of the darkness to join us. There are curious locals from Chennai, and visitors from Hyderabad and Bangalore. All want to know more about these mysterious sea-beings, the turtles.

We finally start walking at midnight. Arun leads. He invites me to join him at the front. We trudge north together. The main group stays thirty yards behind. Arun holds a torch and sweeps the sand in front of him in quick, efficient arcs, like a detective working a crime scene.

I think he's looking for turtles, but really he's looking for tracks.

The sand shelves steeply down to the surf. In the dark, the slope feels steep enough to slide down. The waves are big, brawling creatures, crashing ashore, surging up the berm and then clawing anything they catch back towards the deep. It is an intimidating sea. What must the Boxing Day tsunami have been like here? I wonder. *The ocean rearing up like a curved wall of smooth concrete . . .*

A young woman comes up to me in the darkness with cupped hands. She opens them to show a tiny fleck of iridescent blue, the bright blue of old glacial ice. It shifts and runs in her palm like a sprite.

'Put out your hand,' she says, so I do, and she pours the quantum of light into my palm.

'Sea-sparkle,' says Yuvan, who has joined us. 'Bioluminescence. Rare at this time of year, but in monsoon the sewage treatment plants get overwhelmed, so you get more of the algal bloom feeding on the nutrients in the effluent, and therefore the sea-sparkle is brighter. At such times, the whole ocean can glitter with it far out from the shore. A degraded magic, if ever I heard it.'

I pass the blue spark on, dabbing it with a finger into Yuvan's palm, and he carries it off in the darkness to give to someone else. Suddenly I'm back in the high clearing in the cloud-forest, with the mycelium shining in that deep equatorial darkness. *You can see* all *the veins of the forest lit up – you can see that* everything *is connected . . .*

'Last year I was for a fortnight or so with the Idu Mishmi people in the north of India,' says Yuvan when he catches me back up, 'to see if I could help their resistance to a mega-dam project planned for their river, the Dibang River. To them, it is a world-ending project: the river and the mountains around are the home of spirits, or *khinu*s. The Lepcha people in Sikkim are also protesting a dam project on their Teesta River; their language is soaked in river metaphors. If their river is blocked, so their language and stories will be also.'

glyaṅ: the human spine; also the course of a river or the flow of time

a-čin: uniting; as do two ridges of hills, or two rivers, or the veins of
   the body

dár: to give birth, to procreate; also to increase as a river does after rain

tsŭn: to join, to meet, to be confluent as rivers are

I hear a faint ringing of little bells. Five glass flasks float in the darkness ahead. Within the flasks, glowing points of white light roam and flicker. Are they fireflies? A man in black clothes materializes out of the night behind them as we approach, holding these strange alembics of light.

An older woman walks towards us, bearing a sparkling silver stick with which she points questioningly at my hands. Yuvan speaks to her in Tamil, gestures to her to walk on.

'She wants to tell your future, Rob. She will tap on your hand with the stick to do so. I told her there was no need.'

I wish now that I had let her do so.

Points of light are everywhere: the stars, the sea-sparkle, the clairvoyant's shimmering stick, the flasks with their fireflies . . .

The smell tells us before we see it. Death is in the air. There it is: the shell and rotting corpse of an Olive Ridley sea turtle. Arun pauses at the body, checks something briefly, murmurs something, strides on.

Yuvan and I stop beside her. Her nictitating membranes have closed over her eyes so they are milky grey. Her shell, bowed out like a conquistador's chest armour, is surprisingly small. There is a split running laterally across its layered hexagons.

'Another trawler strike, Rob. Either hull or the propellor. An impact death. You can see that this one has been counted by the Patrol. They tie a line of cord around a front flipper to show she's been added to the tally; that's what Arun just stopped to check for. Olive Ridleys are passive swimmers. They swim only just below the surface as they come in to breed. The fisherfolk can see them, and steer around them. The trawlers: no chance. They just plough right over them.'

We walk on. A second dead turtle. The sand around it is patterned and pilled. The ghost crabs – the clean-up crew – have begun their work.

'In the stories of many oceanic cultures,' says Yuvan, 'it's sea turtles who first taught humans how to navigate the sea and to wayfare its immensity. And now . . .' He shrugs in sadness.

To our right, the Indian Ocean stretches vast, black and illimitable. The night wind is strong, gusting across us, almost cold.

'Out there,' says Yuvan, 'not at all too far from shore, are deep-water canyons. These are sperm whale breeding grounds. Sperm whales sleep vertically in the water, as you'll know, Rob, and the fisherfolk have told me that once or twice they have reached the canyons in their boats and found there the grey noses of several sleeping sperm whales sticking out of the water – "like pillars of stone in the ocean", they said.'

I try to imagine the wonder and surprise of drifting in those vividly coloured wooden boats among those barnacled grey stones, that hanging sea-henge. I remember the British Navy's practice, during the age of wooden warships, of sewing the bodies of the dead into linen bags, each with a cannonball at the foot of the corpse, such that they were carried down to the ocean floor and there stood upright, buoyed by the gases of the decaying bodies but tethered to the seabed by the iron weight: swaying sea-ghouls, sometimes dozens together after a big battle.

'The fishers have also told me of an Indian Air Force fighter jet that crashed off this shore in the 1960s. The fisherfolk saved the pilot and now the wreckage has become a kind of coral reef, encrusted with life! They know to fish there, for the plane gathers species to itself.'

A third dead turtle, down on the wrack-line. This one is almost fresh, and there's no mark of a strike upon her. Her body is intact. She is perpendicular to the waves. Her flippers seem to have halted in mid-stroke. She might be alive – except that her eye-sockets are empty of their eyeballs.

Suddenly, the many deaths of the foreshore overwhelm me with sadness. I speak a spontaneous wish to myself: *Please, of all things, let me die before any of my children dies.* This eyeless traveller has made such a voyage to lay her eggs here, but she didn't even reach her nest before perishing.

'She still seems to be journeying, Yuvan,' I say.

'Yes, she is caught in that posture, here in the in-between. She still has places to go.'

'She's "seen the deep",' I say. 'That's the opening line of *The Epic of Gilgamesh*: "To those who have seen the deep, who have looked into the abyss." I've brought a copy of it with me for you. The "deep" is death, of course – or at least the unknown which lies beyond life.'

Yuvan is silent for a while. Then he says: 'There has been, I think, a narrowing of relatedness.'

I cannot tell if he is speaking of his sister's death, or some vaster attenuation, or both.

'To be is to be related,' he says. 'We must hugely widen the space of relations.'

He points skywards, out over the ocean. 'The Pleiades. They're my favourite constellation. It's an open system, you see. Usually when stars form they do so in a globular cluster – there's a main centre, and then smaller stars around. That's how gravity works. But the Pleiades, well, the cluster has seven sisters and a weak centre, so it's not concentrated around one point. It's a differently political star system.'

I laugh. 'An anti-hierarchical feminist assemblage?'

'Exactly!'

Then: 'There's Venus,' he adds suddenly.

'And there's Jupiter!' I say, pointing.

Yuvan pulls out his phone and summons a star app. He aims it skywards and whistles.

'Rob! There are *six* planets right now aligned in a near-perfect arc over us! Venus, Jupiter, Mercury, Saturn, Uranus and Mars. Mercury on the horizon, Mars at the zenith.'

The ocean is colossal to our east, the night sky cavernous above. We walk on beneath the great arc of planets.

It takes a further two hours before Arun stops and raises a hand to halt progress behind him. I wouldn't have seen it, but to Arun it is as clear as a path of light. There is a track in the sand: a central drag-line, with short, angled strokes to either side.

We follow it inland. The track weaves faintly between boats, and past heaps of rubbish tangled in fishing nets.

Where the sand is dry, Arun stops. He hands me the torch, takes out a thin metal stick, two feet or so long, and begins to probe the sand. On the third probe, he stops, drops to his knees and begins to dig with one cupped hand, scooping the sand behind him like a dog. I hold the torch-beam steady on the site. The shadows its strong light casts show a shallow indentation in front of Arun, roughly oval in shape and perhaps four feet at its longest and three at its widest. It is where a mother turtle has dug her nest.

Arun proceeds gently but steadily. He is up to his elbow in the sand, then to his shoulder, his head turned sideways. Now he has broken through into the cavity where the eggs lie. Now he smiles and lifts out two crinkled, sandy ping-pong balls, which roll together in his palm. A cry goes up from the group.

'Two!' says Arun. 'Rob – come here. You retrieve the rest of the eggs.'

I take Arun's place, kneeling on the sand, one hand flat for balance, reaching down with the other into the hole he has dug. A jolt of wonder pulses up my arm. I can feel dozens of eggs there, gritty, flexible and still warm. I bring one up, place it in the sand beside the hole. Akila, Arun's co-leader at the Turtle Patrol, puts it into her cloth bag.

'Three!' she calls out, counting them in.

'She can only have laid an hour or two ago,' says Arun. 'The eggs are still soft. In older nests the shells have begun to harden; it is more difficult to bring them out intact. Now – you must bring out two or three in each handful, Rob, or else we will be here all night! There are more nests to find, we must hope.'

I take over the count as I lift out the eggs. Each is a miracle to me. 'Sixty-six, sixty-seven, sixty-eight . . .' The count climbs. 'One hundred and twelve!' I use my hand to check around the sandy walls of the nesting cavity. No more – but what a haul!

We trudge on. Arun finds another nest, then another. The weight of eggs in the cloth bags grows. A young man falls into step beside me. We talk as we walk. He works inland, in a forest up towards the Deccan Plateau. He plants young trees, avoids snakes and tries to prevent the illegal felling of the old forest. But in the first months of each year, he comes to live in Chennai and becomes nocturnal: he walks all night, five nights a week, on Turtle Patrol.

'Why do you do this?' I ask him.

He looks puzzled at the question. 'For life,' he replies simply.

We trudge on. The sand ahead of us trembles with movement: hundreds of ghost crabs shuttling out, then scuttling back. We pass a man sleeping and a man shitting.

We reach a ruined turtle nest, dug up by dogs. Dozens of eggs are shredded in the sand, which is sticky and orange with their yolk. We find fifteen intact eggs and save them.

Half a mile further on, we pass a beachfront temple with a powerful white light on its spire. Lines of footprints fan out from the gate to the temple, leading to the sea, where they disappear. Littering the sand are chrysanthemum flowers and curved pieces of dark-red clay.

'This is where I've scattered the ashes of my stepfather, my uncle and my sister – all three of them,' says Yuvan. 'After cremation you come to the temple, bringing the ashes and bones that survive. You bring them in a terracotta urn, and you throw them into the sea. You must make sure the ashes dissolve into the sea, and then you must return without turning back. You *must not* look behind.'

A bat flutters out like a piece of charred paper from the temple, snatches a moth in the beam of white light.

'I find so many funerary practices, especially in the Hindu tradition, meaningless,' says Yuvan. 'But mixing death with the life of the ocean – well, that makes sense to me. You give life to the sea, and let the dead move again. Here in the intertidal zone is where the false opposition of life and death is undone.'

The riptide is audible: a sucking, swooshing roar.

'In the last couple of weeks of her life, when my sister was in a hospital room, moths would come in and rest on the walls there,' Yuvan says. 'She would ask me the names of those moths. Now, those moths don't have common names, and so I told her their scientific names. "I'm sorry I asked!" she would say. "Don't these moths have nice names you can tell me, not unpronounceable ones?" So I began to make up names for them, and for two or three of her last days I told her those names.'

He pauses.

'Then, during her funeral, I saw around twelve to fifteen species of moth which I've seen before, but which just oughtn't to have been there. They were on her photograph. Some were deep-forest species – *Trabala sp.*, *Thyas coronata* – they *shouldn't* have been at the ceremony, right here on the shore, so far from trees. I told myself: *Perhaps the garlands which people are bringing are attracting the moths?* But I've been to many other funerals, and that has never happened. For the next three days after I gave her ashes to the ocean, there were always moths around and on her photograph.'

It is darkest before dawn. Then the first light shows in the east. The moon starts its fade to a transparent silver hangnail. I dig out nest after nest, still awestruck by the task. The cloth bags bulge with eggs. Only a few of the original group are still with us now, including little Mithul, who is somehow still reverberating with energy and excitement.

We haven't seen a single live turtle, though we have dug out nearly a thousand eggs from ten nests. I am oddly pleased not to have met one of these secretive creatures: admiring that these slow-moving mothers have somehow ghosted their way between us, evading our patrol before slipping back into the night waters, their work on land done. That seems right.

To end the night, Arun, Yuvan and I decide to walk up the beach to where the River Adyar meets the sea. That seems a good place to finish this long river-journey we have taken. Maybe there will be a mother turtle there, I think.

The upper arc of the sun is rising red as a Coke can over the ocean.

The chromium-black waters of the Adyar lap and whisper.

The pumps of the upstream tanneries chug their effluent into the river's slow flow.

In time zones around the globe, members of the UN delegation are travelling to their gathering in New York, in what world leaders are calling 'the last chance for the oceans'.

We reach the final sweep of strand, where the sand is curved by the outflow of the Adyar as it reaches the ocean, salt mingling with fresh.

There, among shards of funerary clay pots, charred sticks, human turds and plastic bottles, we find two more intact turtle nests. I dig one out, my head swimming with tiredness now, my eyeballs gritty as if rolled in sand, but the marvel of it all still sending tingling charges up my arm as I lift eggs out of the sand, again and again.

When I look up, a man is wading across the Adyar estuary towards us, up to his waist in water. He is shirtless, wears a turban, and a bag is perched atop the turban.

'Those will be turtle eggs on his head,' says Arun. 'We sometimes get people like him finding a nest and knowing what to do. They come from very far, often at the end of a night's work, to bring the eggs to the hatchery. Such people ask for nothing.'

We trudge to the hatchery. It's an enclosure, fenced with finely woven wicker mesh, perhaps twenty yards long and ten yards wide, with a small hut in the corner. Little white posts with date markers on them are stuck into the ground in regular ranks. In the back right-hand corner are five plots with upturned willow baskets placed on them.

The hatchery resembles a small cemetery, but its logic is inverse: here, burial breeds life.

We hand-dig new nests in the sand for each clutch. It is painstaking, time-taking, loving work.

As I dig, I think back over what I have seen of water's journeys here in Chennai. The blue, braiding channels of the inland rivers, nourished by the monsoon rains. The vast bird-city at Vedanthangal. The poisoned marshes, the murdered Cooum, the dying Adyar, the brutal sacrifice zone of Ennore Creek. River ghosts and river monsters, with angels fluttering around them. Now this: the ancient creaturely rituals of the coast, taking new form.

And so much life, such resilience! The mudskippers on Ennore's shore. The fruit bats improvising new roosts. The urban forest springing back out of nearly nothing. Yuvan's apartment, thrumming and humming socially with insects. What had Yuvan told me? *There are more than four thousand, two hundred species recorded within Chennai's limits, Rob. Life finds a way . . .* And here on the beach – where the Adyar reaches the ocean and Yuvan has strewn the ashes of his sister, his uncle and his stepfather – the sea turtles weave between outboards and piles of net to nest and lay, driven by instincts developed in the Cretaceous.

I have learned a new kind of water literacy from Yuvan: a terraqueous one in which the opposition between river and land is undone, replaced with a metamorphic vision of 'river' as a shape-shifting being, never only itself – now ghost, now monster; now vanished, now resurrected – and always in conversation and interanimation with both earth and human body. If the chief mode of the cloud-forest was branching or reticulation, then that of Chennai's water is surely circulation, I think. What would *its* grammar of animacy look like? Metaphor would be at its core, surely: the trope which transforms, joins like to unlike. It would need to be a grammar of the ecotone and the interzone, rich with transitives and reciprocities, trembling always on the brink; one in which flowing and knowing are indissoluble – a mode that gives on and gives back, rhymes and echoes, moves in arcs and crescents, works with words which lend sounds each to the other, blend water and ground, share weather, shift together; a liquid language, restless and deliquescent.

The binary-breaking Tamil water-words Yuvan has told me ring in my mind: *seru* (slush, especially of dark organic sediments), *sadhuppu* (marsh), *paraval* (floodplains), *uppalam* (salt pans), *eer nilam* (tidal flats). There's something here, I think, something in the work Yuvan and his friends are doing – in their egalitarian, uncategorical reimaginings of water and life – in which I might place faith. How we imagine the matter of water *matters*. To recognize its ceaseless migrancy is to recognize that we live in a fundamentally decentralized world, engaged always in multiple forms of relation – and that power can be crucial in determining the capacity of those relations to animate or to exhaust their participants. The hydrological cycle comprises violence as well as vapour, injustice as well as precipitation. Chennai has complicated my sense of what Los Cedros had shown me: that the 'aliveness' of a river or forest isn't endogenous to the object, a property possessed by a bounded body; rather it is a process which relocates 'life' to the interface and within the flux of which, at best, we understand ourselves to be extended generously outwards into a vast community of others. How had Yuvan put it? *My own spiritual observation has been that a small 'self' suffers and causes suffering, that a love of the living world lets single identities and selfhoods expand and encompass other beings, entities and whole landscapes, such that the self becomes a spacious thing . . .'*

There on my hands and knees above the egg nest I'm digging, I cry secretly into the sand.

It takes an hour for Arun to be satisfied with our new nests. Then we lift the eggs from their bags, lower them down in twos and threes, and back-fill gently with sand – as the mother turtle would do – being careful not to collapse the space beneath. We count the eggs back in, as we counted them out.

I'm filling the last of my nests when I hear Arun call: 'Rob! Come here – see!'

I look up. He's crouched by one of the upturned wicker baskets in the back right of the hatchery, peering through the lattice.

'This is where the first eggs of the season were buried, forty days ago exactly, Rob. And now . . . look!'

He lifts off the basket with the flourish of a Parisian waiter raising a silver cloche for a favoured guest.

And there is a single turtle hatchling, struggling free of the sand, flippers clicking like a wind-up bath toy.

'Oh!'

'Our first of the year, Rob! You're just in time to meet her. Go on – pick her up!'

I lift her tentatively onto my palm and she swims there on my skin, every aeons-old instinct in her minutes-old mind urging her seawards and into the deep.

She is a perfect miniature of the adult sea turtles we have seen on the beach – except that she is alive. She's four inches long, gun-metal grey, and every detail of her is present and finely picked out. The texture of her skin is medieval, like tunic leather. I carry her in cupped hands out of the hatchery and towards the tideline.

'Don't take her into the surf,' says Yuvan. 'It's vital that hatchlings use their flippers to find the way; it helps them gain crucial strength to swim.'

I set her down on the wet sand. The red rising sun turns the sea to lava. I feel tears come to my eyes again, and dip my head to hide this from Arun and Yuvan.

'Don't get too excited, Rob,' says Arun. 'She'll probably be gull food within the hour.'

She drags herself seawards over the wet sand. The first wave carries her back up the beach, and deposits her further inland. She struggles seawards again. The second wave does the same. Then the third.

I move to intervene, but Arun stays me with the lift of a finger.

'She'll get there. Don't worry.'

The fourth wave comes at an angle, picks her up, then sluices her down the slope. The fifth lifts her and backwashes her into the break. I catch the last glimpse of a tiny grey shadow in the inner curl of a wave – and she is gone.

Yuvan, Arun and I wander back from the ocean, towards where the city laps at the beach. I'm stunned by tiredness and happiness.

The Adyar sweats in the rising heat.

In Pulicat Lagoon, several hundred flamingos stand in their own reflections, doubled like playing-card queens, blushing the water pink.

Far out to sea, thousands of mother turtles are swimming with silent certainty towards the beaches of Chennai.

In Yuvan's apartment, Margaret steps into Yazhini's room to lay fresh flowers before her photograph.

Terns scissor past us, all knifepoints and origami folds.

We walk through the main street of the fisher village, passing between two huge speakers mounted on poles. The speakers are booming out a medley of music and prayers: a dawn reveille.

Wake up! Wake up!

The Springs

(Spring)

It's spring at the springs. Weeks too early, but that's how things are these days.

The cherry plum was the first to go, in mid February – the crack that started the blossom avalanche. Now the blackthorn's getting in on the act, and the bird cherries too, and miles of hedgerow are slo-mo exploding in white and pink, a fortnight-long firework display of carpel and pistil. Someone says to me: *If all the trees did this for one day only each year, the whole city would stop what it was doing and come to watch, wouldn't it?* Yes, I answer; yes, they would. Soon enough the hawthorn will be blossoming too, with that strange, sweet smell of rot and riot all at once. Suppuration or celebration? It depends on your mood on the day you smell it.

Since I returned to England from sun-parched Chennai, there's been rain: drenching, river-making rain. Every morning, we open the curtains to find rain pinstriping the air. March will be the wettest in forty years.

In Lewes, in the south of England, the council passes a motion recognizing the rights of the River Ouse. The councillor proposing the motion says: *People feel they are not being heard, and in particular that the* river *is not being heard.* The councillor says: *This is a way of giving the river a voice as a single entity, from source to sea.*

One Sunday, the rain dries up and the sun shows itself. 'Will you come with me to Nine Wells Wood?' I ask Will. 'I want to show you something.'

He looks wary. He hasn't wanted to go to the wood since last summer, when the springs had nearly died.

'It's a good thing,' I say. 'Trust me.'

'OK, Dad. Can we cycle?'

Will has learned to ride a bike late, and it's still a big thing for him. He's ten now. He's eager and proud that he can cycle, even on a bike that's too large for him and makes him seem littler to me than he is.

A strong wind; clouds racing eastwards. A red kite bucks and judders as it yaws into the gusts.

There are seven magpies in the grass of the field, bouncing and beady-eyed, bent over something red and glistening. *Seven for a secret never to be told.* An eighth magpie on the path ahead of us cocks its head, watches our arrival. Will tings his bell at it and it flaps off, cackling.

'I was worried about running it over, Dad.'

'Don't worry about magpies. They know how to handle themselves. They're total pirates.'

I've recently been sent a map showing where archaeologists have found knapped flints on the lower slope of White Hill, right next to the springs, and dated them to as long as nine thousand years ago. I tell Will about it as we cycle. 'Before we go into the wood, let's find some prehistoric flints,' I say.

So we field-walk, slow-paced, hinged at our waists, heads down. It's a Mesolithic treasure hunt. Will holds my hand at first, then shakes free and starts to hop about in the mud, picking up every flint he finds, running to me for identification. I explain how hard it is to tell what's been made by human hand and what by chance; about how the strike of a plough or a hoe on a flint nodule can produce shards that look similar to knapping. White Hill has been farmed for thousands of years since the hunter-gatherers were here. I promise him I'll send photos of the flints we've found to the archaeologists, to see if they can give us a positive ID.

Pockets clinking with flint flakes, we walk into the wood. The needle-song of a wren stitches the air. In the wind and sun, the wood is a light box. The big beeches, with their early green leaves, form a roof made of stained glass: a Gothic church interior, constantly shifting and reconfiguring itself.

'You go ahead, Will,' I tell him. 'Go see how the springs are doing.' He runs off along the path towards the hollow in the chalk. He stops at its edge, looks back, smiling. He gives a double thumbs-up.

'There's so much water, Dad! And it's so clear! You can't even see it.'

It's true. The springs are flowing well. The water level in the pool is up. Continuous light-ripples stir its surface at the edges, marking the spring sites. The centre of the pool is still as metal, though, and reflects the sky above. As we watch, a crow seems to swim across it.

We slither down the steep bank to the edge of the pool. The chalk and marl have turned to sticky clag in the rain. There are deer slots in the mud.

'Look,' I say. 'This is what I wanted to show you, Will. The springs are running again.'

I dip a hand into the water, and a volt of cold runs up my arm. Then – an uncanniness. A blue palm in my palm, fingers of water meeting and lacing mine. A fluttering, an encounter; a single spring, making itself felt.

'You try,' I say.

He does.

'What does it feel like?' I ask him.

Quick as a flash: 'Life!'

I laugh.

We launch little leaf boats onto the riffle where the spring rises. I try to rig one with a tiny hawthorn mast and ivy-leaf sail, but it sinks almost immediately and Will mocks me. He launches one of his own, a curled-up brown beech leaf which sits on the water like a coracle. 'Float, you scallywag!' he says to the boat. It obeys orders.

'That one's going well,' I say to him. It's pushed by the current of the spring out into the centre of the pool, where it begins to turn downstream.

We make three more leaf boats, and Will places them on the water one after the other, giving a cry or *ha!* of encouragement for each as he launches it.

The springs pulse on. The leaf boats spin in the current.

PART III

The Living River

(Nitassinan/Canada)

We've always known the river is alive.

Rita Mestokosho (2022)

Time isn't just a linear arrow, but rather a swirling stream — so at any point 'in time' a river can also connect us to its past and our futures . . .

Anne Poelina (2021)

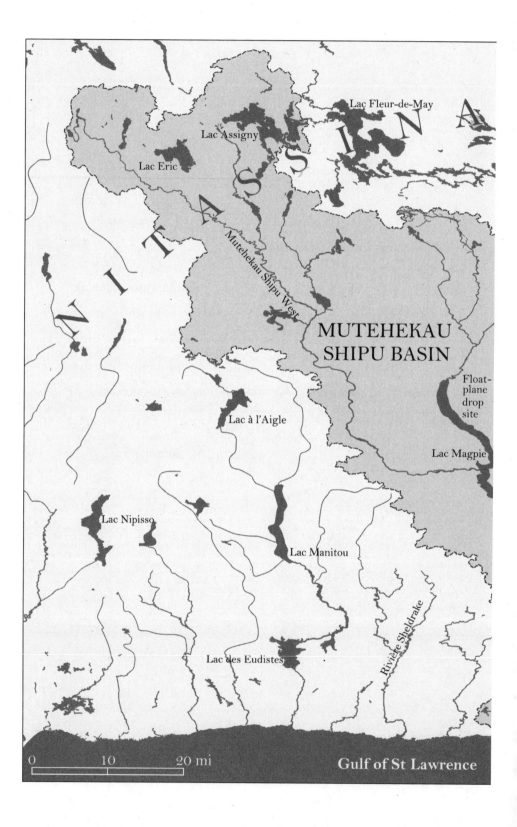

Lac Fleur-de-May

Lac Assigny

NITASSINAN

Lac Eric

Mutehekau Shipu West

MUTEHEKAU
SHIPU BASIN

Float-
plane
drop
site

Lac à l'Aigle

Lac Magpie

Lac Nipisso

Lac Manitou

Rivière Sheldrake

Lac des Eudistes

0   10   20 mi

Gulf of St Lawrence

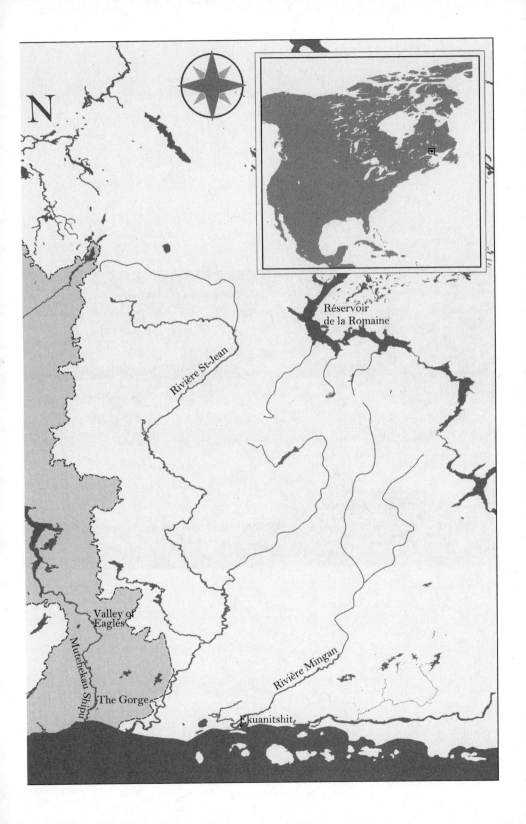

Spruce, pine, alder, rowan. Waxwings on the rowan.

Goldenrod, bear's tails, asters.

In fifty-three miles, keep straight on.

Blue ridgelines. Silver wisps of fireweed seed star the air.

Rivière Ste-Anne. Unnamed river. Rivière du Sault. Rivière du Gouffre.

Porcupine, dead on the hard shoulder: a chequerboard pancake with quills shuddering in the side-blast of each passing vehicle.

Rivière Malbaie. Rivière Noire.

Haze in the air out to sea. No wind now. The Gulf of St Lawrence stretches away in a gleaming silver sheet to the south, sea phasing imperceptibly into sky. It seems like we could hang a right and just motor out across the water and straight off the edge of the world.

In forty-two miles, keep straight on.

It's August, and I have travelled to eastern Canada to meet a living, threatened river who flows south from deep in the roadless boreal forest up near the Quebec–Labrador border, down to the sea at the Gulf of St Lawrence. With me is an old friend, Wayne Chambliss. Our plan is to follow that river – in kayak and on foot – for a hundred miles or so south through the forest, to its mouth at the sea: a hard journey of ten to fourteen days, if all goes well.

To the Innu people of the little coastal township of Ekuanitshit, close to its mouth, the river's name is Mutehekau Shipu, which may be translated either as 'the river who flows between square, rocky cliffs' or 'the river of sharp rocks and steep banks'. This is the name by which I will call it. In English, the river is known as the Magpie.

To reach the mouth of the Mutehekau Shipu, you must drive east and fast for thirteen hours from Montreal, along the straight highway that hems the north shore of the Gulf of St Lawrence.

At Saguenay Fjord, after four hours on the road, we roll onto a car ferry. The air is bright as tin.

On the lower vehicle deck a man prowls agitatedly round and round his soft-top car. WELCOME TO THE NEW WORLD ORDER is stencilled along the back of its trunk. The rear windscreen is thick with stickers bearing weirdly prudish redactions: F*CK YOU GRETA THUNBERG. F*CK LEGAULT. F*CK TRUDEAU. Centre bottom of the windshield is a black Christian cross, atop which sits a black Prussian Iron Cross. It's a grim gumbo of hate.

The ferry-wake churns milk in the blue water of the fjord. Two eagles spiral the thermals that rise off the rock cliffs. Then – a white lozenge, shifting with great speed below the surface of the water, three hundred yards away.

'Wayne! There!'

A second lozenge, then a white fin breaking the water. A third, further to the south. Other people on the viewing deck are turning now, pointing and wowing.

Beluga whales: three of them, surfacing and sinking, keeping the ferry company. Cream in the water, forming and re-forming.

I'd heard belugas might be in the fjord, but I still can't credit the marvel of it in the moment. A creature I never thought I'd see in my lifetime – a white whale, a being of Arctic waters, fellow traveller with leopard seals and narwhals – right here, casually cavorting off the starboard bow of a diesel-stink car ferry four hours east of Montreal. My heart's in my throat. My belly tumbles with the joy of it.

We roll off the car ferry.

In one hundred and eight miles, keep straight on.

Rivière Portneuf. Rivière du Sault aux Cochons. Rivière de Papina-chois. Lac Muskrat. Lac à Tabac. Low Lake.

Pale whalebacks of ice-smoothed rock surface and vanish in the shallow bays: deep-time belugas.

'What would happen,' says Wayne, 'if we could record and under-stand the songs of the whales, extending back to the deepest antiquity of their species? Would their songs be bardic or historical? Would they document the rises and falls of ocean levels? Would they be carto-graphic, mapping the routes of these immense sub-surface canyons and mountain ranges through which whales must steer on their subma-rine wanderings?'

'Whale-cries as . . . song-maps?' I ask.

'Absolutely. We know for certain that whale communities teach one another. There's the now-famous example of the orcas in the Gibraltar Straits who have shared both the knowledge of, and at some level the purpose behind, attacking the keels and rudders of sailing boats in the Straits. Or the example of sperm whales in the early decades of whal-ing, who taught each other to flee from whaling boats after the first few seasons of slaughter, and who then developed their counter-strategies not only laterally within social groups but also intergenerationally, with parents teaching calves.'

Wayne and I have both been reading new findings about whale song and whale speech, coming out of a research group called Project CETI, the Cetacean Translation Initiative, where marine biologists have used AI to analyse datasets of whale recordings, and begun to isolate language units, building and corroborating both a possible syntax and lexis for whale speech.

'It feels,' I say to Wayne, 'as if we're on the brink of a great and long-overdue unlearning of supposed human superiority in terms of language. That we're close now to opening our ears to the countless idioms and dialects, the vast broth of other species' speeches, within which we've unwittingly lived and moved since the beginning.'

'Just imagine if we *do* become able to "speak whale",' Wayne says.

'What new responsibilities would declare themselves to us? Speaking whale – or any other species' or genus's language – would ask many hard questions both about how we act as interlocutors and about the existing forms of communication within a given species or community.'

'Like, do whales tell jokes?' I say, flippantly.

'That is a *very* good question,' replies Wayne, seriously. 'For if they don't, if they only speak either sincerely or instrumentally, then might the humans who are newly able to "speak whale" actually *introduce* the concept of irony *to* the whale world, setting into motion a further twist in the Viconian spiral of time?'

Wayne pauses briefly, then rip-raps on.

'Has that already happened for the whales? Do they already have a venerable and sophisticated culture in this immense Atlantis that they prowl around in, one which is rich in jokes and ironies – or will that be something that *we* introduce from without, contaminating their communication system, helping to turn them against one another? In what ways would our human intervention as whale-speakers disrupt the minds of these creatures, who we're only now *dimly* coming to recognize as possessing a full, robust cognitive alternative to our species?'

Wayne's cooking now. Conversations with him often run like this. A largely rhetorical question: the setting of the riddle. A slow build-up of thought-speed. Then a gathering of momentum, accelerating into a careening, connection-making riff. Especially when he's got momentum up, but also most of the time, Wayne's speech is almost devoid of the hesitations, the *umms* and *ahhhs* and *likes* and all the rest of the verbal lint that sticks to most of our tongues. Talking with him is a wild ride.

Unlike many very good speakers, Wayne is a very good listener. There are also long periods of silence, which may last upwards of an hour. Words pour from Wayne, and then they don't.

Other times, something more like 'Wayne Radio' occurs: the mouth-vent opens and psychic convection currents start bringing up weird exfluvia from his brain's core–mantle boundary: funny noises, repetitions of words, bizarre accents, abysmal puns, arcane trivia, fragments of old poems, etc. A mental Mulligan-stew monologue, to which I am more than happy to provide an audience, especially on long drives.

We pull over in a sidetrack to stretch our legs. A bird with a voice of water trills on, unseen. Vast triple-wagoned trucks thunder eastwards, shaking earth and whipping tree branches with their back-blast. They're contractor transports coming in from Quebec City and other points west, heading for the Romaine Project: the vast hydropower construction being completed on the next big river east of the Mutehekau Shipu. Another thunders by, setting a little spiral dust-devil roaming briefly on the hard shoulder.

The forest hustles tight to the edge of the road. The understorey is so dense with branch and creeper that it would surely be impossible to move through. I think of how hard it will be if we have to abandon our descent of the river in an emergency, and try to move on foot.

We drive in near silence for thirty miles or so. Johnny Flynn comes on the sound system – *All that I have is the river, the river is always my home* – and I'm back again in high camp in the cloud-forest, firelight tigering the clearing.

A southerly wind has risen over the hours we've been driving, and now it's whipping up blowhole snorts and spouts of wave on the rocky shores.

Suddenly, Wayne Radio blurts out: 'The 1811 and 1812 earthquakes in the New Madrid Seismic Zone rang bells in Boston, threw graves and the bodies they held up to the surface, and caused the Mississippi River to temporarily flow backwards.'

'I call bullshit on the Mississippi fact.'

'You are incorrect,' says Wayne, reaching for his phone.

With Wayne I always am.

Lac Éden. Salmon Hole. Ruisseau des Chouinard.

Then the dams begin.

Réservoir Pipmuacan. Réservoir aux Outardes-2. Réservoir Manic-1.

~

You might think it impossible to drown a river – but a dam can do this.

Since the 1880s, the complex hydrology of Quebec – a province more than eight times the size of England – has been steadily converted into a vast electrical machine, which now generates, stores and releases power from reservoirs that are the graves of rivers. The largest of these reservoirs is around 770 square miles in area, and floods the circular impact crater left by a vast asteroid which slammed into the Earth some 214 million years ago, splashing rock around like water. The James Bay hydroelectric project in north-west Quebec involves a land area the size of New York State, re-directed four major rivers into new watersheds, and created a chain-reservoir so vast that it has changed not only the weather but also the climate of the region, altering annual rainfall patterns, affecting cloud formation, delaying growing seasons and bringing harsher Arctic weather to south-central Quebec.

Hydro-Québec is the state company at the head of this biome-scale repurposing, and it is presently the world's fourth-largest supplier of hydro-power. In May 2011, Hydro-Québec and the provincial government announced the multi-billion-dollar 'Plan Nord', or Northern Plan: a twenty-five-year scheme to 'industrialize the remote region north of the 49th Parallel' – one of the largest intact ecosystems in the world.

Among the problems with the Plan Nord was that the entire territory under consideration was unceded territory, belonging primarily to the Innu, the Cree and the Inuit. Indigenous presence in the region dates back some eight thousand years: rivers have throughout that time been the blue highways of the region – routes of travel running roughly north to south, made of ice in the long winter and of water in spring, summer and autumn. Rivers have also been larder, pharmacy and 'school without limits' since early in the Holocene: a time when the remnants of the great Laurentide Ice Sheet were still present in the region as pulsing, shrinking blue islands of ice, besieged by warmth; a time when the land itself, depressed for well over a million years by the weight of the ice sheet, began its slow, terpsichorean uplift in a process known by geologists as 'isostatic rebound'.

Of the sixteen rivers in Quebec listed officially as 'large rivers', fourteen were dammed by 2012. By 2020 the unceded territory of the Innu people – called 'Nitassinan' in Innu-aimun, meaning 'our land' – contained fifteen hydro-complexes of varying size.

One of the smaller hydro-complexes was located on the Mutehekau Shipu. In 2005 a forty-megawatt hydro-project was approved for the river, sited around five hundred yards upstream of its mouth. Construction of the dam and associated infrastructure took three years. The project was formally opened on 20 June 2008. It created power for distant cities and, temporarily, jobs and income for local municipalities and townships. It also significantly raised the river's level for two miles upstream of the barrage.

After constructing the first dam on the Mutehekau Shipu, Hydro-Québec began to target the river in its strategic planning. It estimated that a multi-dam project on the Mutehekau Shipu could add 850 megawatts to the network – and so it proposed building two big additional dams on the forty miles or so of the lower river, south of the vast natural lake, Lac Magpie, which breaks the upper from the lower Mutehekau Shipu.

A vision of what this multi-damming would do to the Mutehekau Shipu was easily available, just sixty miles or so east, where the immense and wild Romaine River once ran.

The Romaine is now the Mutehekau Shipu's ghost sister.

In 2009 Hydro-Québec began the construction of four rock-filled retaining dams on the lower 125 miles of the river, along with four new power stations, four vast associated reservoirs, a ninety-mile-long access road driven through the boreal forest, and huge transmission lines and pylons running westwards for hundreds of miles through forest and muskeg, in order to move the generated energy to the centres of need. Labour camps with gyms and supermarkets were built deep in the boreal forest to house, feed and entertain the thousands of workers involved in the construction.

Today, the bulk of the lower Romaine River lies beneath those four reservoirs: the Grandes Chutes, which once roared below the Romaine-1 hydroelectric station; the salmon spawning beds; the traditional portages, campsites and fishing grounds used by Innu people for millennia – all drowned. Sustained protests against the Romaine Project by Innu river defenders were ignored or suppressed. 'Find their river and slit its throat,' writes the Mojave American poet Natalie Diaz in her poem 'exhibits from The American Water Museum'.

In the 1940s and 1950s an American geoscientist called Arthur Newell Strahler developed a means of numerically measuring the branching complexity of streams and rivers. That method is now known as the Strahler Stream Order, and is based on a hierarchy of tributaries. In effect, Strahler reimagined all rivers as trees: arborescent structures in which the mouth of a river is the root-point of its central trunk, with each significant branch, then branch of a branch, then branch of a branch of a branch, adding a number to the value. A stream with no tributaries, running directly from source to sea, therefore has a Strahler number of 1. The Amazon scores 12 – the highest of any river. The Romaine River had a Strahler number of 7, just one fewer than the Ohio River, which is more than three times its length.

A tree is a river, bound in bark.

In the summer of 2023, after fourteen years' work, construction on the Romaine began to wind up. At the opening of the Romaine-4 dam, the Band Chief of the Innu of Ekuanitshit, Jean-Charles Piétacho – a man widely respected in the region for his integrity and long-term leadership – addressed workers and Hydro-Québec executives. He acknowledged the money and jobs that had flowed to Innu people as a result of the Romaine Complex, but he also cautioned against the drive for more dams, and the costs that the death of a river had brought to his people.

'I would have liked to invite the elder of our community here,' said Piétacho, 'because her home and the home of her children was flooded by the dams. But it would have been too uncomfortable for her. I, in fact, am the last who walked and portaged this river. I want to recognize your engineering genius – but we also have our own geniuses in our nation. Our rivers, the forest, the mountains: they are our monuments – our monuments to protect.'

Hydro-Québec's Declaration of Commitment to the First Nations and the Inuit Nation says: *We salute the resiliency of Indigenous peoples.*

The winding-up of the Romaine Project substantially increased the threat to the life of the Mutehekau Shipu. Transmission lines from the Romaine dams crossed the Mutehekau Shipu: the means of moving the power to the centres of need already existed. It would also be highly cost-effective to break down the Romaine construction camps, and then relocate them westwards to the Mutehekau Shipu, rather than to build them from scratch.

Hungry corporate eyes watched the river from boardrooms in Quebec City and Montreal. Two more dams would turn the entirety of the lower Mutehekau Shipu into a series of chained reservoirs. The preparatory forestry work needed for those reservoirs, and the construction of the labour camps, would require the creation of main support roads thrusting deep into the forest. Off those main highways would come tributary roads, and off those tributary roads further tributary roads. This arborescent road network would have a Strahler Number of at least 3.

Hydro-Québec's New Social Acceptability Framework says: *Your concerns are evolving, and so are we!*

The proposed multi-dam complex would triple-kill the Mutehekau Shipu. It would flay its banks, drown it and entomb it – and would radiate its grey pall of damage outwards into the forests and mountains that surround the lower river.

From 2009 onwards, Innu communities and others in the region watched the slow death of the Romaine and its catchment. Corruption allegations and scandals enmired Hydro-Québec and its contracting processes. Though employment levels rose significantly in the region during the construction of the Romaine Project, so did crime, divorce, social inequality, homelessness and sexually transmitted infection rates.

Over the years, a resolve began to build among both Innu and settler communities to resist Hydro-Québec's damming plans for the Mutehekau Shipu. They would save the river's life.

In 2018 the defence of the Mutehekau Shipu began in earnest, spearheaded by the small Innu community at Ekuanitshit – and a new-old idea moved centre-stage in the struggle.

~

Wayne and I drive on, towards the Mutehekau Shipu, towards the Romaine – towards the living river and the drowned river.

Hour after hour on the grey ribbon of road. Always the forest to our left, always the sea to our right. I have a growing sense of the immensity of this country, and the delusion of resource inexhaustibility, of infinite damage-absorption, that its scale must induce.

Pylon lines marching over the hills, carrying their interconnectors in each metal hand. Boulder archipelagos on a silver-mirror sea. A brass sun. The St Lawrence turning from river to sea; fresh dying slowly into salt.

I'm fading. Wayne seems inexhaustible. Light from the lowering sun pops and flares in the rear windscreen.

There's spray-can graffiti on the roadside rocks where dynamite boreholes show the blast-history. *Love you Jan! Young Innu Mental Health! Merde & LOLs!*

Cars thinning out. Houses thinning out. Always the forest, a massed presence of dark spires to the north. Rivers increasing in frequency, falling steeply off the escarpment to the north in tea-tinted foam. River after river, drawing our eyes uphill and inland.

Are all these rivers alive? They sure as hell look it.

The rock over which the rivers crash is called the Canadian Shield by geologists. The Shield has the oldest surface rock in the world. Two of the most ancient rock samples that exist were taken from here: one dated to 4 billion years ago, the other to 4.8 billion – a mere 300 million years younger than the planet itself.

Moose fences line the road. 'Have you ever seen a bull moose?' I ask Wayne.

'In the Chernobyl Zone of Alienation, yes.'

'Of course in the Chernobyl Zone of Alienation.'

I can't now recall exactly when or how I first met Wayne. I do know that his mind is one of the two or three most unusual I've encountered; that he is always turning perspectives inside out, or holding ideas upside down and shaking them, to see what falls out of their pockets. I am confident that he is the only person in history to have been buried alive on opposite sides of the planet. On one of those occasions, he was inhumed while wearing a suit of mithril armour previously used in the filming of Peter Jackson's *Lord of the Rings* trilogy, in order that a portrait might be made of him in the medium of ground-penetrating radar.

Wayne has a steel-trap intellect and a frankly supernatural memory. He once began reciting a four-hundred-line poem to me which he'd last read on paper twenty years earlier. He reached around line 220 before hesitating for the first time – and was furious with himself for doing so. Both of his shoulders are shiny white with knife-cut keloid tissue, more scar than non-scar, from a period of his life to which he alludes only rarely and briefly. He's the son of a Marine Corps fighter-pilot, so as a kid his family shifted around from air station to air station. He moved home fourteen times in eighteen years: no stability, no permanence. The military-nomadic upbringing sank deep into Wayne's bones. He's the most restless person I know. He once spent a year living in a motel. He reckons to have accrued over a million Hertz points in rental vehicles. Sometimes, those rental cars have served as his mobile home.

The one place to which Wayne developed a strong attachment in his childhood was Naples, where he went to high school in the Phlegraean Fields, known in Italian as the 'Campi Flegrei': a large and geologically active caldera comprising numerous craters and fumaroles. This is a landscape subject to ongoing bradyseismic liftings and lowerings, as the magma chamber of the caldera fills and empties over many thousands of years, in a kind of slow, orange earth-breathing. Uplift events in particular produce there what are known as 'earthquake swarms': hundreds or thousands of small seismic events occurring in rapid sequence. It was Campi Flegrei that seeded in Wayne a life-long fascination with the intersection of geology and geography.

Wayne is fifty or so now. His eyes are rheumy; they've seen a lot. In a wind they weep, but not with tears – he says he hasn't cried since he was fourteen. He's got no spare flesh on him. He looks somewhat like Christopher Walken: the same slow-lowering eyelids, shield-shaped face and at times what seems to be an air of restrained menace. He dresses pool-hall shabby: grubby jeans, a hoodie, a threadbare baseball cap. If you saw him in a seminar room, sitting quiet and scruffy at the back, you might think he's hanging on to the class by his fingernails. That would be a great mistake. He's a man who would like to know everything there is available to know – Leibniz in a hoodie, Pliny in sneakers – if only to be certain that he'd scouted the full perimeters of the humanly knowable, but without the faintest presumption that this might be all there was to comprehend about the world.

If you met Wayne cold, on a bad day, you might think there was a meanness to him, and you'd be wary. You'd be right and wrong. He is mean – but only to himself. He *scours* himself for weakness. He runs full system-scans of his body, his mind, persistently humming away in the background of the principal functions. If he finds a flaw, he castigates himself for it and drives it out. He has the loyalty of granite to his friends. As far as I can tell, demons circle Wayne in holding patterns, though he rarely allows them opportunity to land, except perhaps in the wolf hours of the night. Mostly, he keeps moving. His body has kept the score, though. He is rasputined with injuries. Those shiny shoulders. Multiple belly and chest scars. Blue-grey stick-and-poke tattoos. The entrance-and-exit wounds in his right leg where the thin spike of a metal security fence went through his calf as he exfiltrated himself at high speed from an abandoned British military bunker complex in Malta, pursued by a squatter with a shotgun.

During his many moves over the past quarter-century, and doubtless during the many moves that his restless life still holds, one constant is a heavy wooden chest which Wayne committedly carries from place to place. In it, he keeps various objects that he considers significant in one way or another. These objects include, he tells me, a bone of unknown species from the oracular complex of the Cumaean Sibyl; sundry talismanic stones, including one from the ruins of Plato's Academy, one from the classical entrance to Hell, and a birthstone (for multicellular organisms) that formed in the ocean contemporaneously with the first eukaryotes, circa 1.7 billion years ago; the knife used to carve a scar-cartoon on his back immediately prior to a situation that resulted, ultimately, in him comforting one of Helmut Newton's models in court; his last and first words as a poet; a postcard of Ingrid Bergman; two dream-catchers, both retired after particularly nasty oneiric episodes; a compass he won in a crooked card game with a guy named Little Elk, just before utterly losing his way in life . . . and so on. Wayne has never unpacked the box for another living soul. His plan, if he chooses death or senses its undeferrable approach, is to burn the chest and everything in it. In the meantime, he finds that his nearly three-decade experience of keeping the chest has disclosed to him a life-rule which he recommends to others, including me: *If you're going to open Pandora's Box, make sure to stand behind the lid when you do so.*

Wayne worked in the GIS (Geographic Information System) industry for a decade or so, visualizing and analysing geographic data. Over the last few years he has become what I can only describe as a 'geomancer'. A 'human-geographer land-artist' would, I guess, be the more conventional label, but that doesn't get too close to what Wayne is doing. He works at and with the conceptual outer limits of Earth systems and processes, trying to find ways of making the planet's larger-scale geophysical phenomena humanly legible, bodily tangible.

He has a long list of projects he wishes to undertake as part of this necessarily endless apprenticeship: the list ranges from the geomantically grandiose to the downright bizarre, and includes harnessing a Fata Morgana to turn the lower troposphere into a general-purpose projection system, repairing hydraulically fractured rock using gold summoned from hydrothermal depths ('landscape-scale kintsugi', as he puts it), and boiling an egg using moonlight.

For the time being, Wayne mostly wants to bury himself naked and alive in the earth inside the caldera at the Phlegraean Fields while an earthquake swarm is under way, allowing the waves to propagate through his maximally seismo-exposed body. Ninety-eight per cent of the circa 31,000 earthquakes shivering the caldera over the past two decades are below 2.5 on the Richter scale, and therefore cannot easily be felt by humans above ground. To experience them in new ways, Wayne plans to dive beneath the surface of the volcanic crater and wait for quakes to occur. In preparation for this prolonged interment, he has been training himself with a series of increasingly arduous 'inhumation studies'. One of these involved his partner, Eva, burying him in the backyard of their house in Austin, Texas, for half an hour while she gardened around him, with only the tip of a snorkel marking his living grave. Another involved two friends burying him in the Mojave Desert and then trying to induce weak seismicity by firing a 16-gauge shotgun into the dirt nearby. I have declined the invitation to be involved in a repeat exercise.

Heterodox, kind, weird, super-smart and tough – I couldn't think of a better person with whom to make this journey. So I'd asked Wayne if he'd like to come along, and he'd said yes and that was that.

Except that wasn't quite that. A few months earlier he'd lost a dear friend, a novelist and writer named Paul, to cancer. Paul was brilliant, a flare in the sky that just hung there and glowed, didn't fade or wink out – until the disease consumed him. He died on a cold January day in Poughkeepsie, and Wayne helped bury him. By the time we left for the river, Wayne was still grieving, curled around a ganglion of sadness.

Not long after Paul's death, Wayne sent me a photo of him and
Paul, taken on film in the high desert, one dusk near the beginning of
the century. Paul stands tall, slender, bespectacled and hands on hips,
wearing an immaculately ironed, white collared shirt and sandy slacks.
He looks shy and wise. He smiles slightly, wryly. Wayne is in a blue
lumberjack shirt, long-haired and already balding, off-kilter, a wild,
flattened look in his eyes. In the background: violet dusk, chapparal
scrub, a barbed-wire fence. It's all slightly out of focus – wind-blurred,
light-blurred – as if the camera had snatched at something fleeting,
which of course it had.

Since Paul's death, Wayne has been preoccupied with the idea of
encountering him again. The *katabasis* – the classical descent to the
underworld such as that narrated in Virgil's *Aeneid* – has long fascinated Wayne: a journey to meet spectres and shades. When he tells me
about this wish, I think of Giuliana and what the river and the Cedar
Forest did to her; how powerfully they healed her. I think of the radical enlargement of the self that Yuvan has found in the oceans, marshes
and rivers of his landscape, since escaping the death drive of his
stepfather.

But when I asked Wayne if our forthcoming descent of the river
might offer the possibility of encountering Paul's spirit in mist or
white water, or might wash some of his grief away, he was non-
committal. 'The fact is, Rob,' he replied, 'that while still capable of
joy, even ecstatic joy, I am almost all grief. Paul's sickness and death
is a part of that grief-being, but so are many, many other terrible
things I have experienced personally or absorbed from or through
others over the last fifty years and continue to carry with me behind
my skull-splitting grin. Whether because of the way I grew up, or
how I taught myself to live afterward, or some quirk of my neur-
ology/genetics, I have not been able to let this stuff go. Instead, I've
become synonymous with it: my work is its work; its, mine. There is
no working it out, except inasmuch as I am of the world, and the
world, mercifully, flows. Braided with and in a mightier river – being

dissolved in it, even temporarily – may be, more than anything, a relief. But I can't be sure.'

~

At last, at dusk, Wayne and I reach the mouth of the Mutehekau Shipu.

A half-moon has risen: a clipped coin.

We pull over, and walk onto the bridge that spans the river. If all goes well, in a fortnight or so we'll paddle under this bridge and out into the Gulf of St Lawrence, completing the descent of the Mutehe-kau Shipu from far to the north.

Upstream, just in sight, is the existing dam: the sheer grey face of the wall, and the generating station off to one side. Power lines crackle and snap. Warning signs shout in red and yellow.

Below us the water is filmy, polished by the last sun into metal gouts and eddies. The river widens to its mouth, where fresh and salt mingle, and current and tide become both, not single. The land sharpens to a last dark-forested point, and beyond it the horizon widens into ocean and the co-motion of sky and water is lost in a white, grainy light, and there the river's last trace is slow-vanishing spirals in the water, shallowing as they slip on; now just faint dints in the water's pewter, now shined flat.

A seal bobs and bottles, watching us through dark, wet eyes.

~

The journey Wayne and I hope to make could not be undertaken if the new dams were built.

In 2018 an alliance to protect the Mutehekau Shipu was formed between four groups: the Innu Council of Ekuanitshit; L'Association Eaux-Vives Minganie (the Whitewater Association of Mingan, but more literally the Living or Lively Waters Association of Mingan), made up of kayakers, hikers and other river-lovers from the area; the Mingan municipal regional council; and SNAP Québec, an influential

Canadian conservation body. Watching over them all was a Montreal-based organization called the Observatoire International des Droits de la Nature (the International Observatory for the Rights of Nature), which focuses on supporting and extending the Rights of Nature movement in North America, and in Canada particularly, as it surges.

In the early days of the alliance, it was agreed between these groups that they would work together towards the joint recognition and declaration of the rights of the Mutehekau Shipu. This vision seemed likely to accommodate plural perceptions of the river's powers and qualities. Together, the regional Mingan Council and the Innu Council of Ekuanitshit would draft and then issue a 'mirror resolution': two differently inflected versions of the same declaration, one Innu and one non-Innu, which shared common principles and conclusions concerning the river's life and future.

Crucially, both resolutions would recognize the river as 'a legal person with the right to live', and as the bearer of other attendant rights including the rights 'to exist and to flow', and 'to evolve naturally, to be preserved and protected'. All of the river's rights would be violated were new dams to be constructed on the lower Mutehekau Shipu.

It was the Mi'kmaq Elders Albert and Murdena Marshall (of Eskasoni First Nation) who coined the notion of Etuaptmumk, or 'Two-Eyed Seeing'. The two eyes in the Marshalls' image are Indigenous and Western ways of knowing, focusing together. Much as Robin Wall Kimmerer weaves strands of scientific botanical knowledge and traditional ecological knowledge – told in part through story – in her book *Braiding Sweetgrass*, so processes of two-eyed seeing draw the best from each tradition, seeking mutual enhancement rather than opposition.

The Mutehekau Shipu resolutions saw with two eyes. To the non-Innu paddlers, river-lovers and conservationists, it made emotional sense to speak of the river as a life-giving force and it made practical sense to recognize it as a rights-bearing entity, able in theory to represent itself and bring suit in court.

To the Innus of Ekuanitshit, the recognition of the river's life and rights offered a means of realigning modern legislative discourse with millennia-old Innu values and relationships. 'For Innu communities,' wrote Uapukun Mestokosho, a young Innu woman who became closely involved with the defence of the Mutehekau Shipu, 'rivers are considered the veins of the territory . . . more than just waterways or resources, they are living beings with their own spirit and agency – and they deserve respect.'

As they drafted the resolution, three key principles emerged for the Innu Council. First, that the river is a living being and relative – at once ancestor and descendant – and, as such, sacred. Second, that each generation has a responsibility to protect the river for those who are yet to be born and those they will never meet. Third, that a continuity exists between the human and non-human lives of the river, and that large-scale damming therefore threatens the whole riverine community, including people.

The Mutehekau Shipu Alliance was encouraged by other river-rights recognitions around the world. In particular, the Innu leaders – many of them women – were 'profoundly inspired' by the decades-long decolonizing negotiations between the Māori people and the Crown in Aotearoa New Zealand, and the resulting recognition of the Whanganui River as both a legal person and a living being. It was decided that, as in the case of the Whanganui, a group of river guardians would be established for the Mutehekau Shipu – drawn from both Innu and settler communities – who might together become, as Yenny Cárdenas put it, 'the voice and the light to protect the rights of the river born in law with the watchful eyes of the world'.

On 18 January 2021, a chilly winter day – less than three years after the alliance was formed, and with the region still gripped tight in the cold claws of Covid – the mirror resolution was signed by the Innu Council. A month later, at Havre St Pierre, the Mingan Council signed its version of the resolution – and the process was complete.

The Mutehekau Shipu had become the first river in Canada to be recognized as a living, rights-bearing being:

WHEREAS since time immemorial and long before the arrival of Europeans, the Innu people have occupied, managed, used and frequented the Nitassinan, of which the Mutehekau Shipu / Magpie River is a part, practicing a traditional way of life and surviving on the area's fauna and flora . . .

BE IT RESOLVED THAT the Innu Council of Ekuanitshit declares that as a legal person . . . [and] a living entity . . . the Mutehekau Shipu / Magpie River and its watershed have . . . fundamental rights, in accordance with the beliefs, customs and practices of the Innu of Ekuanitshit.

Right at the heart of this success was an Innu poet and activist called Rita Mestokosho.

~

Ekuanitshit sits in a sandy curl of land with a river to its north-east, the sea to its south and the main Côte-Nord road passing along its edge. Pinewoods press on the inland borders of the township, as if waiting their chance to reforest the land. Down on the road there's a gas station and a big, airy *Innu mitshuap uteitun* – a 'House of Innu Culture' – built elegantly out of pale wood and curved steel. The town's population is a little over six hundred people. The houses are all detached and substantial, many of them are new, and some of them have red threads tied around their door handles. Nailed onto a telephone pole at the village's eastern end is a handwritten, two-word sign: *Remember Kamloops*.

The morning after our long drive, in the atrium of the House of Innu Culture, Wayne and I meet Rita.

Light floods the space – a silver light which can only be made by the mirror of the sea. From a loudspeaker in the corner of the room comes the sound of geese in flight: honk of calls, creak of wings.

An older white woman is sitting in an armchair in the high-ceilinged room. Her eyes are closed. There is a look of pain on her face. Her brow is locked into furrows. She clutches her handbag on her lap. Her mouth is slightly open. One of her trouser legs is rolled partway up her leg, showing a pale shin which shines where the bone is.

Around the woman in the chair moves another person. This is Rita. She is slightly built, and somewhat bird-like in the precision of the way she moves her hands and head. There is a decisiveness to everything she does – not in the sense that her actions have been premeditated, just that each is absolute in the moment of its making. *Kairos* again, I think.

On the table in front of the armchair is a bobbin of red thread, the ash-grey wing of a large bird, and a bunch of dried sage, still holding some of its green.

Rita is shaping the air around the woman's skull and body with her hands. Her head is tilted at a quizzical angle, like that of a robin. Standing behind the chair now, Rita bends and whispers into the woman's ears. A question?

The woman's eyes flutter. '*Oui*,' the woman answers, softly. The word is fragile, easily wounded.

Rita's hands are moving faster now; she seems to be catching invisible things from the air around the woman's head – pulling them off and throwing them away as if they were wisps of straw.

The woman sinks deeper into the armchair, looks calmer. Rita bends and whispers to her again.

'*Oui*,' the woman says again, a little louder now. Her mouth falls further open. Her eyes remain closed.

There is great tenderness in Rita's movements: the touching of the woman's hair with her fingertips, very faintly; the touching of her face, very lightly.

Loon cries echo from the loudspeaker, haunting and molten.

The woman holds her handbag tighter to her belly. Her knees are pressed together. She has slipped her shoes from her feet. Rita lays a palm on the woman's forehead, where it is cool. The woman's hands begin to tremble.

Rita is clearing the air around her head faster now, and then without warning she begins to sing. An electric shock crackles through the room. Wayne and I start upright in our seats. Rita's voice is high and strong. She sings in Innu-aimun, a chant-like song, with long, sustained, bold notes, cascading then rising again. The volume is extraordinary, so too the vocal control.

As Rita sings, she lights the bunch of sage, the smoke of which tendrils the air like honeysuckle. As she sings, she passes the sage around the woman's head and upper body. Then she picks up the wing from the grey bird and uses this first to scoop the air around the woman, then to flick away towards the east of the room, as if flinging off some invisible residue.

After perhaps five minutes, Rita stops singing. The echo takes seconds to die away in the room, years in the ear's memory.

Caribou calls come from the speaker: odd growls and grumbles.

The woman's mouth is fully open now, as if in quiet amazement. The frown has gone; her brow is unknitted. Rita beckons to the corner of the room, and an older man walks hesitantly across. It's the woman's husband.

Rita beckons his head down to the level of his wife's. She leans in and whispers something to them both. Then the man takes his wife's hands, helps her up from the deep chair. She struggles to rise. He holds her hands still as she fits her feet into her shoes. She struggles to walk. He takes one of her elbows, supporting her. She is murmuring: sounds, not words, shaking her head.

Outside, a heavy-goods vehicle thunders past, windows down, pulling a comet's-tail of music: Bill Haley on full blast.

When the woman and her husband have left, Rita turns her attention to me and Wayne. She knows we have come to see her; that we are going down the river. Her gaze is calm, intense, assessing. A LiDAR scan of the soul: a green line flickering up and down the length of our bodies, mapping, fathoming, testing.

She sees a man who lives too much in his head.

She sees a man who keeps his heart in a locked wooden box, a chest in his chest.

She invites us to sit.

'Did you just . . . heal that person?' I ask Rita in French.

'I don't know what I did,' she replies. Her tone is severe, almost admonishing. 'I just followed my heart, and I listened to her soul.'

'How did you . . . decide she needed this?'

'I have not decided anything.' Her responses are quick and sure. 'It was the Creator. We decide nothing. The Great Spirit, the Invisible, the Mystery, the Great Mystery, whatever you want to call it, was the decision-maker. We look too much with our eyes, and not enough with our spirits.'

Her gaze swivels to Wayne, who is trying to make himself invisible. Not a man to duck a stare, he looks right back at her. She speaks in English to him.

'What is your name?'

'Wayne.'

'What she felt,' says Rita, gesturing towards the east, 'is the same feeling you will have on the river, if you give all you have during your journey. I see something in you, Wayne.'

'What's that?'

'Perhaps I will say more later. You have something inside you that you don't need, Wayne – that you don't want to think about in your life. When you go to the river, you must give to the river what you don't need, and call instead on freedom.'

Wayne considers this commandment for a few seconds. Then he says: 'I will.'

~

Rita Mestokosho was born in Ekuanitshit in 1966, and her early years were spent largely living in a small camp near to the coast. Her parents and grandparents continued a close connection with the land, even after the coercive state policies of the late 1950s and early 1960s which compelled many Innus to abandon their established patterns of transhumance – following the rivers up into the interior of the land in winter, then returning to the coast in the summer – and to settle in townships.

Rita remembers the 'real silence' of that first period of her life, a silence filled with the sounds of the sea, the rivers and the trees. It was, she says, where her task as a poet 'who comes into the world to witness life' was forged. She went to school in Quebec City and Montreal, then studied political science at the University of Quebec before returning to Ekuanitshit to begin her life's work as an activist, healer, guardian of Innu culture and language – and poet.

Rita sees no distinction between her poetry and her activism; they form a continuous terrain. Among numerous other campaigns, Rita was part of the Dakota Access Pipeline protests; she and other Innu people travelled there to show solidarity with the other water defenders, and brought with them a *shaputuan* – a big, two-doored tent with a wooden frame – to shelter people during the brutal winter of 2016–17. She was also a significant figure among those Innus campaigning against the damming of the Romaine, to the extent of filing suit against Hydro-Québec.

She writes her poetry in both Innu-aimun and French. Sometimes her poems translate one another; the Innu-aimun original on the recto page, the French version facing it on the verso. Sometimes she braids the two languages together, in a cento or interlace pattern: a line of Innu-aimun, a line of French, a line of Innu-aimun, and so on – the open vowels of French nestling beside the softer *sh*s and *ch*s of Innu-aimun. I cannot read Innu-aimun, but I can read Rita's French, and I have been doing so in the weeks before coming to Nitassinan. Her poetry is greatly affecting to me; it is heartfelt and heartbreaking. Anger burns quietly through some of her poems; a deep sadness pervades others; beauty hovers in them all. 'My people wrote while walking / they had the library of the land with them', runs a poem in which tense matters greatly:

My people wrote millions of books
scattered upon the land
encyclopedias of rivers
dictionaries of mountains
geographies of forests

Rita also, in her words, 'speaks the language of hope' – and that language is a watery one. Rivers flow through Rita's poetry. One of her books is dedicated to all her 'grandmothers who have walked close to the water and learned to listen to it'. She is both water-thought ('The river plunges in my dreams') and water-bodied ('free [. . .] / to feel the water in my veins'). She speaks of the sky as her father, the river as her mother. She figures poetry itself as a river. There is a powerful sense throughout her work that she is speaking with – being flowed through by – natural and divine forces greater than her individual self; indeed, a sense that the idea of the individual as an island or singular unit is irrelevant, even deceitful. In Rita's poetry, humans are part land ('my heart is made of pine branches') and subject to sudden transformation; to skin-slipping and shape-shifting ('I will become salmon'). Often in her poems, the rivers, the land and their beings *speak*. Caribou listen to and address the reader. A bear is a grandfather, and wolves are great-uncles. Streams whisper, the sky utters, and rivers murmur the name of an Elder who has passed away.

Flow matters to Rita. In her collection *Atik^U utei: Le cœur du caribou*, not one poem has a full stop anywhere in it.

'We all', she writes there, 'have a river who calls to us'.

~

Rita snap-switches her focus from Wayne to me.

'Maybe two weeks ago, an Elder of our community passed away,' she says in French. 'He is now in the spiritual world, but I can see that he is also now in the river. His soul, his spirit, is in the river. His name is William: William Napess. A fortnight ago, he departed for the spirit world. William's hunting territory is where you are going tomorrow, very far up the river. I tell you – his soul and spirit are there. I will ask him to help you on your journey down the river, to guide you and keep you safe.'

'Thank you.' I think of my friend Barry Lopez, who loved the Canadian north, crossing the river to the other world on Christmas Day three years earlier. What was it Rita had written? *I have crossed the last river / the current has borne me away.*

Wild geese honk from the speaker again; the recording is on a loop. Rita looks intently at me.

'To you, Robert, I would say this: don't think too much with your head. Forget your notebooks on the river: leave them behind.'

I gulp, then decide to defer the issue of this notebook ban for now, and examine it more closely later in the privacy of my own conscience.

'When you are on the river you must think of her, the water, you must think *like* her,' says Rita, tapping her foot in emphasis. 'Like William. He is a spirit, and above all he is now free. You' – she points a finger at me – 'you speak of birds in your writing, yes? Well, *be* a bird. Be a tree. Be a river. Yes. On the river, *be a river.*'

'I don't know how to do that, Rita.'

'Each day, give something to the earth, tobacco perhaps, or even just a word, a prayer, a song. Every day, give something. I will give you a pouch of tobacco to give to the river. It's very important that you do this. The *true* reason for why you have come to the river? Well, you will come to know this during your time on the river. We have more need of her, the river, than she of us.'

'I've no doubt of that.'

I give Rita a present I've brought for her: a copy of Nan Shepherd's *The Living Mountain*. I tell her about the book and its vision of the mountain as a vast, compound, living entity.

'Thank you,' says Rita. 'That is good of you. How old are your children?'

'Ten, seventeen and nineteen. Will, Tom and Lily.'

'My son is thirty-three. His name is Mishta Napeu, which means "Great Man" in Innu-aimun, and his sister is called Uapukun, which means "flower" in Innu-aimun, "flower in the water". He is in prison.' She toggles back into English. 'Do you have a family, Wayne?'

'Not a conventional one,' says Wayne. 'My friends are my family.'

'Do you have children, Wayne?' she asks.

'No, he doesn't,' I blurt out, stupidly.

'I do have children,' says Wayne, calmly. 'They're just not my biological children. They are my kin, though, and many of them will have children in turn.'

She pauses, speaks to both of us.

'Where you are going on this river, everything is possible. I think you will see a bear there.'

Wayne shifts interestedly in his chair.

She pauses, then speaks again to me in French, with quiet force and precision.

'You need to pay attention to the river, Robert. The important thing is to wake up not the consciousness but the heart. Rather than you speaking *of* the river, it is the river who will speak to you.'

'I hope so.'

'The Mutehekau Shipu, she is not enough known. We *must* recognize again that she is more than "only" water. She wants to flow, to flow freely, and she helps us when she is like this. *She* helps *us*.'

'Rita, may we have your permission to follow the river?'

'Of course! But the person you really need to ask is the river. She may have a different point of view!' She roars with laughter.

'Just please give the tobacco to William when you are at the north of the lake. And collect me some water. His people are from the Rivière-St-Jean area, like my maternal grandfather. My paternal grandfather came from much further north. He was the brother of Mathieu Mestokosho. In the summers, everyone would come south to this exact spot, before any houses were here, to make canoes. *Here.*'

224

She taps her foot on the ground again. 'In the winters, they would head to the north of Quebec for caribou, for everything . . .' She trails off, then suddenly says, 'I think that when you are on the river, it's there that you will be transported by the river — who will speak through you.'

Rita is right, though of course we do not know it then. She is *eerily* right.

Her instructions continue. I feel thankful for them: for their clarity and firmness, amid the uncertainty of the days ahead and the roil of my thoughts; for the generosity this evidently remarkable person is showing us.

'When you are on the river, you must always pitch your tent facing east, so that the first thing you see each morning is the sun.'

'Eastwards. OK. Yes. We will.'

'And — you must gather me leaves of Labrador tea, from the river, and bring them to me here in ten, eleven, twelve days' time when you are off the river. We will drink it. It helps sleep, it's good for breathing.'

'Got it. I always need help to sleep.'

Two little boys on BMXs with high handlebars pedal past the windows, whooping and laughing, their tyres slipping in the sand.

'Now, on the river,' Rita continues, 'you will have *one question* you can ask of the river, or that the river will answer. Listen to me — most of the questions you will think of at first will be about your loved ones, your family: will your daughter grow up to be good, or rich? That kind of question. But the question you can ask of the river is *not* about family. No, it must be a question *for you, from you, to the river*. One question for the river each, no more. And the answer? The answer will most probably come on the days that you fast. You should fast for between twenty-four and thirty-six hours when you are on the river. This will help you get an answer to the question.'

'I have a question for you, Rita. Often in your poetry you write of a sacred tree, or a sacred forest, *l'arbre sacré*. What is this? It reminds me of a sacred forest which is at the heart of the oldest written story we know, *The Epic of Gilgamesh*.'

'Ah yes. The sacred tree. In each forest there is always a tree that, you could say, occupies all of the space. A tree which shines brighter; one which, when you walk in the forest, you will see its soul. When we built the Cultural House here, there were no trees here, so we planted them. I knew that there would be a sacred tree among them. That is the silver birch.' She gestures out of the window, at a young birch on the roadside. 'The same is true in any forest or place.'

She reaches forwards and picks up the bobbin of red thread and a pair of scissors.

'Hold out your wrist,' she says to me. She measures a length of the thread against my left wrist, snips it, then deftly knots it around my arm like a bracelet. She does the same with my right wrist, but using a length of thicker red cloth – then she does the same to Wayne's wrists.

'One of these you must tie around the sacred tree when you find it on the Mutehekau Shipu. You will find the sacred tree, or it will find you. It may not be the greatest or the tallest, but it will . . . blaze out. The other bracelet you must leave on your wrist. Only time or the river, which are the same things, can remove it.'

'I understand.'

'You have come from very far away, Robert,' she says. 'You heard the river, and you will do something for it, I know.'

'I'll try my best.'

'I sense that you are afraid, Robert. Because in your manner of seeing things, you put people here, and rivers over here. You think in hierarchies. This is not a criticism – it's a fact. Instead, you need to seek the current, the flow.'

'But this is exactly the hierarchy I want to escape from – that I've been trying to escape from for years now with rivers.'

Rita doesn't respond. The conversation is drawing to an end, I sense. Wayne senses it too; but there is something he needs to ask before we leave. He sits up, leans forwards, speaks quietly.

'Rita, what did you see in me?'

'Are you ready?' she asks, eyeing him.

'Yes, I'm ready. And I don't mind if Rob hears what you have to say.'

'When I first saw you, I saw a little boy with his grandfather. The grandfather gave the child a box, a chest. You keep your emotions in this box, tightly closed, Wayne. Sometimes you need to open the box and feel those emotions. You will be changed by the river, but in a good way. No one will judge you if you want to cry. It will be important on the river to cry, because we are a drop of the river, you and me both. Please cry for me at the river. Don't be afraid of what will come out of the box.'

If you're going to open Pandora's Box, make sure to stand behind the lid when you do so . . .

'The sun will protect you every morning when you wake up with the door to the east, Robert and Wayne! In the north, on the river, you will be reborn. There is something in the north which is not present where you are from. There are few other humans. You will return transformed.'

I have to find a sacred tree, I think. *Better keep my eyes peeled.*

I have one question for the river, I think. *Better make it a good one.*

~

Coming down the Mutehekau Shipu with me and Wayne are two river-people: Raph and Danny.

Raph is a young French-Canadian with the fine surname of St-Onge. He speaks a fluent, accented English and is keen to practise it with me, which saves both of us the pain of my rusty French. He's spent years learning his craft as a back-country guide, and has a deep passion for and knowledge of this northern land. He has a quick mind, a quick smile — and when he's in his kayak, I'll discover, he seems to fuse with it, becoming an aqueous equivalent of a centaur, with the torso, head and arms of a man, and the lower body of a fish.

Danny Peled is older than Raph; a little younger than me, I guess. He grew up in Montreal, and from early on knew he wanted to work in and with rivers. He's paddled big rivers all around the world, but keeps coming back to the water of his home province of Quebec. He's an expert in back-country safety and emergency response. He's a big man, broad-shouldered, large-handed, very strong and technically superb in a kayak or on a raft. Generosity is an instinct in him, and he navigates cultural differences with the same deft skill as he does a Grade IV rapid. He's trusted by the people of Ekuanitshit. Over the years, he's taken many of the younger members of the Innu community to the river, in order to forge or renew their relationship with the Mutehekau Shipu. Danny dislikes praise, preferring to just get on with what he does, and do it well. He loves ice hockey – but it's the huge northern rivers and their immense forests that really light him up.

The evening after Wayne and I meet Rita, the night before we're due to leave for the north of the river, we drive out with Danny and Raph to a scatter of houses set in a patch of coastal woodland, a few miles from the mouth of the Mutehekau Shipu, to stow some gear with a fisherman named Ilya Klvana.

Ilya's front yard at first sight seems to have been partially destroyed by some kind of explosion. Three canoes lie thrown at angles across one another, one with its tip in a tree. Two wooden kayaks are wedged against a telephone pole. Plastic crates are lodged in the crowns of trees. Webbing and ropes dangle from branches. There is a thirty-foot lorry trailer, open at one end and part buried in the earth, as if it has only recently ploughed to an emergency halt, losing its cab in the process.

Danny gestures at one of the kayaks. 'I think that's the kayak Ilya built himself, which he then solo-paddled across Canada, aged twenty-one or so. And when I say "across", I mean from the west coast to the far east in Newfoundland. Alone. A truly jaw-dropping journey. About four thousand kilometres.'

We follow a path into the wood. Different trees seem to have different storage functions. At the base of one are a dozen or so hand-made children's gliders, painted in bright colours and polka dots. From the branches of another hang about twenty rusting drag anchors, like industrial baubles on a Bauhaus Christmas tree. In a small stand of pines are forty or fifty pink fishing buoys, heaped like oversize sweets, as if mounded over the body of a Playmobil king who has passed.

If you came across this place in deep forest, you'd think a sect practised its rituals here, and you'd run for your life.

Between the trees, lining both sides of the path, are numerous fridges and chest freezers, some of them defunct and their doors lolling open, others humming away. Mossy wires lead away from them towards the house, which is itself an extraordinary structure: tall and thin, perched on a billow of exposed bedrock, right above the sea.

Smoke is coming out of a tall, thin silver chimney. The house seems as if it might just creak to its legs at any moment and stalk off into the forest. It looks very like Howl's Moving Castle.

A flash of movement inside. A face at the window by the door, moonish and pale. A cry of surprise, and a figure running up the stairs inside, wearing very little clothing.

A minute later, the front door opens, and there is Ilya, now sporting green shorts, a broad smile and a 'Perroquets de L'îles de Mingan' T-shirt in the style of Hergé. My first thought: *What a kind man he looks to be.* My second thought: *What power!*

Ilya is a ginger bear of a man. He has a head of red hair, shaved close to his scalp, and long, pale-orange eyelashes. His hands are hard-skinned and scarred from labour, with split nails. Though he's shorter than me by several inches, I have no doubt he could pick me up and toss me like a crash-test dummy. His shoulders and biceps are enormous. His neck's girth approaches, at a rough estimate, the circumference of my thigh. There is no discernible change of gauge where his neck meets the base of his skull.

Ilya laughs – a big, booming laugh. 'You caught me by surprise

there! I was only in my underpants. Sorry about that.' His accent in
English is a distinctive mash-up of Québécois and Czech.

He embraces Danny and Raph, shakes hands with Wayne and me.
A huge ham of a mitt, enfolding mine.

'Hey, how's it going, Ilya?' says Danny.

'Oh, not bad, not bad. I've just acquired two new fishing licences,
and they came with a boat and gear I didn't really want, so . . .' He
gestures at the chaos of the wood behind us, and shrugs helplessly.

'My parents are Czech, you know, they left after the Soviet invasion. And Czechs never throw *anything* away. That's how I was
brought up, anyhow, and I don't seem able to change it. So I now have
four boats' worth of fishing gear. And all of this – well, clearly I find it
hard to throw things away! But I live in a little village, and so I guess
it's adaptive too, because there's always a neighbour who can make use
of a thing.'

Ilya is about my age: second half of his forties or so. He's a halibut
and whelk fisherman, and he lives with his partner, Amélie, and their
two young boys in this little house Ilya has built for them, perched on
the clifftop, overlooking the sea. His fishing quota is filled in just a few
days each spring. The rest of the year, Ilya picks up bits of short-term
employment here and there: harvesting bilberries, or putting in a week
or two on a construction project.

He speaks Québécois, Czech and English. If you ask him a question
of any kind, he will pause before answering, crook his head slightly to
one side as he thinks, and scratch his stubbly skull. Early in our
acquaintance, I sense someone very moral. I also sense someone who
has been born into the wrong century.

We wander around the side of the house, and onto the decking area
that Ilya has constructed. A set of Ilya's underpants, leggings and thermal vest are laid flat on the wood of the decking, like the shed skin of
some broad creature. I remember the passage in *A River Runs Through
It* when Norman Maclean describes a woodsman who lives for so long
in his leggings that his pubic and leg hair grows right through the

fabric, binding the garment to his body so tightly that eventually it has
to be shaved off him with clippers, hair and cloth alike, much as a sheep
is shorn.

Looking south there's nothing but sea, shimmering calmly away.
The land falls steeply from the back of the house, down to where lazy
evening waves slop the rocks. Pools of light gleam and slip on the distant water.

The decking is unfenced, and the drop from its edge is about eight
feet into brambles and rocks. 'Amélie tells me I really must put some
railings up there,' says Ilya, peering thoughtfully over the edge, down
into the prickly hoops of briar. 'The problem is that our oldest boy
walked off the edge one night when he was taking a pee in the dark.'

Ilya shows us down into the basement. It's here we'll stow our gear
while we're on the river. There's an odd-looking woodpile outside the
glass door, with stacked slabs of weathered, brown-grey timber.

'You've flattened the floor, Ilya!' says Danny. 'Good work.'

We're standing on raw bedrock, I realize.

'Wait,' I say, 'you cut out the bedrock? Canadian Shield? The
oldest, hardest rock in the world?'

'Yeah,' says Ilya, rubbing his hand over his head, pensively. 'I must
say, it became one of those jobs you wish you'd never started. It took a
long time. Used diamond-tipped cutters. Went through a few of those.
Cut it into lengths, then dragged the rock outside, chucked some of it
over the cliff, stacked the rest there.'

He gestures towards the glass door. What I'd thought was a wood-
stack is in fact a rock-stack, with each baton made of 1.6-billion-year-old
stone. This particular formation had survived countless glaciations,
but it hadn't survived Ilya.

'You needed a river, Ilya,' I say, 'to do this job properly. Or a glacier. Not a diamond-tipped saw.'

He considers this. 'That would have taken a bit too long,' he replies.

Then he says: 'So, going down the Magpie, then, are you? You
know river politics aren't simple here. Not just dam against river.

The Romaine Project had *big* consequences in this region, and some of them were good. Lots of employment. When I was teaching at the Innu school then, lots of my students would grab jobs that were freed up in the communities here because others had gone to the Romaine.'

'They call it the "Beaver Complex",' says Raph. 'You know, the Québécois compulsion to just *keep* building dams.'

I speak spontaneously, on a hunch. 'Ilya, why don't you come with us down the river?'

He itches his scalp reflectively. *Scratch-scratch.*

'Well . . . I suppose I could. I could, I suppose. When do you leave, anyways?'

'Four a.m. tomorrow morning. Seven hours' time.'

'How long for?'

'Ten days, maybe twelve?'

'And the plan is: a drop-in by floatplane to the north end of Lac Magpie, then paddle out from there? I've never paddled Lac Magpie in its entirety,' says Ilya ruminatively, rolling the idea round his mouth like the first sip of a good wine.

He looks around him. The house is in chaos.

'I'd need to tidy this place up a bit. But, yeah, I think I can. I'd like to. If it's OK with you, anyways?'

'Yes!'

It's almost incomprehensible to me that someone could decide to go away for ten days with seven hours' notice. But I'm happy it isn't incomprehensible to Ilya. I whoop silently in my soul: something tells me this is a very good thing.

'Well . . .' says Ilya. 'It won't be an easy journey. The river's very high. Running at two hundred and seventy-five, I heard. All the rain.'

My stomach pancake-flips. Two hundred and seventy-five cubic metres per second: the average flow-rate for the river at this time of year is around one hundred and twenty.

'It's a big river. Not easy for beginners. As the old joke goes, there are so many rapids on the Magpie that even the trout have portage trails.'

There are firecrackers in the dark that night in Ekuanitshit. A boy bounces on a trampoline in the dark, *creak, creak, creak*, near where the forest begins.

I lie unable to sleep, burning up, my head pounding. I think I have a fever.

~

Four thirty a.m. A lake a mile inland from the coast. The float-plane base.

A single star. A thin line of orange light to the east, smudged by rain. Three loons on the water, calling now and then. A strong northerly wind.

The only way to the upper reaches of the Mutehekau Shipu is by floatplane. An old De Havilland DHC-3 is tethered to a makeshift pontoon pier. It's an Otter – the legendary workhorse of the north – and its riveted red and silver skin is scored and scarred from seventy years of hard service in hard country. The wind isn't a problem to a plane like this, but visibility is.

We wait to see if the rain will clear sufficiently to allow take-off. My nerves are jangling.

Six a.m. A furnace cracks open far in the east. Molten gold and smelter orange pour out.

Seven a.m. The lake is filled with silver light. It brims like mercury. The air is clear now. The wind has dropped a little. We can fly.

'I always carry a knife and a lighter on me on floatplane flights,' says Danny.

I do the same. Doing what Danny does is a good rule of thumb in life, I have decided. Everything else is stowed in dry-bags, shoved in the belly of the plane.

The plane's propellor chugs, spins, speeds to a blur and seems suddenly to rotate back against itself before the pilot increases the throttle, steers the plane into open water, points its nose due north, and accelerates. The engine roars, we're pushed back in our seats, struts and wings begin to judder under the strain, the floats thump on the water – and then suddenly we lift off into smoothness and white noise.

We are gods, birds, lookers-down.

Bronze of the rivers, gold of the sandbanks, red-green sphagnum tapestry.

Distant veils of rain, drifting like candle-blacking far to the north-east.

Sun falling to the west, lighting up valleys and ridges beyond number.

An antlered moose stumbles across a fording place in a winding river, silver rings splashing at his knees. Hundreds of little lakes pock the green, joined by an intricate natural drainage system of creeks, streams and channels. It looks like a neural network. *There is more water than land here*, I think.

The land puckers into long, shallow ridges and shoulders. Grey-green patches in the forest, where the spruces have died in their hundreds of thousands from old diseases enjoying vigorous success in the new climatic regime.

The Otter will drop us and our gear at the northernmost point of the immense Lac Magpie, which separates the lower Mutehekau Shipu from the upper. From there we will paddle south: for several days along the fifty miles or so of the lake – and then onto the river itself for a week or more.

If all goes well, we will reach the sea. If anything goes wrong, escape will be challenging.

Ilya leans forward, cups his massive hands, shouts into my ear and points east to where a wide river wanders in big meanders. 'That's the St-Jean River,' he yells, 'a traditional highway used by the Innu to reach the Labrador plateau. From there they'd cross the land all the way to the upper Romaine, because the Mutehekau Shipu and the lower Romaine were too rough to ascend, even when frozen.'

I'm unprepared for the sheer scale of this landscape. We have been flying for forty minutes, and there's been nothing in sight but river, forest, muskeg and lake. The immensity is both intensely beautiful and frighteningly, blazingly indifferent.

My first sight of the Mutehekau Shipu itself catches my breath.

A world-snake in the green.

Cliffs dropping near sheer to water.

House-sized boulders on the banks; time-falls from the rock faces above.

Water blue-black and glossy in the deeper, calmer runs; peat-brown where it is stretched towards and away from rapids; churning green, gold and cream in the rapids and falls.

Seen from above, from this height, the river appears static, and has the texture of impasto, gouache, as if smeared into place by a palette knife. I press my forehead against the cold glass of the window, feel excitement and worry singing in my back, my neck, my belly.

How the hell *will we descend* that?

'There's Lac Magpie!' shouts Danny, pointing between two ridge-lines on which the rising sun has laid emerald light through a break in the clouds.

A slate-slab of grey water, plucked with white arrowheads.

'Further up, you'll see the West Magpie River flowing into the west coast of the lake,' yells Danny.

You know a lake is big, I think, *when you speak of it having coasts, rather than shores.*

We pick up Lac Magpie about three-quarters of the way down it. The pilot lines up with the lake's central axis, and settles back, letting the topography do the nav. On the lake goes, and on. How on earth will we paddle this – let alone the river who roars from its southern end?

'Big wind down there,' grunts Ilya, gesturing at the white-caps.

'Better hope it doesn't swing against us, or that lake alone will take us a week.'

The wind is funnelled by cliffs at the lake's pinch-point, and even from this height we can see two- or three-foot-high white horses in the waist. If the wind rotates round to the south, as it's forecast to do, it will be tough to make progress. We have enough food for ten days, possibly eleven.

'I intend to gnaw on your thigh if things get desperate,' Wayne calls reassuringly to me.

Twenty minutes later the floatplane banks, then begins a long, slow hypotenuse glide down to the northern shore of the lake, where the upper Mutehekau Shipu curls into it umbilically.

From this height, I can see how the land holds the memory of the river's wanderings over time. It reminds me of Fisk's maps of the Mississippi, writhing with their ghost rivers. I can see remnant oxbow lakes, infilled meanders – a whole archive of the river's previous routes, as it has roamed back and forth across the valley it has harrowed over thousands of years.

~

In 2017 two young Innu activist-artists from Ekuanitshit – Rita's daughter, Uapukun, and Shanice Mollen-Picard – made a short film called simply *Shipu* ('River'), in which they speak of their relationship to the rivers of Nitassinan. It is a melancholy and loving testimony: a three-way conversation between Shanice, Uapukun and the water.

'We pay homage to our rivers, the veins of our territory,' Uapukun and Shanice say in unison. 'We wish to pass on the memory and the tradition of our waterways . . . The rivers belong to no one. We are only passing through. We own nothing . . . We want only that future generations may also follow the current.'

Watching their film before coming to Nitassinan, I felt anger rising in me: fury at what has been done to the Innu people – to their land, their children, their rivers. Anger, among other things, at the sheer inconsistency of it all. In Ekuanitshit, there is a 'boil-water advisory' in force. Though Ekuanitshit is surrounded by rivers, streams and lakes, though Hydro-Québec can spend billions of dollars building hundreds of dams to harvest the water as energy, though eminent domain law allows the state to build oil pipelines and trans-connector pylon corridors through Indigenous lands across North America without proper consultation or consent, that same state cannot muster itself to provide drinkable water to a township of six hundred or so people.

One of the young people from Ekuanitshit who Danny took on the Mutehekau Shipu in the early years of his work in the region was an artist and activist called Lydia Mestokosho-Paradis. She is Rita's niece, and has guided on the river. When I asked Lydia about her relationship with the water, she gave an answer which beautifully joined ideas of the river's life with that of her own, her ancestors and her descendants-to-be:

It seems crazy that we give a corporation that's ten years old rights, but we won't give rights to a ten-thousand-year-old river. Water is life. Water is the medicinal plants. Water is the berries, the fish, and all the other animals that drink the water. If you don't have water, everything else dies around it. The river *is* life – it's like when you see a place, but the colours there are not bright. But when we see the *river*, when we're near the water, the colour is . . . *popping*! You know – that's how we feel. When we go to the river, I feel more alive. I see the people more brightly. The land is healthier.

When I go to the Mutehekau Shipu or any water in the land, I feel like I am hearing my ancestors whispering: *We have been here, we know how you feel, we know how you fear.* I always say that the rivers are the highways of our ancestors. Because we are in the time of a lot of anxiety or depression, so they, the ancestors, are sharing with me: *It's*

*going to be OK. We've been here. We know you are doing a lot of work in
terms of transmission and protection.*

She – the river – has a memory of the people. I see her like that. She
has a memory. And when you are connected with her, you can be connected with the ancestors. If you are respectful with her, she will bring
us food and she is travelling with us, she is just helping us – so we have
to give her the same protection that she gives us.

I see the river like a person in-between, who makes connections in
time and space.

~

At the north end of the lake, we chain the gear off the floatplane, stack-
ing it on a shingle beach curved like a cuticle.

A milk-pale daytime moon hangs over a forested ridge.

My headache is awful: biting and mobile, acid slopping in a
cauldron.

The floatplane pilot has hard eyes and a droopy long moustache,
like the Gaulish blacksmith in *Asterix*. He didn't greet us when we met,
hasn't told us his name, didn't speak to us as we fly and, when we've
offloaded, he doesn't say goodbye. He just pulls himself up into his
cockpit, guns the engine, reverses away from the beach, turns the plane
through 180 degrees so it faces south down the lake, revs, accelerates,
lifts off – and the plane dwindles first to a paper dart, then a silver star,
then a dot, then gone.

I'm aware of a long, rigorous journey ahead. There is now nothing
between us and the Gulf of St Lawrence except a hundred miles or so
of lake, river and forest.

We're each in a single kayak. Fore and aft we stow waterproof bags:
for now, on the flat water of the lake, we can just wedge them across
each boat's bow and stern. When we leave the lake in several days'
time to move onto the river itself, though, we'll take to lashing the
bags down with fingernail-ripping tightness, cinching them into place
with haul-straps, so that in the event of what Danny nonchalantly

refers to as a 'swim', the boat will bear itself and our belongings safely down to calmer water.

Everything we need we carry. We have no fuel with us – just pots and a griddle. All cooking will be on driftwood fires.

We need to get moving. First, though, we must collect the lake water for Rita, and give our thanks to the river and the land.

We push off from the shore and paddle north in a loose line, towards the western shore. Five bright ducks in a row, Danny leading, Raph sweeping at the tail, Ilya keeping an eye out. The inflow from the northern branch of the Mutehekau Shipu pushes and nudges our boats, like the nose of an unseen whale.

A river births a lake, a lake in turn births a river, I think. *Who is the parent and who the child?*

I find it hard to stop my boat spinning in the current. I dig deeper with the paddle, feel the first burn of lactic in the shoulders.

If it's like this where the river sluices into the lake, what will it be like in the full force of the river's current?

We reach a shingle bank where a big deadfall tree has been beached by the spring flood. We haul the boats up with a crunch and climb out onto the shingle, and I dip and fill a small bottle with water for Rita – water from William Napess's hunting ground. I speak a greeting in my head to the lake and the river-to-be. The water says nothing in reply.

If you interrogate a mystery, don't expect answers in a language you can understand.

Wayne and I take pinches of tobacco from the pouch Rita has given us, and scatter some flakes on the land and some on the water. The wind gusts them over the lake. I murmur gratitude to Rita for her blessing of our journey, and I ask William Napess for his guidance and care during the days ahead.

Suddenly, a surge of relief and relaxation runs like a tidal bore from the top of my scalp to my feet. The pain in my head instantly lessens, as if the acid is draining away, gurgling off down a hole. My eyes widen in surprise. It's a welcome moment: a grounding. I'm *here* at last. I'm fortunate in my companions. Rita has approved this river journey and given me clear instructions on how to proceed.

We push off from the shore, point the noses of our boats south, and bend to our work. Hour on hour of paddling. Pain rising in the shoulders, the arms, the flanks. But the wind for now a hand on the back, pushing, pushing. *On you go. Keep moving.*

Light flickering from grey to sudden bolts of gold as the big wind drives sooty cloudbanks separated by blue rifts of sky.

Ridge upon forested ridge. I learn to read the patchwork. Where fire has passed through, or waves of disease have felled the evergreens (spruce, pine, balsam fir), the broadleaf trees (birch, aspen) have crept in to fill the gap. Their colour is both a brighter and a greyer green.

Ilya points towards a hillside where the conifers are dying, standing grey across a square mile or so of slope.

'Caterpillar, beetle – I don't know which, but they're dying for sure,' he shouts to me. 'Give the birches time and they'll fill that space. But give the evergreens time and they'll creep back and crowd out the birches in turn.'

I remember the clacking branches of tens of thousands of ash trees on the South Downs in England, all brittled by ash dieback; the sycamore seedlings starting to colonize where the ashes were dying. Tides of trees, moving back and forth in symphony with each other's fates over decades, centuries. If you pull the temporal lens back far enough, you come to see that trees are migrants too. They walk, move, shift their boundaries. They suffer plagues and pandemics, like us.

The northerly wind rises. Ilya and I push on ahead, paddling hard, using the blades to grab great wind-roused gouts of water, as if pulling ourselves along on fistfuls of cloth. We traverse a big bay on a line that puts our boats perpendicular to the wind. The cross-gale buffets us, tries to spin us, tries to flip us. My heart rate is higher now; little butterflies take flight in my belly. *I could go over here. Not a good place to flip.*

But then we're across the bay, have turned into the lee of a shingle point and instantly the wind fades, the chop drops, and we leap out of the boats and run them up onto the finely graded shingle of the spit with a hiss of gravel and cries of relief.

Raph gets a fire going with crisp curls of birch bark for tinder, then feeds it with sticks of driftwood that we help to gather. The driftwood is barkless, weathered, silver. Its flowing grain-lines stand clear.

Ilya drives a forked stick into the shingle by the fire, then leans a longer stick into the V. From the point of the longer stick he hangs his soaking shoes over the flames to dry-roast.

'Shoe leather for elevenses, Ilya?' I ask. He looks enigmatic.

The gravel of the spit has been graded by the water, the patient, tireless sorting-machine of the waves ranging the biggest to smallest pebbles near perfectly. Long humps of glacier-smoothed gneiss bed-rock rise from the shingle, intruded by quartzite veins that glitter in the sunlight. *More stone whales*, I think, *surfacing and diving across millennia, slow and gentle in their manoeuvrings.*

Blisters are already forming on the inside of my thumbs where the paddle pivots with each stroke. I'll live with them, bleeding and raw, for the rest of the river.

Flies. Alder. Willow. Smoke blue-grey in the clear air, plumed off the fire by the wind. The tiny blast-furnace of the fire's heart.

'Lac Magpie is rare in its extremity,' says Danny. 'It's so long and so steep-sided – this is an unusual combination for a lake, even in this part of the world.'

'The lake's really high right now as it is,' says Raph. 'We may find that most of the possible camping spots are flooded.'

Ilya and Wayne sit close, talking. They've hit it off immediately. They will become thick as thieves during our days on the river. It makes sense. Both are naturally itinerant, restless; both are driven by impulses they find hard to name.

'During the pandemic I couldn't sit still, so I drove thirteen thousand miles around the continental US,' I overhear Wayne saying.

'Hey, that sounds like me!' says Ilya, delighted to have encountered a fellow wanderer.

Ilya starts a story about the accidental conflagration of the jetty at Mingan, several years earlier. 'I was outside skinning a porcupine with a friend of mine . . .' he begins.

'Ilya, how do you kill a porcupine?' interrupts Wayne.

There is a long pause.

'Well . . . I've killed quite a few porcupine in my life,' replies Ilya eventually. 'Do you mean how did I kill the most recent one?' He likes to be precise.

As we rest and eat, the wind drops and the sun comes fully out. The sky is cloudless now. Then it's back to the toil of the paddle.

Mile after mile. Our little line of boats spreads out again. We each enter a private cell of labour. Time and space begin to do odd things, expanding so that each hour seems surely two or three, each mile seems surely ten. The water is working on me. I am learning to recalibrate my eagerness, to settle into a present-tense state of not-anticipating, of not-knowing.

The vastness of scale is defeating to my English imagination, though. None of the metrics make sense. This lake's length is the same distance as that between my home in Cambridge and central London. It holds a billion litres. It would take a year to drain. *It holds a water-year.*

Sun volleys off the waves, scorching me from all directions. My shoulders are permanently fiery now. My elbows feel locked at a crook. When I stop paddling and try to straighten my arms, I find I can barely do so.

I pick a point on the shore, a mile or two distant, and make for it. Then another. Then another. I begin to discover a ritual aspect to the labour, a metronomic pleasure in the pain.

We paddle all afternoon. As dusk approaches, we are all tiring. It is one of the tougher days I have known, physically speaking: a 4 a.m. start, then some twenty miles over flat water. Yet we seem barely to have moved within the vastness of the lake and its self-repeating patterns.

The high sky steadily fades to milk at its edges, blue in its arches, soot at its summit. The air close to us greys, then charcoals.

We cannot find a place to beach and sleep. Raph has a map on which he's marked possible camping locations, but neither he nor Danny have ever been this far north on the lake. Each site we reach either is flooded by the unusually high water or simply doesn't exist.

The precipitous west coast of the lake, along which we are skirting, offers little hospitality. Vast scree-slopes fan beneath shattered cliffs, their run-outs rubbled with giant blocks that tumble down to the shoreline and into the lake. Where there is no rock, there is forest, massing and intimidating. Pines, alder and birch-scrub run right to the water.

So we must paddle on.

Dark is falling. Wayne is far behind me now, invisible in the shadows. He is struggling. My own arms feel numb with use. I don't know if I can make the next few miles. I wonder if we will somehow have to sleep in the boats, tethered to the shore.

Then we round a promontory of rock and enter a new world.

Here, three-hundred-foot-high cliffs rise vertically from the water. They are thylacine-striped in rust and black, and lightning-struck by quartzite.

The wind suddenly drops to utter stillness. Water is sleek and calm as oil. Air is shocking in its silence after the day-long roar of the gale. The dusk is huge.

I follow the line of the cliffs, keeping thirty feet or so out into the lake in case of rockfall. The water now seems molasses-thick and black as treacle. My paddle stirs it into spirals. The water-whispers of my blade echo back at me from the cliff walls.

I feel the uncanny tranquillity that comes from a tired body and a tired mind. I feel I could paddle on into this never-ending dusk for ever.

Then a northern diver, a loon, begins to call – a haunting, tremulous cry which echoes off the rock walls and my shoulder blades, my jawbones, my spine. It keeps calling and I feel each bone clear in me, as if the sound is X-raying me.

The loon is a few hundred yards to my south. I can only see the bright-white band on its neck – a snow-dash, gathering the last of the light to it. The rest of its dark-feathered body is lost in dusk water and dusk air. It cries and cries, seconds-old sounds meeting billion-year-old rock.

We turn past the last of the western cliffs and a vast bay opens, a mile or more from shore to shore. This is the inflow of the West Magpie, a river far too wild for us to paddle, a river who drains a basin of hundreds of square miles to our north-west. The West Magpie has cored out this bay – and it has also created a long, raised bar of sand on the bay's south-western edge. There, for sure, we can camp. I can see the bar glinting across the bay: a thin layer of yellow where the darkness of the forest meets the darkness of the lake.

The sun falling over the river-mouth sets spools of golden light whirring across the lake towards us. They reach Ilya first, who is perhaps five hundred yards ahead of me. He is caught first, struck and spun in gold. I see him look towards the light, lay his paddle across his boat, and sit in silence, drifting in that end-times radiance. Then the golden spools catch me in turn, spiral me into themselves and carry me on.

The loon calls and calls. The world turns to other metals. The calls are liquid mercury, wobbling over the steel water. The forested slopes and ridgelines of the eastern shore are islands of bronze, footless in shadows of ink.

Far ahead I see Raph reach the sandbar, leap from his boat, haul it up and – a shadow on a play-stage – begin to gather wood for a fire. By the time I finally beach my boat, the sun is a red rim of under-light on a single reef of cloud and Raph has the fire going. I drop to my heels by it in the soft sand, warm my hands, stare into its dancing heart, feeling shattered and wild. The smell of woodsmoke fills the air.

Wayne and Danny arrive twenty minutes later. Wayne staggers stiff-legged and white-faced up the beach towards the fire. I rise and make the mistake of trying to embrace him, but he shies away and pushes past me wordlessly. His eyes flash blades. There's anger in him; I can see it burning hot. Anger at what he perceives as his own weakness. He's tired to the marrow. He's worried that his body won't bear him right through this long journey.

The fire steals the dying sun's colours.

The flames gather the darkness into themselves, hauling in the night in ropes and sheets.

Wayne and I pitch our tents facing east, as per Rita's orders. White sand spiders, each the size of a finger-pad, scuttle and hiss where the light-pools of our head torches fall.

I lie in my tent, my bones and flesh made of water now, all shifting side to side, rocking and slopping.

That night I dream of a stone whale surfacing out of black water beneath my kayak, nudging me up into the air until I and my boat are briefly balanced on its mineral back.

That night a moose wanders through our camp, unknown to any of us, its breath snorting from velvet nostrils in the cold night air. It leaves cloven prints the size of dinner plates in the sand between our tents.

~

We wake into a windless, cloudless morning. I unzip my door and the early sun floods me.

Cold air. We are cloud-makers with each exhalation.

Ridgelines of forested hills fold together at the visible head of this endless lake, blued by distance.

Wayne is already sitting by the fire. He has been up since five. I'll learn that he does this every day we are on the river. I figure he finds it better to face his wolves in pre-dawn light while upright and with a cup of tea in his hand. Each morning he will be there when I rise, looking into the fire through the half-light. Each morning the same quiet greetings.

Hey, man.

Hey.

Rituals next. Tobacco for the water, tobacco for the land.

We triple-check our site to make sure we have left no trace behind, then slip the boats into the still, clear water.

Lacustrine calm. The kayaks wrinkling the smoothness. Everything mirrored. Double the trees, double the cliffs. Clouds crossing the water before us with huge slowness.

The water forms millions of shifting lozenges of light, through which we slide. Close to the shore, where the water is shallow, we pass over fields of lake grass, lying on the underside of the surface in green ribbons. Their alignment shows the flows of current and wind.

Again, we sight for a point, a spit, a ridge dipping down to meet the water. Paddle for the point. Choose the next spit, the next point. Paddle for it. A rhythm settles in. The pain in my elbows is tremendous, a red-hot needle thrust into them with each stroke. My headache prowls the perimeter, looking for a way in. Nothing to be done but pull on, distracting myself with dreams and conversation.

I realize again, though, that along with the exhaustion a deep, strange serenity, unlike any I have known before, is emerging, as if I am somehow being . . . slowly flooded from within. That is the best account of it I can find. *As if I'm being slowly flooded from within.*

We pass the inflow of a river to the west. It reaches the lake in a churning white rapid.

'That river drains Lac de la Mine,' says Ilya. 'I've been up that on skis. My son Theo was with me.'

'How old was he, Ilya?'

'Oh, around eight, I think? Yes, eight. We'd skied up to this part of the lake from the coast over a few days, and then we wanted to go exploring, so we headed up that river.'

'The rapids were frozen solid?'

'Mostly. There was always a way through or round them.'

My brain boggles at the thought of taking an eight-year-old on a multi-day winter trip on skis, into frozen country as far from help as this.

'And then?'

'And then, well, I got a bit distracted by the excitement of the new places we were finding up the river, so we went a bit far, and dark caught up with us. We only made it back at eleven p.m. or so to our camp on the east side of the lake.'

'So the last, what, *six hours* were in total darkness? In winter?'

Ilya scratches his head.

'Maybe the last seven hours,' he says.

'At least the going must have been good when you got back to the lake?'

'You'd be surprised. A lake this big? Its surface is rarely smooth. When it freezes, the wind forms, how do you say it, sastrugi? The snow-ridges? They were difficult that day. Theo did well.'

'I remember coming out of that river in summer once,' Danny says thoughtfully. 'We pack-rafted it. Getting in was tricky, I recall. We had to abseil in.'

I have come to think of Ilya as the Bear, for his huge power, his bristly beard and scalp, and for his ambling, shambling nature. And if Ilya is the Bear, then Raph is surely the Salmon, for the part-liquid way in which he moves on and with the river. His kayak is an extension of him, and the water an extension of his kayak. And Danny? Danny is the Boss, no doubt: a natural, gentle leader of people.

There's no way Wayne and I could be here without the Bear, the Boss and the Salmon. They're the ones who make this hard, long jour-ney possible. They teach us, look after us. Expeditions form odd, small families, temporary but tight-knit. Here, Wayne and I are the children.

~

On that long, tranquil second day on the lake, the water helps grow confidences and intimacies between near strangers. Raph and I paddle together for an hour or so, shut into our own chamber of closeness. He tells me about a shocking, sudden trauma his partner's family had suffered.

I nod, murmur heartfelt *so-sorries*. There is nothing else to say.

Another diver cries ahead of us, whirling and elegiac. Raph and I ship our paddles and drift, listening to it cry. Then its smooth body tilts briefly up, like a surfaced submarine hit by a torpedo, and it dives forwards – slipping beneath the lake's brim and leaving scarcely a spiral.

Late that afternoon we spot a flat curve of sand on the west coast of the lake, backed by a little terrace of bedrock, no more than ten yards at its widest between water and stone. A few yards to its south, a small creek gurgles out of alder scrub.

It's an irresistible campsite. We beach our boats in a line, like hauled-out seals, and set up camp. The sand is too shallow and soft for pegs, so we weigh our tents down with rocks, placing one inside each corner. To meet Rita's requirement that we face our tents east, Wayne and I must orient our tents towards the bedrock terrace. So be it. This is not an instruction I plan to ignore. My tent is perched on the last taper of sand, just a foot or so from the waterline.

The Bear disappears into the woods on an undisclosed mission, perhaps to hunt a porcupine or wrestle a moose.

He emerges twenty minutes later, striding from between the spruces, stripped to his orange underwear, with a pair of swimming goggles strapped to his forehead. He gets into his kayak, pushes off, and paddles out thirty yards or so to what looks like deeper water. There, he stands up in the boat, snaps his goggles over his eyes and without hesitation dives in, letting loose a bellow and a roar as he goes.

'I think the water may be shallower there than Ilya thinks,' says Danny.

The Bear surfaces almost immediately. He has a big smile, though, and he taps his skull with his palm to indicate, as far as I can tell, that he has struck a rock with his head. I pity the rock.

That evening, when the wind drops, the first wave of blackflies hits us.

I notice a small, shiny, bulbous-bodied fly crawling on my hand. It looks rather sweet – like a stubby winged ant. It's a miniature child's toy of an insect. I peer at it.

'Is this the notorious blackfly?' I ask, unimpressed. 'It doesn't seem to be a biter.'

The Bear shifts uneasily, and scratches the stubbly top of his head, making a sound like a boot-scraper.

'Yeah, that's a blackfly. And they do bite.' He pauses respectfully. 'They make quite a team with the mosquitoes. The blackflies crawl around a lot; the mosquitoes buzz around. The blackflies like sun; the mosquitoes like shade. The blackflies disappear after dusk, and the mosquitoes take over. The thing about blackflies – well, one of the things about blackflies – is that you don't really notice them biting you until after the damage is done.'

There are quite a few blackflies on and around us now, I note with interest. I look over at Wayne. He's bleeding from his forehead.

'You're bleeding from your forehead, Wayne,' I say. He must have clipped it on a branch while foraging for firewood, I think.

'You're bleeding from your neck, Rob,' he says. 'Really quite a lot.' I must have clipped it on a branch while foraging for firewood, I think. Strange, I didn't feel it. Nor did I go foraging for firewood, now I think about it.

'That'll be the blackflies,' says the Bear.

Blood is now flowing from ten or twelve small points on Wayne's forehead. It looks like he's been raked by a miniature Uzi, stitching a line of minute bullet-holes from temple to temple.

I raise a hand to my neck. It comes away red. The surface of my neck now feels as if I am running my hand over a small volcano-chain on a relief-map of a crustal plate-zone. It is repulsive.

'Blackflies in number have been known to kill mules,' says Ilya.

'Nothing kills mules,' says Wayne.

'An atom bomb couldn't kill a mule,' I say. 'Mules are the shopping trolleys of the ungulate world: fundamentally indestructible. They are what will be left standing after the nuclear warheads rain down: still there, still idly cropping tufts of irradiated grass.'

'Blackflies can definitely kill mules,' says Ilya with certainty.

I pat a lot more blood off my neck. I am starting to think that blackflies can probably kill shopping trolleys too.

An hour or so later, Wayne walks over to me. 'My head's topography has been substantially reshaped by these bites,' he says.

I examine him, and whistle. He is right. Where Wayne's temples had been, there are now thickened domes of flesh, histamine-taut and shiny. All the wrinkles on his forehead have vanished. His cheeks are beginning to bulge up and out, impinging on his sight.

'At least what they've done to you is symmetrical,' I say.

The late sun bronzes forested ridgelines to our south.

A half-foot-long dragonfly slips briefly out of the Jurassic era, then vanishes again.

The moon rises just shy of full, glowing buttery yellow between the black pines, above the orange of the fire.

The river smelts moonlight to silver.

Overnight, I wake to feel that the wind has swung round to a big southerly, plucking the tent canvas, shifting its frame. I am glad of the rocks that are holding me down. It will be a hard day paddling into this tomorrow.

~

The law is a storied thing, and as such can be re-storied.

The consequences of recognizing the Mutehekau Shipu as a living, rights-bearing being have quickly rippled outwards. Itself influenced by earlier Rights of Nature declarations, this declaration has in turn inspired new actions. The story of the Mutehekau Shipu, writes Yenny Cárdenas, 'is now a story to tell across Canada and many countries. Narratives are a powerful way to change Canadian law.'

On 5 May 2022 the modestly named, philosophically disruptive 'Bill C-271' was given its first reading in the Canadian House of Commons. It is the draft of an Act which seeks to 'give legal capacity to the St Lawrence River' and to establish a council of eleven river guardians to oversee its protection.

The bill, observed Ross Montour – Chief of the Mohawk Council of Kahnawake – would merely formalize the guardianship role that Indigenous people have performed with and for the river over millennia. But he also welcomed the Indigenous perspective, which he saw as actively dissident towards Western legal framings of the St Lawrence: 'All things on the Earth have a spirit and a life whether they are inanimate or not. That spirit is what is specific to that resolution. If it's a legal person, it's protected, and we know that Quebec is not going to do it.'

On the shores of Lake Erie, sixteen-year-old Anellah Orosz and her younger brother Deklan heard the news of the Mutehekau Shipu victory, and were inspired to campaign for Lake Erie – the southernmost of the Great Lakes; poor, wounded, algally poisoned Lake Erie – also to be recognized as a being with rights and personhood. 'We believe water and nature deserve protection and respect,' they said, 'rather than treating [them] as something that we can own or as an exploitable resource.' These youth activists want their First Nation to adopt a Band Council resolution which recognizes the lake as 'a living entity under Indigenous law' – and then they hope to get other First Nations to follow suit.

Dozens of communities in the United States have now used the

Rights of Nature as a means to protect water, soil, mountains, streams —
and even particular species. In Orange County, Florida (Seminole
Territory), for instance, the rights of Lake Mary Jane have been
asserted. The White Earth Band of Ojibwe has campaigned for the
rights of manoomin (wild rice); the Sauk-Suiattle Tribe has successfully fought for the recognition of the rights of Tsuladxw (Pacific
salmon); and a major campaign to recognize the rights of the ecologic-
ally stricken Great Salt Lake was under way until the Utah State
Legislature, rattled by the campaign, passed a House bill prohibiting
the granting of legal personhood to any natural entities. In New York
State, the town of Potsdam has recently passed a resolution acknow-
ledging the inherent rights of the Raquette River and committing the
town council to pass binding law as a result; the town of Canton, New
York, is presently preparing to commend a similar process. In 2020 the
Tsilhqot'in Nation in western Canada documented rights and responsibilities in the Sturgeon (Fraser) River. These irruptions of ecocentric
legislation in North America have predominantly been local in origin
and scope – but change brought from below is often the most durable.

Geographies of natural rights are beginning to match up; pieces of
jigsaws are being pushed together, their edges meeting, forming continuous areas of resistance to one-dimensional definitions of rivers.

~

Sunrise.

Scent of pine resin in the cool air.

Mist in a three-foot layer a hundred yards or more from the shore,
twisting like a troupe of little acrobats.

The southerly gale has dropped to nothing. The morning is still; the
lake is foil.

'A funny thing happened in the night,' says Wayne from his tent.
'My eyes swelled shut. I've had to spend about half an hour massaging
them, just in order to be able to see.'

He emerges. '*Whoosh,*' I say. Wayne's head looks like a pumpkin. His eyes are arrow-slits set in masonry of hard-swollen flesh. His eyelids have turned into duvets; his cheeks are grapefruits.

'Are you laughing at me, Rob? I can't really see if you are. But it seems like you might be.'

Tobacco for the water, tobacco for the land, antihistamine for Wayne.

Squirrels chitter their alarm-calls as we move around the camp. We only have ten miles or so left to paddle to the point where the lower Mutehekau Shipu flows out of the lake. Today, I think, we will meet the river – we will make the phase-shift from flat water to moving, from mirror to current. I'm eager for this transition. I realize I have no headache for the first time in over a week. It's been washed away.

I leave before the others, wanting to paddle alone in this marvellous stillness.

Fifty yards ahead of me, the water is gold, and it is gold for as far as I can see down the lake. *Just the light, surely?* No, it can't be the light, for the band of gold doesn't correspond to the morning sun's border with shadow.

I reach the band, pass into it and understand.

The gold is pollen. Billions and billions of pollen grains which have been knocked from the trees by the big southerly overnight and then blown out onto the water to form this gold-dust surface. Not light, then, but life.

As I paddle through it, the gold swirls, parts and then re-closes behind me like a zip being pulled, so that my wake is only ever a yard or two of open black oil.

Ahead I can see huge spirals and spurs of gold curving out towards the lake's centre. Seen from above, it must look like the marbled endpapers of an eighteenth-century book. Ahead of me, tall rocks shaped like watchful grey knights line the shore. I pass these sentinels slowly.

The first sign of the change is the appearance of long, low waves that start to cluck and glug against the hull of my boat. I pause paddling, puzzled. There is no wind and no current, and so there should be no waves. It is inexplicable, unsettling.

The waves increase in breadth and regularity, now passing under me and lifting me like speed bumps. Then I realize: it's the outrider of the wind – the new southerly that has been promised. Miles away down the lake, that wind is rising and driving water ahead of itself, which I am meeting as waves but not yet as wind.

I turn a crook in the lake, where it straightens due south, and here the wind reaches and touches me – first just a hand in the chest pressing me gently backwards, fingers lightly kneading the flesh of my cheeks. Within a minute, though, the water is standing up in little karate-chop waves. I have to paddle harder both to keep a course and to drive the kayak forwards.

My pulse quickens. The wind is a jet-engine roar now. Paddling the remaining length of the lake directly into it will be surely impossible. Raph is a few hundred yards away. He gestures urgently to the distant eastern shore. I understand. We must traverse the open lake to where cliffs fall sheer to the water; we can hug that shore and creep along in the wind-shadow of the cliffs, hiding as best from the gale as we can.

It's a tough pull across the open water. The waves rise to a height of two feet, hammering on the boat with gauntleted fists, slapping my arms and splashing my face. *Thunk, slap, thunk-slap.* Fear in my chest – partly the waves intimidating me, partly the knowledge that we'll meet the river and its force soon, which will make these waves look like babies.

It's running at two hundred and seventy-five. All the rain.

Raph and I reach the eastern cliffs, pull tight in – and the wind-profile is transformed. Sound also changes instantly, like stepping off shingle and onto sand. We raft up and bob together to wait for Danny and Wayne.

'The air's hazy today,' says Raph. 'I think it's the smoke from wild-fires being blown in by the wind. But the fires may be hundreds of miles away.'

The fire weather in Canada this year began five months ago, in March: before the snow had melted from the boreal forest, before the spring floods had filled the northern rivers. Disease had bulked out the fuel load with blowdowns and brash. The previous year's drought had dried the lichen and sphagnum, turning the understorey to tinder. Once a wildfire started, the spread-rate from the point of ignition was very high. Strong winds from the north and east drove the reaction zones onwards. The wildfires shifted like creatures, crested ridges, leaped rivers. By May there were more than a thousand fires burning across Canada, from British Columbia to Newfoundland. Viewed from space on satellite images, the smoke-plumes flowed laterally from their origin-points, widening as they extended. They looked like plumes from the deep-sea vents where life was born. They looked like hundreds of bad new streams and rivers, rising as thick white water and refusing to follow the contours of the land.

In early June the prevailing winds had swung round to the northwest, driving the smoke from Quebec's wildfires for hundreds of miles south across the Gulf of St Lawrence and into upstate New York. The skies above Manhattan were tinted a pale orange. The wind persisted. The air coppered.

New Yorkers shared photographs of the reddened skies online, *#EverydayApocalypse*, *#LifeOnMars*.

Welcome to our world, Californians replied. *Welcome to the glorious Pyrocene!*

~

It is almost a mythical idea to me that this vast lake, this inland sea, might possess an end. But over the course of that afternoon, as we sneak a leeward line down the shore of the lake, the flanking ridges begin to bunch and narrow towards one another, and the blue hill-line which end-stops both water and eye does not recede as others have.

Then, faintly, I feel it: a current, the slightest of pulls – *follow me please, come this way* – and long before I can see the mouth of the Mutehekau Shipu I can sense it, for I am suddenly now in the threshold where flow takes over from flat, and I call back to Wayne with a whoop – 'Can you feel it too? Can you feel it?!' – and an involuntary shudder of force moves through me, and the current's pull becomes stronger, less negotiable – *you will come with me* now – and then it is as if the lake has somehow tilted such that I am now sliding down its slope, and the water ahead is behaving strangely – *a funny piece of water, that* – for it looks deckle-edged and cockled, forming a tangle of movement and shallow turbulence, but then amid that turbulence I see, lying puzzlingly clear, a huge arc of silver-smooth water, a flat-fallen slice of moon over which lines and coils of foam are sliding seemingly without friction, in perfect laminar flow – *like ice riding its own melting on a cast-iron stove* – and my boat bumps over the stipple-line that marks the boundary of that shining moon-slice, and I *know* I have crossed the event horizon, the frontier beyond which all things tend towards the river, and a charge pours up my arms from the water and tingles my trunk and crackles my scalp and neck – *as river births lake, so lake must birth river* – and then the true mouth of the river is there, here, where the lake slips over its own rim and down, a point of astonishment that is also a point of enlivenment, and having longed for days for the lake to speed us on, now I long for the river to slow us down, for I can feel its immense and frightening will, and then I understand that at some level I must surrender agency to this incomprehensible presence.

The river is born and it bears us . . .

The first big rapid is right round the river's first big bend. We meet the outrider waves first: little fins and spikes standing up – *a porcupine's back, a nursery of sharks* – striking a high percussion from the hull, rabbit-punching at my legs as I go over them, and then I see the rapid in all its terrible beauty and my mouth dries instantly with fear, for it's a huge milk-churn of a rapid, thunderous and magnificent: a creamy, narrowing tongue of green-glossy water that begins in the left-hand channel of the river, between the bank's bedrock and a river-central block of boulders, then plunges fast down a short, steep slope into a big, yellowish standing wave, just under four feet high, ceaselessly toppling and rebuilding itself, and from there the flow follows a huge sweeping arc turning nearly right back upon itself, and along this arc are ranged more standing waves, smaller but also green and cream, and yellow in their centres, and then the current pulls even further round beneath a flat-faced rock wall where another big standing wave waits, and it seems absurd that I'm about to paddle this, unthinkable that the river will not flip me, spin me, drown me, bury me there, body and head . . .

'Stay left, catch the tongue, let it take you,' calls the Boss calmly as we approach the edge of the rapid, as we are *drawn* irrevocably into the rapid, like space-debris caught in a black hole's pull. 'Steer for where you want to go. Meet the tall wave head on, plant the paddle hard like a stake and haul on it as you enter the biggest water.'

I glance back. The Bear has a big grin on his face, I see. Happiness radiates out of him like a sun. He is sitting up very straight now in his kayak, his back ramrod-straight, the paddle gripped before him like a toothpick in his immense hands. *He looks like a chauffeur*, I suddenly, absurdly think, *driving a Bentley or a Rolls-Royce, with impeccable posture*. Wayne appears nervous but determined. The Boss leads, the Salmon hangs back, last in line, ready to sweep up casualties and swoop to the rescue, moving effortlessly with the flow.

And then I'm into the rapid, hard into it, the water now vinyl-tight under my boat, and I'm accelerating as the river enters the channel before the block, the golden rocks on the bed of the river are fleeting beneath me, and time is stretching in the way it does at certain moments of terror and exhilaration, so that in the thirty or so century-long seconds it takes to run the rapid, I can see in isolated and shining detail each water droplet and boiling pool, and I slip nose-first over the sill and skim like a ball-bearing on a metal slide down the slope of the tongue and – *bang!* – straight into that big polar-bearish standing wave, and the nose of my craft crashes into its snowy front face which fills it and me with river, and I must *surely* be flipped or buried by the wave, but somehow, perhaps because I have hit it so straight, the nose of the kayak shakes itself free of the impact, and the boat bucks beneath me and begins to rise right up and over first the point and then the ridge of the big wave, and *surely* I must fall backwards out of the boat or be flipped, and then I am punched full in the face by a fist of water but it is the standing wave's valediction and I'm through and upright and the elastic curve of the current pulls me round the 150-degree bend and I can hear Danny yelling something behind me and Wayne is whooping, great belts of sound that rise over the roars of the rapid, and I'm thumping over the smaller green-cream-bronze waves and then I'm under the flat-faced rock wall – *goddammit but this last wave isn't going to flip me if the biggest one didn't* – and I plant the paddle as Danny told me and pull on it like I'm trying to uproot an iron fence post and the pull boosts me into the last standing wave, the sneak-wave right under the rock wall, but I don't hit it at the perpendicular as I had the biggest one and so it shrugs me off its right-hand slope and the boat cants sideways and my stomach lurches and I call out and begin to roll sideways but some amygdalan part of my brain tells me to lean uphill not down and I re-right and then I'm over the blast-wall and into the long black pool below the rapid where the Boss and the Bear already wait, grins on their faces and shouts of congratulation, and Wayne is through too without flipping, and the Salmon swims up to us and my heart is piston-block pumping and Wayne says something like, *Living right, my friend, living right!* with a manic smile on his face, shocked and exhilarated and enlivened.

We flow on.

Late that afternoon, a mile or two down the river, we reach a place to camp. It's an area of flattish ground, brinking a big side-bay to the river, just upstream of a thunderous rapid. A hill rises behind the camp, its slopes dappled an odd red-white pattern.

We will stay here for two nights. Rain's coming; we can feel it building in the air and the pressure on Raph's barometer-watch is dropping steadily. The sky is bruised to our north, but for now the sun shines and the river is a wild, shining blue-black. We pitch camp fast, flies swarming us, tents facing east.

'I could scarcely see the water ahead of me in that rapid,' says Wayne. His face is still grotesquely swollen from the blackfly bites. When he smiles, his crow's-feet crease up so he looks like a pillow trussed with baler twine. 'Near-blindness was OK on still water, but it made the churn hard,' he says.

'It occurs to me,' I say, 'that your injuries are an odd fulfilment of Rita's instruction that we mustn't use our eyes too much, mustn't look too hard when we're on the river.'

As dusk falls, Danny, Wayne and I climb the hill behind the camp. There is no path. Underfoot are bilberries in ripe profusion, which I rake out in handfuls, gather in my palm and throw back like purple pills, clapping my palm to my mouth, relishing the bloom of fresh taste.

Then we are into the plush red-green embroidery of sphagnum bog, and between the bog are wide bands of an ice-white brittle lichen I have never seen before, ghostly and delicate, forming millions of tiny trees, each two or three inches high, which together tessellate the bog into panels. These little trees crunch beneath our feet with each step, like ice crackling on a glacier during the dusk refreeze, and I feel an unease at each stride taken, each shattered print left.

The wind rises as we do. The summit of the hill is cold, bare and raven-haunted; a single black feather caught in lichen, gobs of bilberry-coloured scat on bedrock. From this height we can still glimpse the southern end of the lake, away to the north-west, and to either side of it ridgelines of forest receding beyond sight. *We passed through that*, I think, *all of it*.

What really draws my eye and holds it, though, is the river itself: now a shining bead of mercury through the darkening trees, pulling the mind downstream, its call a low, hushing white noise. Even at this distance, it exerts an immense — my tired brain fumbles for the word — *charisma?* No, that's not quite right. An immense . . . *presence?* That will have to do for now. The river, so long anticipated, has already begun to dominate my attention, my perception, my waking thoughts, already begun to frustrate language's short reach.

I can scarcely remember the lake. The river has us now.

Mare's-tail clouds whisk the northern sky. The weather change is coming fast.

Back at the camp, in the last light, I kneel on a smoothed rock at the river's edge. I feel again I should somehow greet the river, but it seems preposterous to do so. If this silver-gold . . . entity *speaks*, it's not going to be in my language.

So instead I plunge my head underwater, and hold it there in the bone-biting cold. I force my eyes open, and rinse my sight clean, then lift my head clear, gasping and dripping, my mind ringing. Red and white fireworks pop in the night of my skull.

We fish in the big side-bay and catch five brook trout. Their golden flanks are spotted with red embers. They are the precious metals of this water, as the hummingbirds were of Los Cedros, and the bee-eaters were of Chennai. We clean them and cook them on the fire.

Ilya sits apart from us at dusk, eating his trout, watching the river intently.

Mackerel-pattern clouds form as the last light crumbles.

I burn branches of juniper. The scent reminds me of fires at camps in the Himalayas, before big days of mountain ascent, in air chill as marble.

Later, round the fire, in the cloak of the dark, Ilya speaks tentatively about his troubles: his depression, his compulsive eating, his recourse to alcohol, so severe at times that he now keeps an entirely dry house. He speaks with puzzlement and clarity: clarity about the difficulties he faces; puzzlement that he is able to identify them but do so little about them. He speaks of his confusion at how the human world has come to do itself and all else such harm, in so many ways. He speaks of how he both meditates and medicates with rivers and wild land.

'When I'm on a river trip like this,' he says, 'I feel alive again. At times, at home, I feel half-dead.'

Wayne listens, watches. In the dancing orange light, with the shadows, his face pale, rounded and swollen, his eyes dark slits of night, it looks as if he is wearing a death mask.

Raph sits by the fire, taking a brief pause from his seemingly endless work of campcraft, advice and help-giving. He's messaging his partner on the inReach satellite phone.

I'm here. It's OK. I'm alive. Alive, still, again.

~

Around midnight the rainstorm comes, and the wind with it.

It rains hard until 3 a.m. or so, then torrentially through to dawn.

The wind bullies the camp, whipping small trees and deforming the tents. I sleep fitfully, and wake cold at 4 a.m. to find my sleeping bag soaked through, and the ceiling of the tent belled down above me by the weight of water which has gathered there, and which is plipping onto me like juice from a wine press. Something has gone very wrong with the tent; the flysheet should not be leaking through to the inner like this, even in rain this heavy.

I pull out a 150-litre heavy-duty black plastic contractor bag and crawl inside it, sleeping bag and all. I shiver there in my plastic sack until dawn, waterproofed but chill to the bone, my mind fixated on the thought of the river rising with this rain, becoming even bigger, yet more monstrous. I feel afraid.

Grey, greasy dawn. The rain has grudgingly stopped. Wayne is by the fire, of course, hunched and silent.

Hey, man.

Hey.

A pinch of tobacco for the rocks, a pinch for the river.

Today Wayne and I will fast, as per Rita's instruction. My body feels jittery, as if it knows tough times are coming.

Sitting together in the wretched light of that dawn, Wayne and I talk quietly about a novella we both regard highly called 'The Willows'. It was written by Algernon Blackwood in 1907 and describes a canoe trip made by two friends – 'the Swede' and a nameless narrator – along the Danube. The adventure begins in eagerness and good spirits, but descends into darkness when a rainstorm strikes, the water begins to rise and they find themselves trapped on a shingle island in the middle of a stretch of the river where millions of willow trees thrive along the banks and on the islands. As the river spates, they realize their island is slowly being eroded by the current.

That, it turns out, is the least of their problems. As night falls, the two men hear an eerie ringing noise emanating around them from the darkness. Then a sound begins to rise: 'a gong-like humming', the 'whirring of wings.' The two men gradually comprehend that they have somehow stumbled into a place where the usual screens are not in place. What they are hearing is the sheer, terrifying presence of animate matter – the river, the storm, the willows – unmediated and therefore crushing.

'We had strayed,' says the unnamed narrator, 'into some region . . . where the risks were great, yet unintelligible to us: where the frontiers of some unhuman world lay close about us.' The noise they can hear, says the Swede, is 'the sound of their world, the humming in *their* region. The division here is so thin that it leaks through somehow.' The men sense that the willows are in some way hunting them; that the trees track them by listening to their thoughts. The only way to go undetected is *not to think*.

'Our thoughts make spirals in their world,' says the Swede urgently to his friend in the darkness. 'We must keep them *out of our minds* at all costs if possible.'

'The Willows' is sometimes called a ghost story, but that description falls far short of both its metaphysics and its achievement. It's an attempt to fathom in prose what it might mean to encounter and acknowledge the anima of the 'non-human world'. It tries to find form for what Blackwood calls 'the early feeling that everything was alive, the dim sense that some kind of consciousness struggled through every form, even that a sort of inarticulate communication with this other life was possible'.

Central to that 'other life' is the river itself. 'The Danube,' says the narrator early in their journey, 'more than any other river I knew, impressed us from the very beginning with its *aliveness*.'

In front of us, as we talk, Wayne and I can see our river visibly swollen by the rain of the previous twelve hours. The smooth rock on which I'd knelt to dunk my head the night before is now half flooded. The wind is strong, harrying. The sun is sunk behind a caul of cloud. My fear rises with the river.

That day, under grey skies, Wayne and I learn first how to interpret the river, then how to move upon it. Danny and Raph are our literacy teachers. It is, really, a hydro-poetics class: an exercise in the close-reading of water from two experts of the art.

We learn how to 'ferry' across the river, chaining eddy pool to eddy pool: how to make sudden, leaning dashes across big channels of current before crossing the eddy-line and holding position in the stiller water, regaining breath and balance, then making the next dash to the next eddy. We learn how to 'peel out' into a channel, and how to 'eddy out' into an eddy. We start to build water-glossaries in our minds and eyes for features of the river: stretches of 'laminar flow', where water is slipping over its own layers in near-frictionless smoothness; also 'tongues', 'boils', 'pillows' and 'standing waves'.

Then Danny runs us through the real dangers, the true killers.

There's the 'strainer': a flood-stripped tree trunk, jagged with shattered radial branches, that gets jammed between boulders on the river. Hit one of those and the boat will puncture, or wrap and buck you out, and you might well get trapped under the strainer, clothes or straps caught in a branch, pressed down by the onrush of the current.

There's the 'sieve': a tunnel or aperture within rocks themselves, into which a boat, foot or body might be jammed and then pinned by the current. Sieves are a plausible risk in limestone rivers; they're unlikely here on the old, hard Canadian Shield, but they do sometimes form where boulders have tumbled over one another.

Then there's the 'hole'. Of all the river-words, this is the one – plain, everyday – that ices my heart. A hole is formed where flow plunges down a slope with sufficient force that it curls constantly back on itself at the zone of impact. A hole can trap an object, a body, hold it in a spin cycle of onwards rush and backwards wash, tumbling and tumbling in that hungry, tireless maw until it has whittled it to nothing or swallowed it whole.

There are countless holes on this river between us and the sea.

Danny schools us on capsize drills. *If you swim, there are three rules. One, don't panic. Two, get clear of the craft. Three, get your feet up, float flat, head upstream. Now say them back to me . . .*

We practise for an hour or so: peeling out, ferrying, eddying out. My water literacy improves. I think I'm gaining in competence and confidence. But then I flip in quiet water and get stuck under my over-turned kayak as I surface – and stay stuck, coming up three times under the hull, feeling the panic surging in me, then at last kicking clear to emerge, spluttering and furious with myself. I recover for a while on the bank, shaking from hunger and cold, trying to disguise my body's response.

Danny thinks Wayne and I shouldn't be fasting, I know.

Amid the fear and the discomfort, I find myself increasingly fasci-nated by eddies and the eddy-line. I thought I knew what an eddy was: a flow of water moving counter-directional to the main current, close to the bank. Simple. I'd dropped leaves and sticks as a child into eddy pools, enjoyed the unexpected movement upstream. Eddies were just a petty sideshow to the main flow.

But it turns out that a river like this one, wild and vast and forceful, is made almost as much of eddies as of currents, and these eddies are immense: wide corridors of whirling, shining water which possess their own rules of entry and behaviour. This is a river that runs *back* on itself, uphill in great sleek surges of volume. And to *be* the stick or the leaf, dropped into one of these eddies – well, this is something else entirely, I am discovering.

Here, the eddy-line is the always shifting boundary between main flow and counterflow. Quickly, I learn to identify the signs that mark it: the ways foam gathers and migrates around it, the texture-change from turbulence to gloss – and above all the spirals which weave and dance along it. Where one current flows against another, spin is produced in the water column, which rises to express itself on the surface as helixes. On a big eddy-line, these spirals can be wide and deep enough to put your fist in and pull it out dry. The spirals are life-bringers: they are what draws oxygen down into the water column, and in rapids they're also what allows migrating fish to travel upstream. Salmon and steelheads seek, find and leap into the vortices formed in the turbulence, knowing they will serve as portals in the flow.

Their thoughts make spirals in our world . . .

The rain builds in the afternoon. I hunch in the tent, taping up my fingers where they're raw from the paddle. Worry and fatigue curdle together in my belly. I've lost all my boldness. The river is breaking me down, fast.

That night the rain is so hard it pours off the hill in streams, one of which runs under the lower half of my tent. My feet and legs float and wobble. I am literally in a waterbed.

In snatches of sleep, I dream old dreams. *A long-shanked figure stalking the evergreen forest. The spiral made by the whirlpool at the world's end, whose current is space and whose counter-current is time.*

I wake at 3 a.m. with vast weight on my spirit, as if pressed by stones.

At 5 a.m. I surface again. There's no sound of rain – and bright sun is pushing straight through the door of the tent. The storm has passed.

I struggle out of the tent into a bright world. The rain has rinsed the air, knocking all the dust from it. With no particles left to impede light or eye, the air is a clear lens. Colours and forms startle and pop. Sphagnum is scarlet, not russet.

Light floods the river and its rock-bones are bronze and gold again in the shallows, its tongues green, and its eddies shimmer tungsten blue.

Wayne is crouched by the fire. He has a faraway look in his eyes. He has fasted for twenty-four hours now. His cheeks have finally lost their puffiness, and dipped in on themselves again. His face looks hollowed and grey, his eyeballs almost bulbous.

'Wayne, are you OK?'

'Something . . . happened to me in the night. Just like Rita said it would, during the fast. I worked out the question I have for the river.'

I wonder if it has to do with his dead friend, Paul. *Will I see him again, ever?*

I'm happy for Wayne that he knows his question, though he doesn't seem too happy himself.

But what's *my* question for the river? I don't know yet. I can't waste it. I get one shot at it.

I wonder if it is to do with fear. Or age. I have old bones now. They ache in the cold.

~

Water can bury you as sure as earth can.

That morning, Wayne and I break our fast, then we all strike camp quickly. We have a huge day ahead: many miles, a portage and many rapids, most of them big enough to have been given nicknames – Porcupine, Snow-White – and last of all, right at the end of the day, if we make it that far, the mighty Marmite.

'You'll like Marmite,' says Danny, with a wintry smile.

The wind has swung round to a northerly overnight. It's a colder wind, but a drying wind also.

266

The light of the rising sun sets the world ringing like a singing bowl.

That morning, we run rapid after rapid. Porcupine is as spiky as it sounds. Snow-White is immense and sustained, and beyond me and Wayne, so we must hand-line the boats down it, wading the margin of the river's left bank, floating the boats on straps, slipping on wet rocks below the surface. The river pulls and pushes our legs, eager to sweep us off and away. My spirits move up and down the octave range.

We flow on.

All the rain has fattened the river. I flip twice, once in big water: dunked and doused and shocked, floating down into a run-out pool, catching my kayak as it bobs past. The river exhilarates and intimidates.

Wayne flips three times. Each time he comes up more clenched, more shaken. He stops speaking. His face goes a greyish-green colour, the colour of fear and fury. I can sense the rattlesnake in him tensing and coiling.

Hot sun. River glitter.

An odd, black-feathered catechism forms in my head, then plays on loop in my skull jukebox:

Who is stronger than Mountain?
  Me, obviously, says River.
Who is older than death?
  Me, of course, says River . . .

Around two o'clock, on a stretch of calm river, we haul the boats up onto a sloped plain of riverbank bedrock. Raph sets a driftwood fire going.

I peel off my dry-suit and wet clothes, down to my shorts. There's a body-shaped hollow worn into the rock and I bask in it, feeling the light hot on my skin above and the rock hot on my skin below. I am wearing both gneiss almost as old as the Earth, and photons fired from the sun eight minutes ago.

There's a thrumming in my body, the source of which I cannot identify. I remember an account I'd heard from a man who was swimming in an Arctic fjord when a pod of orca approached him. He sank beneath the surface and drifted, in order to seem less like prey. A female orca circled him six times, looking at him throughout. *I could feel her echolocation through my whole body . . .*

The river is starting to feel like that orca – as if some vast and unknowable other life-way is scanning me, echolocating me, clicking away on frequencies far beyond the hertz range of human ears or minds.

Tiny red-hot-poker lichens burn like matchsticks in the sunlight. Thousands of silvered pieces of driftwood have gathered in clefts in the rock: an ossuary of water-worn river-bones. The grain of this wood is intricate and whorled into currents and eddies. *Everything is becoming river.*

Wayne finds a piece of driftwood perhaps four inches long and three inches high, and unmistakably in the shape of a bear – as if its outline had been drawn by the hand of one of the painters of Lascaux or Chauvet, though the artists of this maquette are water, gravity and time.

Ilya gestures at the trees behind us on the bankside: alders, pines. Many seem to have been ring-barked, some of them to death, at around the same height. 'What do you think did that?' he asks.

'Moose?'

'Nope. Guess again.'

'Bears?'

'Nope. Ice. That's the winter high-water mark.'

Good God. The thought of this river in winter and the spring spate brings into perspective its relative summer kindliness. The river six feet higher than now, its swollen current crashing sharp shields and plates of ice into those trees, cutting and rotating round them like a season-long churn of axe-blades . . .

Far to our north move grey-black rain veils, drifting over distant ridgelines.

We flow on.

The sun slides down its bidden arc to the west.

We hear it before we see it.

A new bass undersong to the forest, though the river ahead of us is flat, and we are spinning slowly down it, talking as we go. The undersong rises to become the oversong.

We see it before we reach it.

A band of white mist, fast-shifting and self-replenishing, hangs above the river horizon, perhaps half a mile away from us and approaching fast. Spindrift plumes up and steams away, forming its own spirals and eddies on a vertical plane. The land beyond is punched down, sunk out of sight, and speaks of a big drop.

The river is falling far and fast, and as it falls it is exploding itself upon rock, is vaporizing itself – and that vapour is dancing like a veil above the brink.

Fear slithers down my throat.

'This is big water coming up,' shouts Danny. 'Marmite! Plenty of four- and five-foot waves.'

We pull into a side-pool and tether the boats to a thicket of alders. This is most definitely a feature we need to reconnoitre. We bushwhack to a spit of bedrock at the head of the rapid.

My mouth has dried to glue. I can feel the river's thunder coming through the rocks. I can hear the boulders it is moving along its belly, within its gizzard.

'Get through this,' says Raph, 'and our campsite is right there.' He points with his paddle to a thirty-foot-deep cleft in the bedrock of the bank, a few hundred yards downstream of the rapid's end.

He might as well be pointing to the moon; it feels at least as distant.

Ahead is a welter of white water, which looks as if it is constantly under bombardment. Water detonates, billows, bellows, shrapnels in all directions.

A green slope of water narrows the main channel of the river straight into a standing wave easily six feet tall from trough to tip, beyond which lie a hundred yards or more of four- and five-foot waves, continuously peaking. The six-footer is the biggest I have seen on the river, crescent-faced and roaring, like Hokusai's wave.

'There's no way I'll come through that lot upright,' I say to Danny. 'Well, maybe a . . . three per cent chance. No, I take that back: a one per cent chance.'

'I hear you. No pressure. We can portage it. Not easy, but feasible. In terms of paddling it, I'll only say that it's not hugely consequential water. If you swim, you should just float down into that big, wide flat-water pool at the bottom.'

If you don't get trapped by something in that mosh-pit, nags my brain, *and held under. This river is to you as you are to a moth.*

Wayne and I confer. There is something cussed in both of us to even consider running this, something stubborn and dumb and probably male, something I need to interrogate further but don't have the time to do so right now.

Then in a *snap* I realize it's too much, too dangerous, I'll need to line or portage my boat past this, and I turn to tell Danny, and then with a second *snap* the grey light of the overcast sun is flicked off as a cloud clears it, and the rocks and my eyes are flooded instead with bright-gold light, and the sudden warmth of that light takes the decision for me – for at the moment of choice, the business of choosing is almost always all done – and so I nod a *yes, let's do it* at Wayne and Danny, and we walk back to the boats as if to an execution.

To run water which is far bigger than your ability, you at least prepare with care. You cinch everything tight; you tuck everything away that might snag. My river shoes have a two-millimetre nylon cord loop-lace on them. It's the thing I worry about most. That cord is more than strong enough to hold my body if it snags on a submerged rock and comes under tension. I tuck the lace away inside the shoe as best I can, tighten straps, buddy-check Wayne.

Then we slip into the water and flow on, and within seconds the first wide green slope has me and I glide over and down it and hit the six-foot-high face of the first standing wave and the tip of my boat plunges deep into it, then lifts up shuddering out of water thick as cream and I begin to rise up the face of the wave but then it picks me up as if I were driftwood and tilts me upwards at 45 degrees and spins me through 180 degrees, so in an instant I am – I realize through a blur of fear – facing *upstream*, against time's flow, and *downwards* into the hole at the wave's base into which I am surely now to be plunged, but then I cannot understand what is occurring because effect has not followed cause; a second passes, then two, then a third, and I am still there, suspended in that same absurd-astonishing position, canted on the tilted crest of the wave which is re-forming itself continuously around me, facing up-time and down-world, and I see that by some prestidigitation of river physics I am being *held* there, unintentionally surfing this monstrous wave *backwards* – no, being juggled by this wave – and all around me from shore to shore are more standing waves, but then suddenly river has had enough of its game and I feel the slide and lift of the back of my boat up and over the vertical and I am staring *straight* down into the hole at the wave's foot and then I'm airborne and slammed into the hole head-first and upside down, I am *exploded* out of the boat on impact as if hurled from an ejector seat down into the white hole, and river is punching fingers up my nostrils and river is ramming fists into my mouth and down my throat, and I'm deep down now but the right way up, so I grab handfuls of water and haul for the surface on them as if they are holds on a cliff or rungs on a ladder, but they dissolve under each grasp and I'm kicking out and feel my feet bang against the rocks on the riverbed and one of them catches briefly – *did the loop come free? If I snag now I'm done, cooked, end of* – and then one of my shins smashes a sharp rock edge – *what the hell is down there?* – but then I'm free and then the flotation device has done its job and bobbed me up like a cork and – *three rules, say them back to me, yes Boss, 1) don't panic, 2) get clear, 3) feet up* – and downstream everything is chaos, four of the five boats are belly up – *where's Danny? Where's Ilya? What the fuck could have knocked both the Boss and the Bear over?* – and only the Salmon is still upright, and he is pounding upstream towards me, yelling at me to swim to a side eddy, and I strike out and somehow traverse the current that's rushing me downstream and there are rocks under my hands then under my elbows then under my knees, and I haul myself out onto the rocks and lie there face down, gulping like a landed fish, then roll over onto my back and shout-laugh at the sky, which is now flooded with a late-day storm-light.

That night the moon is full and huge and made of egg yolk, and bright enough to read by. The trees cast moon-shadows across our tents. Spruces living and dead stand in silhouette. The wind has gone, and it is cold enough to see my breath plume inside the tent.

We burn pieces of driftwood, and the flames lick them while loons chain-call up and down the valley.

The river runs flow and counterflow in my brain. I see spirals forming everywhere: on the eddy-lines, under the pull of our paddles, in the grain of the driftwood, the licks of fire, the sky-gyres of a watchful osprey.

Far upstream, gold-dust pollen swirls atop a dark deceleration of water at a bend of the river, like a star map.

Far above, the ongoing helical collision of the Andromeda and the Milky Way galaxies, which began 4.5 billion years ago, spreads across the dark sky like pollen on water.

I fish the run-out pool below the rapid, and catch six trout.

The Bear toasts his socks on the fire. Earlier, he disappeared into the forest, and returned with pockets bulging with bolete mushrooms. Now he's frying them in a bit of butter, while toasting his socks. He stirs the mushrooms with a metal spoon, and adjusts his socks with the same spoon. Then he places the buttery spoon down in the sand, mistaking it for rock in the shadows. Wayne and I watch, mesmerized, as the Bear realizes his error, picks up the spoon – which is now thickly coated in sand – considers his options, puts the spoon in his mouth, licks it clean of the sand, swallows, and returns to stirring the mushrooms and tending his socks.

'Do you have a gizzard you need to furnish with grit, Ilya?' asks Wayne.

The Bear eats three platefuls of the mushrooms, eats my uneaten food, then Wayne's, then eats until there is no more to eat.

Wayne and I sit up late by the flames. His face is its usual impassive mask in the shadows.

I think about having been spun to face upstream and held there for three seconds that were aeons as the river destroyed itself over and over again at my feet; how I became a ludicrous plastic parody of Walter Benjamin's 'Angel of History', face turned towards the past, but the current irresistibly propelling me into the future to which my back is turned, while the pile of debris before me grows skyward.

'I've been wondering,' Wayne says after a while, 'whether it might be possible to engineer an encounter with the eidolon of my friend Paul; to meet a holographic ghost of him beyond the Gates of Hell and attempt to embrace it.'

He pauses, continues. It is clear he wants to talk about this.

'I think I figured out how to do this on the river today, in a way that would recapitulate the whole history of optics, from the camera obscura to a Neural Radiance Field animation based on photogrammetric 3D modelling.'

'OK. I think I get the basic idea, at least,' I say, 'if not the specifics of the tech. But the "why" is perhaps even more interesting to me than the "how". Why would you want to do this? And I must ask, with the best of intentions – would Paul have wanted this? Do you need to seek his permission before you do it?'

Wayne considers this carefully. 'Among the many triple rhymes that connect the *Odyssey*, the *Aeneid* and Dante's *Divine Comedy* is a scene in each where a living interloper among the dead thrice tries and thrice fails to embrace the shade of a loved one: mother, father and friend, respectively. In the Campi Flegrei near Lake Averno, where as you know I've been spending a lot of time underground recently, there's a site I'm confident Virgil used as the model for the cave-mouth through which the Cumaean Sibyl led Aeneas, down into darkness and across the Styx.'

He pauses.

'Aeneas, of course, had the Golden Bough to get himself in and out of the underworld. All I have is a bright-yellow folding set of twenty-four-inch bolt cutters. It's through that door, as close to the banks of what locals regarded as the River Styx as I can get, that I'd want to try to embrace Paul again. I don't know quite why. Maybe this is all just grief or guilt talking. Whatever Paul preceded me into, he is irretrievably lost. The eidolon is only a memory, a thought-image, a shade: mute unless blood-fed, and insubstantial evermore. *Katabasis* among the dead is about the living finding a way to live. As for the question of permission, I'll give it serious thought.'

He pauses again.

'I mentioned Vico's vision of history to you in the car. According to Vico, history isn't circular but helical. Viewed from above, it might look like ripples propagating laterally in a pond into which you've lobbed a rock, or like tree rings – but if you follow it down or up, it's actually Dantean, which is to say, a spiral.'

There are a thousand stars, a hundred thousand. I wish I knew more of the constellations.

The moon is round and silver as a coin.

~

We wake early into thick, shifting mist – and a diffuse, lemony sunlight.

The river is covert and mysterious.

Far above us, the sunlight makes nacre in the alto-cirrus. Far to the west, the sunlight pinks the cloud bellies. We can see none of these, for we are soft-packed in mist and that is the limit of our world.

River, rock, forest, mist. A raven, hexing.

Invisible to us, a buzzard glides overhead, looks down from its great height, sees that the mist follows the river, is *made* by the river, and does not hang over the forest, so that from above it seems a white mist-river now winds through that vastness of trees for dozens of miles.

I clamber through brush to a knoll of bedrock by the snowy fields of the rapid that had spun and undone me the evening before. I sit alone for a quarter of an hour, watching the river. My shadow is cast upon the mist and shimmers as a Brocken spectre – until the mist thins and my shadow is cast upon the water, which will not bear it.

Wayne joins me.

'Do you know what a Pepper's ghost is?' he asks. I shake my head.

'It's another trick of the light, you could say. An illusion first described by the sixteenth-century Neapolitan polymath Giambattista della Porta in his book *Natural Magick*, that got popularized – and given its name – in the nineteenth-century English theatre. It works like this: the image of an off-stage figure, illuminated by a hidden light source, gets projected at a forty-five-degree angle onto an invisible surface, so that an apparition seems to appear directly in front of the audience. The key is that you need something transparent for the screen: a plastic film, stretched tight, say, or a plate of glass.'

'Or mist?'

'Or mist. Maybe.' He pauses. 'You can adapt the technique to make people or things seemingly materialize out of nothing, or vanish into empty space.'

I remember the hologram-likeness of Yazhini, Yuvan's sister, laser-etched into the plastic cube that rides the dashboards of the family's cars.

We leave an hour after dawn. We have many miles to go before we sleep. There are two portages, several big rapids – and we must pass through the Valley of Eagles.

The water in the river's bays seems solid as zinc. Everything gleams in this light. There is a happiness in me that I cannot control and do not wish to. Sound travels fast and wide over the water.

A mile into the day, a kingfisher dives from a spruce branch: an arrow shattering a mirror. Two sandpipers flick low along the shallows, passing in and out of visibility against the shadows of the forest as they turn; passing in and out of the given world.

The sun beats down. The river glistens in the heat.

Here the river is wide and without rapids. We float fast, carried by the current, paddles shipped across our laps, our boats spinning whole, slow circles, watching, talking, dreaming. How different the metaphysics of lake- and river-travel are: on the lake, you must effortfully pull the horizon towards yourself, hand over hand, spiral by spiral, and the surprising thing is that this graded, repeated effort *works*. But on the river, time's flow bears you along, sweeps you seawards, vessel and host.

Cliffs of rust-black rock start to rise on both banks. We are entering the Valley of Eagles. Bird cries echo off the crags. The river is wide and sleepy. It has, with vast patience, found and ground its way between these cliffs, opening its path to the sea.

The valley is monumental. The highest cliffs are eight hundred feet or more. We do not speak much. The mist has fully burned off now, and we revolve in circles of spilled light.

I think about triple rhymes: between the *Commedia*, the *Aeneid* and the *Odyssey*, and also the triple rhymes of death, life and revival that bind the three places to which I've travelled, and the people I've met. The forest and the river drawing Giuliana back to life, back into her uncanny powers. The rivers and the sea healing Yuvan after the brutality of his childhood and the loss of people close to him; him bearing their ashes in clay urns, one after the other, to the sea. And now, here, Rita's dreams of freedom on and for the river, and Wayne's wish to embrace his departed friend one last time.

I try to fathom the deeper relations between these things – but they shift and tangle mistily with one another. I know it's something to do with the animating power of flowing water, with the capacity of rivers to bring both the dead and the living back to life.

Don't think too much with your head, don't look too much with your eyes.
I still don't know the question I must ask of the river.

We flow on. It feels as if we have been on the water for weeks.

There is almost no birdsong in the Valley of Eagles. I wonder at the silence of the forest, how it holds so much life we cannot see or hear: the cryptic, secret lives of bear and moose and lynx, grey owl and wolverine. I don't sense the woods to be lonely or empty, just wary, watchful.

Then I see a familiar profile in the sky. 'Osprey! Osprey!' I cry out, pointing. Not an eagle in the Valley of Eagles, then, but an osprey, and – *there!* – a second, and then we see the nest, set on the crown of a spruce with the trunk's tip growing through it, like a watch-platform atop a ship-of-the-line's foremast. The ospreys wheel and curve and mew, watching us, assessing our threat level. I'm glad when we have drifted beyond their zone of anxiety, and they can return to the nest.

At Tiptoe Falls, a rapid too big for any of us to run straight, we do the first proper portage.

I find it shockingly tough work: unstrapping the bags, chain-hauling boats and bags up the steep bank out of the water and into the forest, where a thin portage trail exists. Then back and forth in shuttle runs, lugging craft and cargo through the forest, over and again. My body, which I've trusted with a lot for a long time, is becoming less able to carry these weights. It's losing its power in the slow downhill trundle to older age. Danny and Raph are so strong. The boats, each of which must weigh thirty kilograms or more, seem like party balloons in their hands.

As for the Bear, well, he simply hoists his kayak into the air, flips it upside down and lowers its centre onto the top of his head, steadies it there with one hand, picks up his twenty-five-kilogram waterproof bag with the other hand, and strides off down the portage trail. I simply can't comprehend the power of it. It's the equivalent of carrying a small fridge in one hand as if it were a sports grip, and a freezer on your head. Through a forest.

The respect I have for the Innus who made these journeys with birch-bark canoes exceeds expression.

We rest at the base of the falls. They are magnificent. I swim in a quiet side-pool, scrub away the grime and fright-sweat of the past few days. We are watching the falls when Danny says, unprompted: 'Of course a river is alive! I mean, to me it's self-evident that that's the case. I've basically given my whole life to rivers. I can't *not* feel them in that way.'

After Tiptoe we run rapid after rapid. Sometimes we take a sneak-route, nosing from pool to pool. Elsewhere we hand-line the boats through hard water.

Wayne flips twice. He speaks less and less. Each capsize is another tack-hole in his confidence, which is hissing out of him now. His jaw is tight. His face has lost all its warmth of colour. I can see that fear is gnawing at him; fear that he might not make it down this river un-injured, might need extracting.

Then, as we are trying to work round a rapid, Wayne follows Ráph down a side-channel which narrows suddenly to a choke point. His kayak grounds its nose on a boulder, the current swings it round, the tail of the boat jams on a second boulder and becomes broadsided in the current, which flips the boat immediately, throwing Wayne hard out onto a third boulder.

I see him land upside down on his lower back, right over the spine and the kidneys, and he gives a terrible cry, and it seems certain to me that he has broken his back, and Danny leaps from his boat and plunges full length into the pool by Wayne to stop him from being swept away, injured, into the big rapid, and Wayne comes up spitting rage, ready to strike, and I know that sympathy will be poison to him for he will take it for pity, and he cannot bear that above all things, and I can see him fighting admirably to prevent himself turning his rage upon others, upon me, and instead with a huge effort he uses the blast-doors of his mind to deflect that rage back into himself and not out upon us.

His back isn't broken, but a plate-sized bruise will slowly bloom black then green on his flank, above his kidney.

Wayne and I hand-line more rapids, keeping river-left. Our feet slip again and again on submerged rocks as we tow our boats, adding new bruises to those I wear on my shins from previous days, earlier rocks. The second portage is longer and harder than the first. *How in God's name did the Bear do this, alone, across all of Canada, in a wooden boat?* I wonder. *Thousands of miles, hundreds of portages. How?*

Whenever I see the Bear on the water that day, he is sitting bolt upright in his kayak, apparently impervious to whatever turbulence he is passing over, riding his craft as calmly as a monarch in a carriage of state.

Late in the afternoon we approach a huge rapid known to paddlers as Saxophone. There the river passes over a sustained series of drops and holes, before funnelling into a deep, fast channel between outcrops of bedrock, then pulling a hard curve to the right and another to the left, and at last opening into a long, deep run-out pool. The rapid's double-bend folds and then flares like, well, a saxophone.

We pull into the bank a few hundred yards short of the rapid. There's a serious puzzle to be solved here. The Salmon, the Bear and the Boss can run Saxophone, but there is almost zero chance of Wayne and me getting through it. An early capsize could be consequential in a rapid of this shape and length; a tumbling body might crash against boulders, and be slammed or even pinned against one of the bedrock walls at the sharp turns.

But lining the boats isn't really an option. The bank ahead is vertical for sustained periods. The forest grows densely to the brink of the rock. And there's no easy water for a sneak-route.

'We could always ghost-boat it,' says Danny after a while.

So that is what we do.

Ghost-boating is where you send a kayak down a stretch of river with no one in it. Raph and Danny will run Saxophone, then pull up in the run-out pool, ready to catch my and Wayne's boats as – hopefully – they emerge from the rapid. The Bear will hang back in case the boats some-how get caught or lost. And Wayne and I will bushwhack the eight hundred yards or so of bank-side forest to reach the lower mouth of Saxophone.

'Make sure you give them a really good shove out into the main channel,' calls Danny as he slips into the flow.

Wayne and I surrender our boats to the current, then clamber our way downstream along the bank: heavy going in thick brush. We're scratched and bitten. After twenty minutes, I see Raph across a calm side-bay of the river, standing on a high dome of bare, tawny bedrock, looking down onto Saxophone itself. He glances back at us and gives a double thumbs-up: *We've got your boats.*

Screw it, I think; *I've had enough of bushwhacking.* I jump off the bank and into the bay, swim across it, and scramble up the rock dome to join Raph. He's looking thoughtful, troubled. Below us Saxo-phone roars through the bedrock channel and westwards out into a wide, straight stretch of river. The river's focused power in the rapid thrums the air around it. The sun is low, and scintillates the water. The old rock glows caramel as whisky. The sound of the rapid is immense and exhilarating.

'This is it,' yells Raph, spreading his arms wide.

'Too right!' I say. I think he's celebrating the wonder of the place.

'No – this is where one of the big dams would go.'

I blink, startled. 'Here?'

Raph points with one hand at the far shore, and with the other at the forest behind us, then shouts into my ear over the noise of the water.

'Right across where we're standing – along this line. They've got their eye on this site because a lot of the hard work has been done for them by geology; they can join up all this bedrock, then drive down into the narrow channel of Saxophone itself, and so create the barrage. It would flood all the way back up the Valley of Eagles, the whole valley. It would create a reservoir all the way to Lac Magpie, *en fait.*'

I'm gut-shot. My mind runs the counterfactual. The huge sweep of concrete here, *right here*, filling the river from bank to bank, the whole valley from flank to flank. The work camps, the exercise gyms, the pool halls, the bars, all here for the years of construction. The wide roads bulldozed up through the forest from the coast in order to service the camps and extract the timber. And everything we have just floated through – the Valley of Eagles, Tiptoe Falls, the portages – all of it flooded, lost within the dozing, sluggish stasis of impoundment.

You can adapt the technique to make people or things seemingly materialize out of nothing, or vanish into empty space . . .

'They will have to log and extract hundreds of thousands of trees due to the mercury problem, I think,' says Raph. 'All of that forest to either side of the river, anything that would be underwater, all the way back to Lac Magpie, would need to be felled and taken out.'

We've ghost-boated our way into ghost-ground, I think. No, not only here – the whole of our journey down the river so far has existed in this spectral space, the pristine present and the flooded future.

I feel sick. I think of Rita and her battle, Shanice and Uapukun, of all that the Innu people have done to save the river from *this*. There has to be another way.

Then Raph shouts and points – there is the Bear, grinning broadly as he shoots the final channel of Saxophone, bouncing on the waves like a rubber duck. He reminds me of a Weeble toy, unsinkable, always refinding his plumb line. The river, for all its tumult, steadies him.

Raph turns to leave the dome of bedrock. 'We've still got a few miles to go before camp,' he says. 'Danny has the boats by the run-out pool.'

I stay for a couple of minutes, wanting to take stock of this bright place and the shadow that lies across it. The sun is low in the sky, and because the river turns westwards here, it's shining upstream towards me.

Then I see it, and it is unmistakable. It declares itself to me just as Rita had said it would – with clarity and intensity.

It's a tiny spruce, no more than eight inches high. It's growing among grass and myrtle, in a handkerchief-size pocket of earth and lichen that the wind has gathered in a hollow on the camel's hump of bedrock on which I'm standing.

In the sunlight its needles shine green-silver. It is a miniature World Tree. It is *l'arbre sacré*. It is resistance.

The river seethes in slow, shiny pools, the dark-green curves of the forests hold their lines, and the tree persists.

Year after year it must have survived inundation, ice, the bitter cold of winter and the brutal floods of spring, holding its ground on this scrape of a home. It could well be decades, even centuries old, though it's less than a foot high. Research into the black spruce trees of the harsh terrain of northern Labrador has shown that some small trees – not even the height of a person, with trunks perhaps only a few inches in diameter – are as much as four hundred years old. So extreme are the conditions that trees may only grow a ring one cell thick in a year. *One cell!*

I snap off the red-thread bracelet that Rita had knotted onto my left wrist, bend down, and tie it as I have been bidden around the trunk of this tiny, sacred tree.

That night we camp on a long beach of river stones, on the western bank of a wide stretch of the river which runs almost perfectly north–south. Walking the beach at dusk, I find my son Will a white stone which has been rolled by the Mutehekau Shipu until it is eggshell-smooth and ovoid.

After dark, the red lights of transatlantic night-flights dot-dash their Morse code messages at the uncomprehending northern forests. The moon-path flutters in the current.

'If they succeed in damming this river,' says Wayne round the fire, 'the suits at Hydro-Québec, I mean – well, there's a line from Tacitus that comes to mind: "They created a desolation and called it peace."'

Somehow, I think, *somehow we need to find new kinds of imagining, new ways of being that will leave us less alone in this world, less the desolate lords of Tacitus' victory field. Our aliveness, as well as all life that lies beyond the human, is at stake in this.*

'Boy, there sure was a lot of water coming through Saxophone today,' says the Bear, gazing happily into the flames. 'If this river gets dammed – well, Danny, can you remind me to start blowing up the dams? When the winters are long and boring, it will give me something to do with the family on the weekends.'

~

A pinch of tobacco for the river, a pinch for the land.

Long days of hot sun and hard work. Nights crisp, and the moon waned by a sliver each time. We flow on. Slowly, we are reaching the sea.

One afternoon we arrive at a vast waterfall, a hundred feet from sill to plunge-pool and two hundred feet wide.

The spray clouding from the falls is so great it creates a permanent rainbow, hovering thirty feet or so out in space. I can see the shifting veils of spindrift passing through the colours, or perhaps it is the colours passing through the spindrift. Whose ghost is being projected from what occluded chamber, I cannot say.

The portage to get the boats down the left side of the falls is steep and strenuous, and takes us an hour and a half. Saucer-sized, lion-coloured fungi litter the moss of the forest floor. I can smell the vinegary scent of apples fallen in orchards, though there are no apples and no orchards here.

From the base of the portage we paddle across the mouth of the bay the falls have formed, and hump our gear and boats up past a subsidiary rapid.

I pitch my tent on an ice-smoothed plane of bedrock, guying it out using chunks of rock. The door of my tent is a foot from the water. The door of my tent faces east towards the falls. If the dams were to be built, the river would back up right to these falls. The bay we're camped in would be drowned.

That evening we sit on the bedrock and watch the river. I have the persistent illusion of relative movement. Looking across the river to its northern bank, I see that the river itself is both turbulent and immobile, and the bank is eddying upstream fast against it: rock suddenly made mobile, transitive.

Watching the current, I notice that there's no focal length available between two poles: you either blur vision and focus on the stasis of the forest background, or catch one detail in the water only to find sight swept away downstream, from where you must haul the eye back up the river and rebegin the slide.

I'm beginning to understand what Rita meant when she told me to 'seek the current'; to feel rather than see my way with the river. My tendency is to believe in the delusion of perception which lies beyond the river's flow; the point from which I might look in and upon the river – might inspect and record it, notebook and pen in hand. But really there is no such point, for the current is *everywhere*. It doesn't stop at the river's banks, but overfloods them, like the winter inundations which leave their ice-marks upon the tree trunks. We are always launched upon the river, already afloat on the flow.

The rapid exiting the main pool is a concatenating series of chained detonations. Powerful eddy-currents prowl up either side. The night grows old. The fire burns down.

~

At first the Gorge is only a sound: a steady big-gun bombardment, rising in volume – mortars and heavy cannon firing on repeat, trying to flatten a city.

Thunk, thunk, thunk.

Somewhere just beyond our sight, a dozen geysers appear to be throwing spouts a hundred feet into the air, over and over again.

Thunk, thunk, thunk.

The event horizon of the Gorge is immense: a blooming arc of pull that reaches at least a mile upstream of its brink. The river is very wide here, but then geology suddenly narrows and drops it in two vast steps.

To go over the lip of the Gorge would be certain death, so we take what feel like absurd precautions. Thousands of spring floods have used logs as battering rams to open up a tapering channel to the right of the Gorge's rim, perhaps two hundred yards across at its mouth. From nearly a mile away, we hug the right bank tightly and proceed in a cautious line.

The water in the flood channel is shallow, and dense with water reeds that make a high, crying noise like a host of tiny ghosts as they brush against our hulls. When we reach the channel's end, Wayne and I haul the boats out, portage them a few yards over a little hump of bedrock – and stop.

One hundred and fifty vertical feet below us and perhaps five hundred yards distant is the Gorge.

I've never seen a rapid of anything close to this scale and power. It is shaped like an hourglass, with the force and volume of the entire river being coned down to a falling waist of river perhaps fifteen yards wide, clamped between two shining jawbones of bedrock.

There is no water that is not white. Even at this distance, the Gorge generates a noise so huge we can't hear each other speak from more than a few yards away. It is a noise you feel on your skin, in your lungs.

At the heart of the Gorge's hourglass is a hole. The white water plunges in a vast tongue between the bedrock jaws, and where it lands it punches a hole in its own substance, before rising back up in huge recoiling boils. A human body entering it would be pressed down, churned back up and then pulled straight back under the tongue to rebegin the whole rag-doll wash cycle.

'That's a hole you'd never leave if you got into it,' says Raph. 'That's an eternity hole.'

The others pitch their tents in a sliver of trees a hundred yards away. Wayne and I pitch our tents side by side on bedrock facing east, which is also facing the Gorge, and we guy them down with stones. The noise of the Gorge alone seems strong enough to sweep us clean off the rock.

We gather driftwood, build a fire of silver, smoke ourselves dry. The ground is thick with bilberries. I pick them until my fingers are purple and eat them until my tongue is too.

'I can eat two litre-tubs of blueberries in an afternoon,' says Ilya thoughtfully, 'but then I need to prepare for hibernation.' His mind is turning homewards.

'You need to know that this is where the other new dam would go,' says Danny.

I'm gut-shot all over again. 'Here?'

'Same logic as at Saxophone: the bedrock has done a lot of the infrastructural work already. It's perfect. Millions of dollars are saved by geology. Where we're sitting now, this would all be underwater.'

'Waterfalls are known in parts of northern England as "forces",' I say. 'Mare Force, Aira Force, and so on. I prefer this term to the more scenic and placid "waterfall". And *that*' – I nod towards the Gorge – 'is one hell of a *force*.'

In the summer of 1802, the poet Samuel Taylor Coleridge walked to see Lodore Force in the north-west Lake District while it was in spate. He wrote a letter that evening describing his encounter with the force: it remains the best description of a cataract I know. 'The mad water rushes thro' its *sinuous* Bed, or rather prison of Rock with such rapid Curves,' wrote Coleridge there:

> as if it turned the Corners not from mechanic force, but with fore-knowledge, like a fierce & skilful Driver; great Masses of Water, one after the other, that in twilight one might have feelingly compared them with a vast crowd of huge white Bears, rushing, one over the other, against the wind – their long white hair shattering abroad in the wind . . .
>
> What a sight it is to look down on such a Cataract! – the wheels, that circumvolve in it – the leaping up & plunging forward of that infinity of Pearls & Glass Bulbs – the continual *change* of the *Matter*, the perpetual *Sameness* of the *Form* – . . . the Precipitation of the fallen Angels

from Heaven, Flight & Confusion, & Distraction, but all harmonized
into one majestic Thing . . .

His letter – with its onrushing dashes, its molten language, its flowing
metamorphoses of matter into other matter – practises something like
a grammar of animacy for a living river. In Coleridge's description,
the river is sentient and animate; it turns the corners 'with foreknowl-
edge', it is made of fallen angels and of pearls and of glass bulbs and,
fabulously, of huge white bears, 'their long white hair shattering
abroad in the wind'. It is always in a state of becoming.

If the cloud-forest was a place of reticulation, and Chennai one of
circulation between waterbodies, the Mutehekau Shipu's mode is,
surely, purely flow, I think, and its grammar of animacy is one of *ands*
and *throughs* and *tos* and *nows*, of commas not full stops, of *thens* not
buts, aura not edge, of compounds and hyphens and fusings, silver-
blues and grey-greens and mist-drifts and undersongs, process not
substance, *this* joined to *that*, always onrushing, always seeking the sea
and here and there turning back upon itself, intervolving, eddying in
counterflow to cause spirals and gyres that draw breath into water, life
into the mind, spin strange reciprocities, leave the whole world whirled,
whorled.

Not, it seems there at the Gorge, that language could come anywhere *close* to representing this river. The history of literature is
littered with the debris of attempts to utter water: a vast Oort cloud of
fragments shrouding a presence which declines articulation and resists
correspondence. Faced with a river, as with a god, apprehension splin-
ters into apophasis; deixis is dismantled. The alien will not be
articulated. Alive, yes, but not in any way we might speak it.

Perhaps the body knows what the mind cannot. Days on the water
have produced in me the intensifying feeling of somehow growing-
together with the river: not thinking with it, but being thought *by* it.
This physical sensation of merging, almost of capture, has occurred
far more powerfully over the past fortnight, I realize, than I've known

before, even during longer journeys in the mountains. *Rivers are running through me*, I think; *I've been flowed through and onwards.*

When I mention this to Wayne, he nods in recognition.

'Oh yes,' he says, 'I've also felt something like this. I think it's important to recognize that this kind of merging doesn't happen as an epiphany; it's a chronic rather than an acute process. Paddling into those headwinds. The appearance of a pine marten at the first river camp. Being slapped and dunked and twisted by the rapids. I've not felt . . . *entirely myself*, as if I've been somehow – and not voluntarily, and not entirely pleasantly – hybridized with the larger situation in which we have been participating during this journey, which includes, perhaps above all, this giant body of moving water with whom we have all been flowing.'

He pauses.

'But as for how the hell you might construct a politics or law out of this kind of apprehension, though? That I just don't know. We scarcely have words full stop to cover even the basic phenomenology of what you're calling "growing-together" with the river, let alone political structures that might accommodate it. That said, it seems to me that the encounter with these hugely *other* beings is where the making of a politics with the more-than-human world has to start. Without any sense of that presence, we can barely articulate *our* end of the politics – let alone that of the river.'

~

That dusk at the Gorge, nighthawks scissor the sky above the spruces and utter high cries. Pale stripes bar their underwings, and their eyes flash ruby as landing lights.

Night falls. The first star shows over the Gorge. Soon the sky is speckled as a trout's flank. The flames fling out sparks like tiny flares, thinning then snapping out to leave scorch lines on the retina.

Round the fire I read out sections to the group from the Innu version of the resolution concerning the life and rights of the river. Here, now, it seems incontrovertible to the point of trivial that the river is alive.

Ursus Major, the Great Bear, glitters to the north. The white bears of the Gorge hoard the moonlight. Starlink satellites tick across the paint-slosh of the Milky Way. The forest stretches immense in the darkness. Its secret life teems. You could walk four thousand miles westwards from here to Alaska, and only cross two highways.

I'm woken once by the thunder of boulders being moved along the river's bed by the huge force of the flow. A muted rumble, like distant rockfall in the mountains. Fear prickles the left side of my neck.

I fall back into uneasy sleep, and wake early into half-light.

Mist wools the river downstream of the Gorge.

Wayne is up already, sitting by the fire in the cool dawn air, eyes fixed on the Gorge.

Hey, man.

Hey.

A pinch of tobacco for the water, a pinch for the land.

'I've been thinking through some of the hard matters raised by the declaration you read from last night,' Wayne says after a while, 'indeed by the whole Rights of Nature movement, and those phrases like "living entity" and "fundamental rights". Behind all of this lurks the surely unanswerable question: how do we know what the river wants?'

'What the river wants is . . . to reach the sea,' I say. It feels like an inadequate response.

'Gravity is not intention, but that doesn't mean there isn't intentionality present. But – a river is not a decision-making entity, Hydro-Québec will say.'

'I can think of few things more decisive than a river.'

'Yet humans still make decisions on behalf of, and with consequence for, this immense being, or force, or presence – or whatever you want to call the river. In fact they *have* to, whether they want to dam it or assert what they've decided is its "fundamental right" to flow freely from source to sea.'

'A god. For now, I want to call the river a *god*. And why should a god make choices we would recognize as choices?'

'Over the course of this journey, I've sometimes wondered,' says Wayne, 'are we a client species for the river? Is Hydro-Québec, in fact, a client entity for the river, performing functions the river wants to have performed on its behalf? The thought-experiment is worth undertaking, if only to jolt the mind out of its usual grooves of proprietary thinking about "more-than-human" presences. But I remain sceptical of the notion of giving voice to or for a river. It strikes me as both insufficient and fraught with the risk of ventriloquizing. Better by far to help the river do as it will, in my opinion, either directly on its behalf (if a credible line of communication can be opened with it at some future point), or else by protecting a context in which it is able to do its own thing, however inexplicably. Which for this river might mean flooding as well as flowing; backing up as well as running on.'

'It's the crux that needs solving, for sure,' I say. 'Not "Who speaks for the river?" but "What does the river say?" These are two distinct questions. And while it's relatively trivial to answer the first of them, it's a philosophically immense task to answer the second.'

'Yup. I sometimes wonder if the Rights of Nature is just serving as a proxy in an asymmetrical power situation that already exists, irrespective of the river's . . . actuality. For it not to be merely a disguised form of political manoeuvring between and among us humans, we'll need to find ways of listening to, and with, these other beings – river gods included. And that obviously needs to be happening not just among Indigenous communities, or among artists and writers and fringe-weirdos like us – but also state actors, corporate actors, industrial actors, the whole cast. The power-holders.'

'I can't tell if you sound hopeful or hopeless about the possibility of all this,' I say to Wayne.

'Hopeful!' He gestures at the Gorge. 'Look – a river like that can cut a fucking *mountain* in half, a mountain made of the oldest, hardest rocks on the planet. Are you telling me that it can't also damage ideological structures; that this *god* can't in some avatar of itself erode at least some of the superstructures of terminal-stage capitalism?!'

The fire's embers throb in the light dawn breeze.

'A hypothesis,' Wayne says: 'earth and river are both gods made of time, but even earth has cause to fear the river.'

'I'll drink to that,' I say, lifting my coffee mug and vowing silently to myself that I'll do everything I can to prevent the damming of the Mutehekau Shipu: for Rita, for the river.

Suddenly, Wayne Radio says: 'The French know every kind of unhappiness; that's why they invented the bidet!'

Later, we leave the boats hauled up at the camp and set off on foot for the brink of the Gorge itself, and that is where it happens.

~

Wayne and I pick a path through the spine of forest in which Danny and Raph have camped, then out onto open ground where thickets of Labrador tea grow amid red sphagnum and white lichen.

We scramble down the side of the ridge towards the Gorge. We are laughing, joking, happy to be together in this place. The light is calm and equable.

We approach the jaws of bedrock through which the river crashes and thunders. The rock is stepped and smoothed, and shines in the spray. We stop a yard from the edge. At our feet the river smashes ceaselessly into a super-massive white hole of its own making, churning and quaking, and I feel queasy and drawn and obsessed. The rock beneath us is juddering from the water's force and the vibrations move through our bodies as if they were tuning forks, so that our bones turn turbulent and our minds also, and now the rock we stand on gleams and is liquid – it also roils and has eddies, though they are too slow for our human eyes to see – and the water is all pearls and bulbs, and the rock is those things too so we must surely fall through it or sink into it, and there are sounds with no source. Spray from the Gorge drifts upon us, dewing our clothes and wetting our eyes, and tiny rainbows roam like iridescent insects, and we talk as best we can amid the uproar and we realize that our speech is speeding up under momentum not our own, is becoming rapid with answers and thoughts tumbling across and into one another, and later both of us will describe the shared sense that somewhere on that almost planet-old rock we stepped across an invisible border and into a zone where the usual locks and screens were not in place.

Then speaking no longer seems tolerable and I am unable any longer to decline the compulsion to move closer to the river, so I step right to the very brink of the Gorge, a few inches from destruction, where water, rock and air are all three glossy, and I glance up and understand that I am looking into a *mouth*, an immense river-maw that pours between the jaws of the Gorge, and I see that this mouth has a *tongue*, a vast green-white tongue which tapers and glides to its tip right at my feet, and I hear speech is tumbling out of this mouth, has been tumbling out of it since the old ice left, and that this is a place where ghost-realms of times past and future overlap with one another, each transparent to the other, and I try to peer right and left into these laminar worlds but the river-mouth and its river-voices hold me in this one *here* and the river's tongue *now* is the tongue of tongues, and the river's song is the song of songs, slipshifting and shapesliding and veering, sung in spirals and stars and roars and other notes beyond hearing, and the voice sings what I cannot understand, however much I long to, and my heart is full of flow and I sit because I can no longer stand and then I have the dim but unmistakable sense at the shatter-belt of my awareness of an incandescent aura made of something like bears and angels but not bears and angels, something that is always transforming, and in that moment it is clear to me that this is the aura of the river-being –

why should a god make choices we recognize as choices?

— and the coast of my mind senses this *force* and I know, *know*, that this is no Pepper's ghost, no projection or illusion or trick, and that the question Rita wanted me to ask of the river is nothing to do with fear or age but is after all and of course the question of life, which is not a question at all but a world —

find the current, follow the flow

— and the river's voices say and sing what I cannot comprehend, and each time I lean my mind out to listen they retreat in the measure I approach them, so instead I start to scrawl the pages you are reading here and the paper glistens with river-mist until I'm just jotting words in ink that's blotting in curls as phrases whirl into the notebook from a source vastly greater than the sphere of my skull and I find tears in my eyes that I did not put there but the river did —

it may involve a great reach outward of mind and imagination

— and for those few seconds, beckoned on and shivered by that hourglass-shaped and silvered force that is a mouth and has a tongue and utters, after miles and minutes and years on the flow and in it, I am rivered.

EPILOGUE

The Springs

(Autumn)

A three-day storm has passed over the south of England. Gingkos on street corners suddenly stand bare-branched in pools of gold.

Up in the hedgerows near the wood where the nine springs rise, spiders sling webs that tremble with droplets of rain, each holding a burnished ember of light.

Look – three people are walking together towards the edge of the wood. A girl, a boy and a boy. No, that's not right. Look again. Look closer. It's a woman and two men. The girl – the woman – clutches a cloth bag in one hand.

A buzzard mews overhead. It's agitated. Young? A nest? At this time of year? Perhaps. Two of the three don't hear the buzzard's cries, or if they do it doesn't register. They've got other things on their mind. One looks up, points at the buzzard, says something. The other two smile. *Trust you to notice, Will!*

There are buildings on three sides of the wood now – and they're close to the springs. Only the slope of White Hill is undeveloped. There are more hospital buildings, and there's a new train station too, to serve the hospital. Tarmac, concrete, bike hoops, a taxi turning-circle, the works. That's OK. It's what the city needs.

But how did all this arise so quickly? The work of decades in the blink of an eye. It was spring only half a year ago up here, wasn't it?

Oh. I see now. That was a different spring. Fifteen springs ago, maybe twenty.

The river has run on and I didn't notice.

Two skylarks plummet upwards over White Hill to become dark

stars, torrenting out a cascade of song that lifts the heart even as it falls.

The circling buzzard watches the three figures approach the entrance to the wood. There's a confidence to their walk, a closeness. There's something in common in their faces, as well, and to their mannerisms. They're siblings: a sister and two brothers.

They're my children, I see that now. Lily, Tom and Will.

These words taste strange in the mouth.

They cross the bridge into the trees.

The three of them wander through the wood, past the clootie rags on the hawthorn – dozens more of them now, like tattered red flowers – to the big spring site at its northern end. It's as full of water as they've ever seen it. So much rain these past weeks! The land itself is slaked, the groundwater has recharged the aquifer and is driving the flow. The surface of the pool is coppered with beech leaves after the storm.

There are grey streaks in Lily's hair and kindness, as ever, in her smile. Pepper and salt in Tom's stubble, and the beginnings of crow's feet at the corner of his eyes. *Sorry, Tom: you got those from me. By the end, mine were deep enough to lodge a penny in!*

And the youngest, Will, well, he's a man now. Six feet tall, and still radiating an aura of lawless merriness. *When you were little, I could never imagine how you would be old, Will.*

I call out to them, but they can't hear me.

They are so beautiful and so vulnerable. I wish I could touch them again, embrace each of them one more time.

I feel a terrible ache of sadness that they exist in the world without me. I feel joy beyond measure that they remain in it, bright and alive.

I wish I could speak with them.

What would I tell them? That the river is time, and we are always within it, even when we think we're standing dry-footed on the bank, watching the current pass.

All nine of the springs are pulsing away. *Dad would be happy*, says Will. *Yes, he would*, says Lily, *he'd like to see this.*

She reaches into the bag, pulls out a soft envelope of cloth, opens it, and offers it round like a pouch of tobacco. Bitter-sweet smiles at the mundanity of it.

Just two little pinches of ash each; this is a sensitive ecological site, after all. The first pinch is for the land: mud, beech leaves, tree roots.

Then one by one they reach out over the pool where a river is born, and let the ash fall like snow onto the water's surface, where the flakes begin to move together, drawn by undercurrents we cannot see.

Death and love and life, all mingled in the flow.

GLOSSARY

adze A cutting tool mounted on a handle like an axe, but with the blade perpendicular to the shaft, not parallel.

aestivate Of an amphibian, insect or fish, to enter a state of dormancy during a sustained period of hot or dry conditions.

agger In Roman road-building, the trench or bank that forms the road's core, usually filled with stone or gravel.

agon The ancient Greek word (ἀγών) for a conflict, struggle or contest.

amygdala A small, almond-shaped brain structure, the chief function of which is to recognize and process emotions.

anchoritic Reclusive, solitary (from 'anchorite': a hermit, one who has retreated from the world).

anima A current of breath or wind; the vital principle; life; soul; that which animates.

animism The belief in an enspirited world; the attribution of life to what others take to be pure matter, inanimate objects.

Anthropocene The (ongoing) epoch of geological time in which human activity is taken to be the dominant shaping influence upon Earth systems.

apophasis Theologically, the attempt to speak of the ineffable only in terms of what may not be said; definition by negation (from the ancient Greek ἀπόφημι, 'to deny').

aquifer A body of rock or sediment that holds **groundwater**.

arborescent Tree-like in form; branching.

aurochs Now-extinct species of wild ox; part of the Pleistocene–Holocene megafauna. Huge in stature, with massive, curving horns.

awl A sharp-pointed tool used to pierce holes, especially in leather.

berm A bank of earth, often used to retain water.

bioluminescence The emission of light by creatures (fireflies, glow-worms, sponges) and more than a hundred species of fungi.

biome A large-scale ecological community; a major climatic region or habitat type (e.g. tundra, taiga, rainforest, desert, savanna).

bistre A painter's brown pigment made from soot.

blowdown A tree uprooted or trunk-snapped by wind.

boreal Of the north.

bradyseism The slow rise and fall of the Earth's crust, caused by deep geological action.

brash In forestry, the lower branches and foliage of a tree, once fallen or cut from the trunk.

bromeliads A **Neotropical** family of plants (including the pineapple) with spiralling leaves, and often the ability to grown **epiphytically** on other plants, taking both nutrition and hydration from the air.

bubo A swollen lymph node, especially one caused by the (bubonic) plague.

bund An embankment or retaining wall.

burin A sharp-pointed tool used for engraving.

cadastral Concerning the value, extent and ownership of land (particularly for the purposes of taxation).

caldera The cauldron-like hollow formed when a volcano erupts and empties its magma chamber, which then collapses.

catchment The area of land in which all flowing surface water eventually converges to a single point (a river-mouth, the debouchment into a lake or ocean); also known as a river basin, drainage basin or **watershed**.

chain-reservoir A sequence of connected reservoirs.

chiaroscuro In painting, an image in which light and shadow, white and black, are represented and contrasted (i.e. rather than colours).

chitin The hard organic substance with which (for instance) beetles make their exoskeleton and crabs their shells.

cirque A steep-sided, amphitheatre-like valley formed beneath a continuous curve of ridges and peaks.

coliform Of or resembling a bacillus (disease-causing bacterium) of the coli group of bacteria, associated especially with sewage pollution.

constitution Of a state or polity, the system of fundamental principles according to which governance proceeds.

copse A small stand or thicket of trees.

coralline Coral-like; having the form of coral.

corrido In Mexico or the south-western United States, a traditional narrative ballad song form, which originally developed as an expression of resistance against the advancing (Anglophone) culture.

cryptid An organism whose existence or survival is unproven by science; 'a living thing having the quality of being hidden or unknown' (J. E. Wall).

culvert A channel, tunnel or drain, usually carrying water and made of brick, stone or concrete.

cuneiform Lit. 'wedge-shaped'; also the writing system of ancient Persia, Assyria, Babylonia, etc., inscribed using the trimmed end of a river reed.

dead-pool Of a river or reservoir, when water levels reduce to such an extent that downstream flow ceases.

deep time The vast chronology of Earth history; measured in epochs, aeons and eras, rather than centuries, years or months.

detritivore A creature which feeds on dead organic matter.

dryad In Greek and Roman mythology, a tree nymph or tree spirit.

ecocide 'Unlawful or wanton acts committed with the knowledge that there is substantial likelihood of severe and either widespread or long-term damage to the environment being caused by those acts' (Stop Ecocide Foundation).

ecotone The transition zone between two ecological regions (e.g. sea and land; forest and prairie), often characterized by an exceptional abundance and diversity of life.

ectomycorrhizal Concerning those forms of symbiotic relationship that occur between certain fungi and the roots of various plant species. Ectomycorrhizal fungi do not penetrate the cell wall of the host plant's root tips, but rather create a latticework of **hyphae** between and around those root cells.

eidolon A phantom, a spirit; the ghostly manifestation of a person.

elytra The hard wing-cases of a beetle or other insect.

endosymbiosis A form of symbiosis in which one organism lives inside another (the endosymbiosis between a cyanobacterium and a **eukaryote** is thought to have been the origin of both algae and plants).

epigenetics Lit. 'extra growth', 'overgrowth'; in biology, the study of changes of cell function and heritable traits which happen without changes to the DNA sequence.

epiphyte A plant which grows on another plant.

erratic (n.) A rock which has been transported to its present location by glacial action.

erumpent Bursting forth.

eukaryote An organism in the domain Eukaryota; i.e. having a membrane-bound nucleus within each cell. All animals, plants and fungi are eukaryotes.

eusociality In biology, the highest level of the organization of sociality, often characterized by divisions of labour between groups or 'castes' within a society and high levels of cooperation and specialism. Eusocial colonies are sometimes viewed as superorganisms.

extirpate To destroy, root out, exterminate.

extractivism The exploitation of natural resources, particularly by mining and especially for purposes of export.

extractivismo The critique of the social formation of **extractivism**, focusing particularly on the territories and communities affected by mining and other extractive projects.

Fata Morgana A form of 'superior' mirage which causes distant objects to appear to float above their actual position.

floccose Woolly or tufty in texture.

fluvial Of or pertaining to a river or rivers.

fly-ash The fine ash produced by burning pulverized coal.

foliate Leaf-like, leaf-shaped.

fumarole A vent in the surface of the Earth, out of which volcanic gases emerge.

funambulist A tightrope walker.

furcation Splitting, branching.

geomorphology The study of the origin and changes of the physical features of the Earth's surface or crust (e.g. the action of rivers or glaciers upon landforms).

gneiss A metamorphic rock composed of quartz, feldspar and mica. Often very old indeed.

Gondwana The supercontinent which formed 600 million years ago and united the landmasses of what are today South America, Africa, Antarctica, Australia and the Indian subcontinent, among others.

groundwater Water present – stored or flowing – underground, in soil and porous or cracked rock.

gyre A spiral, whorl or circular turn.

headwater The source or sources of a river or stream.

hydrophone A microphone used to detect or record sound underwater.

hydrosphere All water on Earth, whether liquid, vapour or ice, below ground, on the surface or in the atmosphere.

hyphae The thin, branching filaments of fungi, which together make up the **mycelium**.

hyporheic The zone under a stream-bed or riverbed in which surface water and shallow **groundwater** mix.

hypotaxis Stylistically speaking, language in which the hierarchy of clauses is organized and clarified by subordinating conjunctions, relative pronouns, etc.; see also **parataxis**.

ISDS Investor–State Dispute Settlement; a mechanism in international law which gives private parties (e.g. foreign companies) the right to seek reparation from a sovereign nation in a forum other than that of the nation's domestic courts, if they feel the state has failed to guarantee the terms of an investment.

jurisprudence The philosophy and theory of law; both what the law is and what it could or should be.

juristic Of or relating to the law, or the study of law.

kairos The right or critical moment; timeliness, the opportune instant.

katabasis A descent, typically to the underworld.

Kichwa The Quechan language spoken in Ecuador, Colombia and parts of Peru. 'Quechua' is the Indigenous language family which is now the most widely spoken pre-Columbian language family of the Americas.

kinkajou A mostly fruit-eating, tree-dwelling mammal found in the forests of Central and South America, also known as the night-walker and the honeybear. Scientific name: *Potus flavus*.

kintsugi The Japanese art of repairing broken pottery or ceramic using a gold, silver or platinum lacquer.

knap To shape flint, chert or obsidian into stone tools (blades, scrapers, axe-heads, etc.).

laminar Relating to or consisting of layers; in fluid dynamics, 'laminar flow' is flow in which fluid layers slide smoothly and in parallel over one another.

lee/leeward On the side sheltered from the wind.

legal person A being or entity (human, corporation, river) who can hold rights, enter into contracts, own property, sue and be sued, etc.

legal standing The capacity of a party to bring suit in court.

LiDAR Light Detection and Ranging: a remote-sensing technology which uses laser pulses to generate precise 3D information about the Earth's shape and surface.

mendicant A beggar; beggarly.

mithril The fictional super-metal found in Tolkien's Middle-Earth books; silver in colour, very light and immensely strong.

montane forest Forest that flourishes on mountain slopes, towards the upper altitudinal limits of tree growth; often characterized by a lower canopy, and high levels of endemic species and **epiphytes**.

more-than-human Of the life, and web of lives, which exceeds the human, and with which human life is inextricably entangled; 'earthly nature'. The phrase was coined by David Abram in his 1996 book *The Spell of the Sensuous: Perception and Language in a More-Than-Human World.*

muskeg Peaty, tussocky **sphagnum** bog, found especially in the Arctic and **boreal** regions of North America (from the Cree word *maskek*).

mycelium The mass of thread-like, branching **hyphae** with which fungi decompose organic matter, absorb nutrients and transport water and other resources.

mycology The study of fungi.

mycorrhizae Symbiotic associations between plants and fungi, with an interface where root-tip and **hyphae** meet.

naiad In Greek and Roman mythology, a water nymph or river spirit.

Neotropical realm One of the Earth's eight biogeographic realms; comprising South and Central America, the Caribbean and certain southern parts of North America.

nictitating membrane The transparent or translucent 'third eyelid' that certain animals possess, allowing them to protect the eye while still seeing (e.g. for sea turtles, while underwater).

numinous Mysterious, quasi-divine, spiritually awe-inspiring: inexpressibly so.

oneiric Dream-like, dreamy.

ontology In metaphysics, the philosophical study of being (often contrasted with 'epistemology', the philosophical study of knowledge and knowing).

Oort cloud A vast cloud of icy plantesimals (small asteroids, comets, etc.) which is thought to surround the Sun at distances ranging from 0.03 to 3.2 light years.

Pachamama Lit. 'World Mother' in **Kichwa**; in Indigenous Andean cosmogonies, Mother Nature, the spirit or deity whose creative force sustains life on Earth.

parataxis Stylistically speaking, language in which clauses are placed next to one another without coordinating conjunctions, or elements are 'listed' one after the other, with only commas, semicolons or 'ands' joining them; see also **hypotaxis**.

phenomenology The philosophical study of experience as it is experienced; of life as subjectively lived and felt.

pileus In **mycology**, the cap of a mushroom/fungal fruiting body.

pinnate A term used to describe compound leaves which have leaflets arranged in two rows on either side of a central mid-rib/stalk. The rowan, ash and walnut all have pinnate leaves.

portage In kayaking/canoeing, the practice of carrying your craft on land, usually to go around an obstacle in a river, or between bodies of water.

protist An organism that isn't an animal, land plant or fungus: e.g. slime moulds, kelps, algae, amoebae.

quaquaversal Extending in all directions from a centre point.

reticulated Like a network; branching and connecting.

rhizomatic Resembling a rhizome; i.e. a non-linear, non-hierarchical network in which any point is connected to any other point.

ring-bark To remove a continuous circle of bark around a tree's trunk, usually resulting in its slow death. This can be done by browsers (e.g. deer), by foresters or by ice/river action.

riparian The edge or bank of a river; something relating to this area.

sacrifice zone Places or landscapes which are subjected to disproportionate environmental harm (pollution, ecological degradation), in order to benefit groups elsewhere.

sastrugi Wind-driven, hardened snow-shapes that ripple and ridge the surfaces of sea ice, frozen lakes, mountain ridges.

scroll bars Ridges of sediment that form on the inner banks of river meanders, as the river's channel shifts laterally over time.

semiotics The study of signs and the communication of meaning.

sicario A hired gunman or killer (esp. used in relation to Latin American drug cartels).

slow violence 'a violence that occurs gradually and out of sight . . . an attritional violence that is typically not viewed as violence at all . . . built on the bedrock of social inequality' (Rob Nixon, *Slow Violence and the Environmentalism of the Poor*, 2011).

sousaphone A vast brass musical instrument with a large flaring 'bell', and a central circle designed to fit around the body of the musician.

sphagnum A genus of mosses, which grows to form mires, bogs and, eventually, peat. Beautifully coloured in greens and reds.

stipe In **mycology**, the stalk of a mushroom/fungal fruiting body.

stridulate Of an insect, to make a high, shrill sound by rubbing the legs, wing-casings or other hard parts of the body together.

substrate The surface or substance upon which an organism lives, grows and feeds; an underlying layer.

sump A pit or pool into which waste liquids are drained; a cesspit; a sewage tank.

supervoid In astronomy, a very large part of the universe containing very little or no known condensed matter (galaxies, superclusters, etc.).

sylvan Of trees and forests.

tailings A by-product of mining; the waste rock and other matter left behind after ore has been processed for its valuable fraction.

terpsichorean Dance-like; to do with dancing.

terraqueous Formed of both land and water.

theodolite A precision instrument used by surveyors to make highly exact angular measurements.

thylacine Aka the Tasmanian tiger or Tasmanian wolf: an extinct carnivorous marsupial native to Australia. The thylacine had rust-red and black stripes on its back and flanks.

transhumance The seasonal movement of people and/or livestock (e.g. between summer pastures in the mountains and lowland winter pastures); a form of nomadism/pastoralism.

trophic cascade The set of consequences in an ecosystem that unfold when a 'trophic level' in a food web is removed; e.g. when humans exterminate wolves, ungulate populations boom, leading to the overgrazing of mountainsides, leading to changes in river-formation and **riparian** species.

troposphere The lowest layer of the Earth's atmosphere, lying immediately beneath the stratosphere.

undersong An underlying song or melody or sound; an underlying meaning.

understorey In a forest, the flowers, bushes, plants and small trees that grow beneath the canopy and above the forest floor; underbrush, undergrowth.

viriditas Latin; lit. 'greenness'. The medieval mystic Hildegard of Bingen (1098–1179) coined the word to mean 'vitality', 'lushness', 'growth', 'the greening power'.

watershed In American English, a river basin or **catchment**; in other English-speaking places, the dividing line of elevated terrain which separates neighbouring catchments.

Yggdrasil In Norse mythology, the vast, sacred ash tree that connects the underworld (roots), the mortal realm of the earth (trunk) and the realm of the gods (canopy).

NOTES

Epigraphs

Pages

vii   '*How can I translate . . . no life without it?*': Natalie Diaz, 'The First Water is the Body', in *Postcolonial Love Poem* (Minneapolis: Graywolf Press, 2020), p. 48.

vii   '*Dear broken rivers . . .*': Alexis Wright, 'We All Smell the Smoke, We All Feel the Heat: This Environmental Catastrophe is Global', *Guardian* (18 May 2019).

Prologue: The Springs

Pages

6   *A purging fury is visited upon the animate land . . .*: I draw here upon Alexandra Walsham's magisterial *The Reformation of the Landscape: Religion, Identity, and Memory in Early Modern Britain and Ireland* (Oxford: Oxford University Press, 2011), *passim*.

7   the rivers, lakes and ocean . . . within their silent depths: George Gordon Byron, 'Darkness', in *Byron's Poetry and Prose*, ed. Alice Levine (New York: W. W. Norton, 2010), p. 245.

Introduction: Anima

Pages

13   '*We are searching . . . forgot to build*': Barry Lopez, *Embrace Fearlessly the Burning World: Essays* (New York: Random House, 2022), p. 385.

15   '*the natural contract*': Michel Serres, *The Natural Contract*, trans. Elizabeth MacArthur and William Paulson (1992; Ann Arbor: University of Michigan Press, 1995).

15   '*Water is speaking*': Nan Shepherd, *The Living Mountain: A Celebration of the Cairngorm Mountains of Scotland* (1977; Edinburgh: Canongate, 2011), p. 22.

17 *In cities where daylighting has occurred . . .*: see Andrew C. Revkin, 'Peeling Back Pavement to Expose Watery Havens', *New York Times* (16 July 2009).

17 *Munich freed the blue-watered River Isar . . .*: for more on the 'Isar Plan', see inter alia 'Munich: The Restoration of the Isar River', Naturvation.eu., https://naturvation.eu/sites/default/files/munich_snapshot.pdf.

18 *the Don River in Toronto suffered such contamination . . .*: for more on the fiery fate and recovery of the Don, see Jennifer Bonnell's excellent *Reclaiming the Don: An Environmental History of Toronto's Don River Valley* (Toronto: University of Toronto Press, 2014).

18 *In the 1990s, Lake Ontario . . .*: see Mary Williams Walsh, 'Looking for Inexpensive Photo Processing? Try Lake Ontario', *Los Angeles Times* (13 November 1990).

18–19 *'The conquest of nature . . . brought under complete control'*: William John McGee, 'Water as a Resource', *Annals of the American Academy of Political and Social Science*, 33:3 (1909), 37–50; 39. I'm grateful to Jamie Linton in his fine *What is Water? The History of a Modern Abstraction* (Vancouver: University of British Columbia Press, 2010) for directing me to McGee's absolutism.

19 *one-dimensional water*: see Herbert Marcuse, *One-Dimensional Man: Studies in the Ideology of Advanced Industrial Society* (1964; Oxford: Routledge, 2002).

19 *'inanimate brute matter'*: letter from Isaac Newton to Richard Bentley on 25 February 1693, *Isaac Newton's Papers & Letters on Natural Philosophy*, ed. I. Bernard Cohen (Cambridge, Massachusetts: Harvard University Press, 1958), p. 302.

19 Bestand . . . *'appears as something at our command'*: Martin Heidegger, 'The Question Concerning Technology', in *The Question Concerning Technology and Other Essays*, trans. William Lovitt (1954; New York: Harper & Row, 1977), pp. 307–42; p. 321. I despise Heidegger's politics, but find it necessary to engage with aspects of his philosophy.

20 *'as a calculable coherence'*: ibid., p. 326.

20 *more than a million barriers . . .*: see *The AMBER Barrier Atlas: A Pan-European Database of Artificial Instream Barriers. Version 1.0* (29 June 2020), the *AMBER* Consortium, https://amber.international/european-barrier-atlas/.

20 hier gaan over het tij . . . en wij: for this detail and more on modern Dutch hydrological engineering and landscape design, see Lizzie Yarini's fascinating essay 'The River is a Model', *Places Journal* (February 2024).

21 *'Resources are not, they become'*: Erich Zimmermann, *World Resources and Industries* (New York: Harper & Row, 1951), p. 15.

21 *'cleaning fluid'*: Ivan Illich, *H_2O and the Waters of Forgetfulness: Reflections on the Historicity of 'Stuff'* (Berkeley: Heyday Books, 1985), p. 75.

21   *'of the deep imagination'*: David Cayley, *Ivan Illich in Conversation* (Concord, Ontario: House of Anansi Press, 1992), p. 246.

21   *'Following dream-waters upstream . . . of their voices'*: Illich, *H_2O and the Waters of Forgetfulness*, p. 7.

21   *'grammar of animacy'*: see Robin Wall Kimmerer, 'Learning the Grammar of Animacy', in *Braiding Sweetgrass: Indigenous Wisdom, Scientific Knowledge and the Teachings of Plants* (Minneapolis, Minnesota: Milkweed Editions, 2013), pp. 48–59.

22   *'Our histories run deep . . . animals who instruct us'*: Elouise Wilson, Mary R. Benally, Ahjani Yepa and Cynthia Wilson, 'Women of Bears Ears are Asking You to Help Save It', *New York Times* (25 April 2021).

22   *You find yourself falling in love outward*: see Robinson Jeffers, 'The Tower Beyond Tragedy', in *Tamar and Other Poems* (1924; London: Hogarth Press, 1928), p. 12.

22   *In Māori, one greets someone new . . .*: see Jacinta Ruru, 'Who are Your Waters?', *e-flux* (26 July 2019).

23   *'Shifting baseline syndrome'*: see Daniel Pauly, 'Anecdotes and the Shifting Baseline Syndrome of Fisheries', *Trends in Ecology and Evolution*, 10:10 (1995), 430.

24   *'The simple truth . . . every river in England is dying'*: Feargal Sharkey, quoted in PA Media, 'Environment Agency "Letting River Wye Go into a Death Spiral"', *Guardian* (8 February 2024).

24   *Shifting baseline syndrome can also function in reverse*: see an interesting pair of Instagram posts on SBS by the excellent Australian campaigning group Revive the Northern Rivers: @revivethenorthernrivers, 7 February and 13 February 2024.

24   *When the Lower Elwha Dam . . .*: I draw for the details of these paragraphs on Jessica Plumb's beautiful essay on the restoration of the Elwha, 'A River Reawakened: Ten Years of Rewilding the Elwha Watershed', *Orion Magazine* (2021); and her superb documentary film, *Return of the River* (2014).

25   *'So what would a radically different . . . a community's view of itself?'*: Christopher D. Stone, 'Introduction: Trees at Thirty-Five', in *Should Trees Have Standing? Law, Morality, and the Environment*, 3rd edn (New York: Oxford University Press, 2010), p. xi.

26   *'Should Trees Have Standing?'*: Christopher D. Stone, '"Should Trees Have Standing?": Towards Legal Rights for Natural Objects', *Southern California Law Review*, 45 (1972), 450–501.

26   *'Each time there is a movement . . . holding rights at the time'*: ibid., 455.

26–7   *'Indigenous peoples throughout the world . . . river-bed and river-bank'*: Jacinta Ruru and James D. K. Morris, 'Giving Voice to Rivers: Legal Personality as a Vehicle for Recognising Indigenous Peoples' Relationship to Water?', *Australian Indigenous Law Review*, 14:2 (2010), 49–62; 49–50.

27   *At the Act's heart . . .*: pioneering as it is, the Act is (inevitably) imperfect. Among other key aspects, it fails to reconcile the fundamental difference between a 'legal person' as recognized within a Western rights framework, and an ancestor or living being as recognized within the Māori cosmovision. These two categories will not fit flush together, and should not be mistaken here or elsewhere as identical – or even as siblings. Nor does the Act substantively redress the matter of Crown property/landholding in respect of the river, initially seized by colonists in the notorious 1840 Treaty of Waitingi/Te Tiriti. For a probing analysis of the Te Awa Tupua Act and points beyond, see Rod Barnett, 'Utu in the Anthropocene', *Places Journal* (August 2021).

27   an '*indivisible and living whole . . . lifeforce*': Aotearoa New Zealand Government, 'Te Awa Tupua (Whanganui River Claims Settlement) Act 2017' (20 March 2017).

27   '*life principle . . . being or entity*': *Te Aka Māori Dictionary*, https://www.maoridictionary.co.nz.

27–8 '*comprising the Whanganui . . . human face*': Aotearoa New Zealand Government, 'Te Awa Tupua Act'.

28–9 '*We want . . . perspective of ownership and management*': Gerrard Albert, quoted in 'New Zealand River Granted Same Legal Rights as Human Being', *Guardian* (16 March 2017).

29   '*those from below*': see Gustavo Esteva, 'The Time for Resistance and Solidarity', *Radio Zapatista* (13 September 2012).

29   '*grassroots groups . . . in the here and now*': 'Hasta Siempre, Gustavo', in 'Weaving Alternatives #07', *Global Tapestry of Alternatives* (2022).

30   '*Right to Flow . . . Free from Pollution*': 'Universal Declaration of the Rights of Rivers', *Earth Law Center* (2017).

30   '*The law . . . and learn from, rivers*': Anne Poelina, Alessandro Pelizzon and Erin O'Donnell, 'Australia's Rivers are Ancestral Beings', University of Melbourne, *Legal Affairs* (18 October 2021). I would urge anyone interested in Australian or global river politics to seek out the work of Anne Poelina, human and river rights advocate, filmmaker and scholar. She is helping to drive a large-scale reimagining of river-presence, especially in the Martuwarra/Fitzroy catchment. See, for instance, her co-written journal paper about the Martuwarra in which the river itself is the first named author: Martuwarra River of Life, Anne Poelina, Donna Bagnall and Michelle Lim, 'Recognizing the Martuwarra's First Law Right to Life as a Living Ancestral Being', *Transnational Environmental Law*, 9:3 (November 2020), 541–68.

30   '*not a machine . . . alive and kicking*': D. H. Lawrence, 'Sex versus Loveliness', in *Selected Essays* (1928; Harmondsworth: Penguin, 1950), pp. 13–18; p. 14.

Part I: The River of the Cedars (Ecuador)

Pages

35 '*One way to stop . . . outward of the mind and imagination*': Ursula K. Le Guin, 'Deep in Admiration', in *Arts of Living on a Damaged Planet/Ghosts of the Anthropocene*, ed. Anna Tsing, Heather Swanson, Elaine Gan et al. (Minneapolis: Minnesota University Press, 2017), pp. 15–21; p. 16.

42 '*inalienable . . . permanent alteration of natural cycles*': Constitution of the Republic of Ecuador (2008), *passim*.

43 *But how did this come to pass?*: for a detailed account of the inclusion of the Rights of Nature in the 2008 constitution, see Fundación Pachamama, 'Experienca: Reconocimiento de los Derechos de la Naturaleza en la Constitucíon Ecuatoriana', *Iniciativa Ciudadanizando la Política Ambiental*, 6 (April 2010).

43 '*all the beings around . . . the spirits of nature*': Carlos Larrea, in *Paraecologists for the Rights of Nature*, documentary short, dir. Mika Peck, Ecoforensic (30 August 2022).

43–4 '*The world is painting still lifes . . . piece of property*': Eduardo Galeano, 'La naturaleza no es muda'/'Nature is not mute', translation unattributed, *Seminario Brecha* (21 April 2008).

44 '*the extirpation of idolatry*': see Father Pablo Joseph de Arriaga, *The Extirpation of Idolatry in Peru*, trans. L. Clark Keating (1621; Lexington, Kentucky: University of Kentucky Press, 1968).

44 '*five centuries of . . . mutilate reality and memory*': Galeano, 'La naturaleza no es muda', 2008.

45 '*These elements . . . sensitive to our feelings*': see (including footage of the purification ceremony) 'La naturaleza también tiene derechos', Fundación Pachamama (2011), https://www.youtube.com/watch?app=desktop&v=PfCszVQD_kU&t=129s.

46 '*We were moving forwards with ideas . . . what we had done*': Alberto Acosta, interviewed on my behalf by César Rodríguez-Garavito (1 November 2022).

47 *the great, wounded Atrato River*: see Constitutional Court of Colombia, 'Decision T-622/16: The Atrato River as a "Subject of Rights"' (10 November 2016).

49 *helped drive global recognition of a third 'F'*: see Francisco Kuhar, Giuliana Furci, Elisandro Ricardo Drechsler-Santos et al., 'Delimitation of Funga as a Valid Term for the Diversity of Fungal Communities: The Fauna, Flora & Fungi Proposal (FF&F)', *IMA Fungus*, 9:2 (2018), A71–A74.

50 *She will be looking for two fungi in particular*: on the extraordinary fungal diversity of Los Cedros, see Roo Vandergrift, D. S. Newman, B. T. M. Dentinger

et al., 'Richer than Gold: The Fungal Biodiversity of Reserva Los Cedros, a Threatened Andean Cloud Forest', *Botanical Studies*, 64:17 (2023), 1–22.

57 *according to the 'Dry Refugia' hypothesis*: see Santiago Ramírez-Barahoa and Luis E. Eguiarte, 'The Role of Glacial Cycles in Promoting Genetic Diversity in the Neotropics: The Case of Cloud Forests during the Last Glacial Maximum', *Ecology and Evolution*, 3:3 (2013), 725–38.

62 *The Los Cedros concession was one of dozens . . .*: on Ecuador, Correa and the complications of eco-socialism, see Thea Riofrancos's outstanding *Resource Radicals: From Petro-Nationalism to Post-Extractivism in Ecuador* (Durham, North Carolina: Duke University Press, 2020).

63 '*infantile left*': Rafael Correa, 'Ecuador's Path', interview, *New Left Review*, 77 (September/October 2012), 88–104; 92.

63 '*odious debt*': see Michael Kremer and Seema Jayachandran, 'Odious Debt', *Finance & Development: A Quarterly Magazine of the IMF*, 39:2 (June 2002), online only.

63 '*Oil contracts . . . and take four*': Rafael Correa, quoted in 'Leftist Correa Claims Victory in Ecuador', *People's World* (1 December 2006).

63 '*by thousands . . . heavy metals into the Amazon basin.*': Liz Downes, 'Neoliberalism versus Justice on Ecuador's Mining Frontier', *Chain Reaction: The National Magazine of Friends of the Earth Australia*, 137 (December 2019), 38–9; 38.

64 '*maintain its cycles . . . what is going to happen tomorrow?*': Agustín Grijalva Jiménez, Judgment No. 1149-19-JP/21, Constitutional Court of Ecuador (10 November 2021).

64 '*The forest helped us . . . swayed the bench*': interview with Agustín Grijalva Jiménez (24 June 2022).

65 '*A river [or] a forest . . . rights inherent to a subject*': Grijalva Jiménez, Judgment No. 1149-19-JP/21.

65 '*This ruling is as important to nature . . . to our own species*': Mika Peck, quoted in Patrick Greenfield, 'Plans to Mine Ecuador Forest Violate Rights of Nature, Court Rules', *Guardian* (2 December 2021).

65 '*the turning-point in the history . . . law of the future*': Mónica Feria-Tinta, quoted in Rebekah Hayden, 'Saving Los Cedros is "Case of the Century"', *Ecologist* (26 November 2020).

70 I keep expecting to hear . . . we have to protect him: interview with Natalia Greene (23 October 2022). In 2008 Natalia Greene – then a young Ecuadorian eco-feminist campaigner and academic – was instrumental in getting the Rights of Nature articles included in the draft constitution, and she has since gone on to become a key figure in the global Rights of Nature movement, including as the director of GARN, the Global Alliance for the Rights of Nature.

74   *Monse brings news of an atrocious event*: on the brutal murder of Alba Bermeo Puin, see 'Urgent Public Statement: Murder of Pregnant Nature Defender in Molleturo', *Alianza por los Derechos Humanos* (24 October 2022).

76   *There is the 'Battle of Junín'*: for more on Junín and the long history of resistance in the Intag Valley, see Malcolm Rogge's outstanding documentary *Under Rich Earth* (2008), https://www.youtube.com/watch?v=QRinnhe-jBIw; and an extended interview with the formidable Carlos Zorrilla (community organizer and anti-mining activist in Intag): 'How to "Stop Mining Before It Starts"': Carlos Zorrilla, interview with Liz Kimbrough, *Mongabay* (4 April 2024).

79   *'Slime moulds mapped the Tokyo subway'*: see for a sparkling description of this experiment, Merlin Sheldrake, *Entangled Life: How Fungi Make Our Worlds, Change Our Minds and Shape Our Futures* (London: Bodley Head, 2020), pp. 16–17.

82   *'enlarge the imagined range . . . move in'*: George Eliot, *Felix Holt, the Radical*, ed. William Baker and Kenneth Womack (Peterborough, Ontario: Broadview, 2000), p. 47.

83   How can you hope to communicate . . . one another: Stanisław Lem, *Solaris*, trans. Joanna Kilmartin and Steve Cox (1961; London: Faber & Faber, 2003), p. 23.

86–7   No way was clear . . . half an inch across: Ursula K. Le Guin, *The Word for World is Forest* (1972; London: Gollancz, 2015), p. 27.

88   *I tell them how, thousands of years ago, a god-king called Gilgamesh . . .*: see for two contrasting translations/tellings of *Gilgamesh*: Stephen Mitchell, *Gilgamesh: A New English Version* (London: Profile, 2005); and Sophus Helle, *Gilgamesh: A New Translation of the Ancient Epic* (New Haven, Connecticut: Yale University Press, 2021).

89   I don't know . . . part of human nature: Le Guin, *The Word for World is Forest*, p. 83.

91   *'double death . . . living presence of the past'*: see Deborah Bird Rose, 'Double Death', *The Multispecies Salon*, https://www.multispecies-salon.org/double-death/.

91   *'shimmer'*: see Deborah Bird Rose, *Shimmer: Flying Fox Exuberance in Worlds of Peril* (Edinburgh: Edinburgh University Press, 2022).

92   *the Anthropocene, the Capitalocene, the Great Acceleration*: on epochal naming variants, see Donna J. Haraway, 'Anthropocene, Capitalocene, Plantationocene, Chthulucene: Making Kin', *Environmental Humanities*, 6:1 (2015), 159–65.

92   *the Eremocene*: Edward O. Wilson, 'Beware the Age of Loneliness', *The Economist* (18 November 2013).

97 'ecology of selves . . . becoming': Eduardo Kohn, *How Forests Think: Toward an Anthropology Beyond the Human* (Los Angeles: University of California Press, 2013), pp. 16, viii, 72.

97 *Kawsak Sacha*: see the Kichwa Indigenous People of Sarayaku, 'Kawsak Sacha – The Living Forest. A Living and Conscious Being: The Subject of Rights' (2012/2018), https://ecojurisprudence.org/wp-content/uploads/2022/08/KAWSAK-SACHA-Declaration-Summary-Eng.pdf.

97 '*from the smallest to the largest . . . its own consciousness*': Beatriz Miranda, '"We Can't Hunt or Fish": The Villages in Ecuador Surrounded by Abandoned Explosives', *Guardian* (18 April 2024).

97 '*alive . . . living, thinking being*': José Gualinga Montalvo, quoted in Carlos Andrés Baquero-Díaz, 'José Gualinga Montalvo: "The Jungle is a Living, Intelligent and Conscious Being"', *Sumaúma* (5 January 2024).

97–8 *to designate the forest's aliveness in this way . . .*: I draw in this section on Marisol de la Cadena's brilliant *Earth Beings: Ecologies of Practice Across Andean Worlds* (Durham, North Carolina: Duke University Press, 2015).

98–9 '*for freedom . . . a sacred territory*': the Kichwa Indigenous People of Sarayaku, 'Kawsak Sacha – The Living Forest. A Living and Conscious Being: The Subject of Rights'.

99 '*a living, intelligent and conscious being*': José Gualinga Montalvo, in Carlos Andrés Baquero-Díaz, 'José Gualinga Montalvo'.

101 '*This monument is to acknowledge . . . if we did it*': the plaque's wording was composed by the Icelandic writer Andri Snær Magnason, and the context is described in his beautiful *On Time and Water: A History of Our Future*, trans. Lytton Smith (2020; London: Serpent's Tail, 2021).

105 '*All that I have is the river . . . I'm done with my dying*': Johnny Flynn, 'The Water', *Been Listening*, album (London: Transgressive Records, 2010).

106 It is time to lose the fear of death . . . the beginning of others: Giuliana Furci, *Let Things Rot*, documentary, dir. Mateo Barrenengoa (2021).

107 Life is as much undergone . . . in the midst: Tim Ingold, *Being Alive: Essays on Movement, Knowledge and Description* (London: Routledge, 2021), p. xii.

The Springs (Winter)

Pages

111–12 Brazil and the planet . . . risks human life: Luis Inácio Lula da Silva, presidential victory speech on 30 October 2022, quoted in 'Lula's Victory Speech', *Brasilwire* (1 November 2022).

113 Every single river in England . . . legal limits: Rachel Salvidge, 'How Clean are England's Rivers?' *Guardian* (25 September 2020).

113–14 Springs are special places . . . people were drawn to it: Finlay MacLeod, *The Chapels and Healing Wells of the Western Isles* (Stornoway: Acair, 2018), p. 7.

Part II: Ghosts, Monsters and Angels (India)

Pages

117 '*The river had to be killed for the city to live*': Yuvan Aves, *Intertidal: A Coast and Marsh Diary* (Delhi: Bloomsbury India, 2023), p. 202.

117 '*Before landscapes die, they first vanish in the imagination*': Bhavani Raman, 'The Curious Disappearance of the Ennore Creek', *The Wire* (13 November 2017). I'm grateful to Bhavani for our conversation about the relationships between language, archive, memory and hydro-politics in Chennai.

123 It's official . . . new water analysis report shows: Komal Gautham, 'It's Official: Chennai's Rivers are "Dead" ', *Times of India* (18 January 2023).

125 '*Cities grow along riversides . . . in the first place: a river*': Aves, *Intertidal*, p. 205.

125–6 '*The news of the remarkable revelation . . . my work then lay*': Robert Bruce Foote, 'Author's Preface', *The Foote Collection of Indian Prehistoric and Proto-historic Antiquities: Notes on Their Ages and Distribution* (Madras: Government Press, 1916), pp. v–vii; p. v.

127 '*unfit for any kind of life form . . . dissolved oxygen*': Gautham, 'It's Official'.

127 '*lakes or water monuments called* Jalasthambam': Yuvan Aves, 'A Tamil Animist: Gleaning Identity, Nativity, and Animate Wisdom from Tamil Culture', *Dark 'n' Light* (March 2022); see also Nakkeeran, *Neer Eẓhuthu* (Chennai: Crow's Nest, 2019).

127–8 '*May they perish . . . cannot be displaced by water*': see Tho Paramasivan, *The Sweet Salt of Tamil*, trans. V. Ramnarayan (Chennai: Navayana, 2023), p. 29, p. 31.

129 '*Once upon a time . . . allow it to flow*': Aves, 'A Tamil Animist'.

129 '*When the rivers were tapped . . . began to die*': Venkatesh Ramakrishnan, quoted in Gautham, 'It's Official'.

130–31 '*We displaced them . . . claimed them as their own again*': Krupa Ge, *Rivers Remember: #Chennairians and the Shocking Truth of a Manmade Flood* (Chennai: Context, 2019), p. 17.

131 '*All stories from Chennai . . . surely something missing*': Aves, *Intertidal*, p. xvi.

133 '*Waiting is the act . . . constraints of one's will*': Yuvan Aves, *A Naturalist's Journal* (Chennai: Notion Press, 2017), p. 47.

133–4 '*He always had this strange . . . rivers, mountains*': Jiddu Krishnamurti, *Krishnamurti's Journal* (San Francisco: Harper & Row, 1982), p. 15.

134 '*Have you ever sat very quietly . . . your mind is like that*': Jiddu Krishnamurti, *Think on These Things* (New York: Harper & Row, 1964), p. 38.

136 *'like a thick, gentle rope'*: Aves, *A Naturalist's Journal*, p. 24.

136 *'the entire abounding community of life around'*: Aves, 'A Tamil Animist'.

136 *'into the long hall . . . these arachnids'*: Aves, *A Naturalist's Journal*, p. 179.

136 *'relating and relationship . . . above everything else'*: ibid., p. 118.

137 *'How does a moth know . . . in an entirely new light?'*: ibid., p. 199.

146 *In late March 2017 . . .*: I draw in this section on Michael Safi's reporting in 'Murder Most Foul: Polluted Indian River Reported Dead Despite "Living Entity" Status', *Guardian* (7 July 2017).

146 *'breathing, living . . . mountains to the sea'*: Uttarakhand High Court, India, 'Mohammad Salim vs State of Uttarakhand & others', articles 17 and 19 (20 March 2017).

147 *'attempting to kill the river by slow poison'*: Brij Khandelwal, quoted in Hemendra Chaturvedi, 'Environmentalist Seeks FIR for "Attempt to Murder" Yamuna River, Now a Living Entity', *Hindustan Times* (26 March 2017).

147–8 *'The natural environment . . . sustainable destruction'*: Madras High Court, India, 'A. Periyakaruppan vs The Principal Secretary to Government, Revenue Department & The Additional Chief Secretary and Commissioner of Revenue Administration', articles 19–20 (19 April 2022).

148 *'Nature's Rights Commission . . . springs and waterfalls'*: ibid, article 21.

150 Rivers remember . . . thrived in: see Krupa Ge, *Rivers Remember*, p. 17.

151 *'I am thankful for the unknowable field . . . in life itself'*: Yuvan Aves, Instagram post, @A_Naturalists_Column (6 March 2023).

152 *'geologian'*: see Andrew C. Revkin, 'Thomas Berry, Writer and Lecturer with a Mission for Mankind, Dies at 94', *New York Times* (4 June 2009).

152 *Ecozoic Era*: see Thomas Berry, 'A New Era: Healing the Injuries We Have Inflicted on Our Planet', *Health Progress*, 73:2 (1992), 60–63; 60. For more on Berry's Ecozoic, see Thomas Berry and Brian Swimme, 'The Ecozoic Era', in *The Universe Story: From the Primordial Flaring Forth to the Ecozoic Era; A Celebration of the Unfolding of the Cosmos* (San Francisco: Harper Collins, 1992), pp. 240–61.

152 *Technozoic Era*: Berry, 'A New Era', 62.

152 *'The Great Work'*: see Thomas Berry, *The Great Work: Our Way into the Future* (New York: Bell Tower, 1999).

152 *'We are talking only to ourselves . . . the great conversation'*: Thomas Berry and Thomas Clarke, *Befriending the Earth: A Theology of Reconciliation Between Humans and the Earth* (Mystic, Connecticut: Twenty-Third Publications, 1991), p. 20.

152 *'a communion of subjects, not a collection of objects'*: Thomas Berry, *Evening Thoughts: Reflecting on Earth as Sacred Community* (San Francisco: Sierra Club Books, 1996), p. 96.

152 '*Earth Jurisprudence*': on Berry's coining of this phrase during a 2001 symposium in London, see Mike Bell, 'Thomas Berry and an Earth Jurisprudence: An Exploratory Essay', in *The Trumpeter*, 19:1 (2003), 69–96.

152 '*Trees have tree rights . . . mountain rights*': Berry, *The Great Work*, p. 5.

153 '*inscendence*': Thomas Berry, 'The Dream of the Earth: Our Way into the Future', *CrossCurrents*, 37:2/3 (1986), 200–215; 209.

154 '*Barrenness is . . . a state of land*': Aves, *Intertidal*, p. 191.

157 Everything is alive and everything is speaking: quoted in ibid., p. 47; see also Siddharth Pandey, 'Emplacing Tasks of Magic: Hand, Land, and the Generation of Fantasy Taskscape in Terry Pratchett's Tiffany Aching Series', PhD thesis, Cambridge University, submitted 2020.

159 *the most ancient three stages were older than the Mississippi River Belt itself*: see Harold Norman Fisk, 'Ancient Courses, Mississippi River Meander Belt, Cape Girardeau, Mo.-Donaldsonville, La.', *Geological Investigation of the Alluvial Valley of the Lower Mississippi River* (Vicksburg, Mississippi: Mississippi River Commission, 1945), Atlas Plate 22, Sheets 2, 3,7 and 9.

159 '*Looking at them . . . and gazed upon the river*': Jason Kottke, 'Just Added! Jason Kottke Intros Two New Vintage Mississippi River Maps', 20x200.com (18 June 2019).

159 *Since Fisk, advances in remote-sensing . . . river, delta or floodplain*: see the spectacular river mapping/visualization work of Dan Coe at https://dancoecarto.com/4k-rivers.

160 '*The idea appeals to me . . . "veins of water"*': Leonardo da Vinci, in Martin Kemp, *Leonardo* (Oxford: Oxford University Press, 2011), p. 93.

161 *Question: how do you make a river disappear overnight?*: for more on this, see Raman, 'The Curious Disappearance of the Ennore Creek'.

163 '*multi-species justice*': see *The Promise of Multispecies Justice*, ed. Sophie Chao, Karin Boldender and Eben Kirksey (Durham, North Carolina: Duke University Press, 2022).

166 Where water comes together with other water . . .: see Raymond Carver, *Where Water Comes Together with Other Water* (New York: Random House, 1985).

166–7 *Archives examined by a Dutch scholar . . .*: see Wil O. Dijk, *Seventeenth-century Burma and the Dutch East India Company, 1634–1680* (Singapore: Singapore University Press, 2006).

170 '*Bodies need water . . . also needs a body*': Astrida Neimanis, 'Hydrofeminism: Or, On Becoming a Body of Water', in *Undutiful Daughters: Mobilizing Future Concepts, Bodies and Subjectivities in Feminist Thought and Practice*, ed. Henriette Gunkel, Chrysanthi Nigianni and Fanny Söderbäck (New York: Palgrave Macmillan, 2012), pp. 85–99; p. 90.

170 '*body is marshland, estuary, ecosystem*': Neimanis, 'Hydrofeminism', p. 93.

170 '*My kidneys are marshes . . . I am primarily hydrosphere*': Yuvan Aves, Instagram post, @A_Naturalists_Column (7 March 2024).

170 Inner and outer merge . . . on all shores: Aves, *Intertidal*, pp. xx–xxi.

175 'glyan: *the human spine . . . to be confluent as rivers are*': see the *Dictionary of the Lepcha-Language*, compiled by G. B. Mainwaring, rev. Albert Grünwedel (Berlin: Unger Brothers, 1898), *passim*.

184 'My own spiritual observation . . . a spacious thing': see Aves, 'A Tamil Animist'; my recollection of it there on the beach was not word-perfect.

The Springs (Spring)

Pages

189 People feel . . . from source to sea: Councillor Matthew Bird, 'Motion – Rights of the River', Lewes District Council Meeting (20 February 2023).

190 *where archaeologists have found knapped flints*: see Steve Boreham, Julie Boreham, Lawrence Billington, 'A Flint Scatter at Nine Wells, Great Shelford', *Proceedings of the Cambridge Antiquarian Society*, 107 (2018), 7–14.

Part III: The Living River (Nitassinan/Canada)

Pages

195 '*We've always known the river is alive*': Rita Mestokosho, quoted in Susan Nerberg, 'I am Mutehekau Shipu: A River's Journey to Personhood in Eastern Quebec', *Canadian Geographic* (April 2022), https://canadiangeographic.ca/articles/i-am-mutehekau-shipu-a-rivers-journey-to-personhood-in-eastern-quebec/.

195 '*Time isn't just a linear arrow . . . its past and our futures*': Anne Poelina et al., 'Australia's Rivers are Ancestral Beings'.

201 *new findings about whale song and whale speech*: see the work of Project CETI; also Tom Mustil, *How to Speak Whale: A Voyage into the Future of Animal Communication* (London: William Collins, 2022); and Elizabeth Kolbert, 'Talk to Me: Can Artificial Intelligence Allow Us to Speak to Another Species?', *New Yorker* (4 September 2023).

204 '*industrialize the remote region north of the 49th Parallel*': see Alexis Lathem, 'Innu Continue to Protest the Plan Nord and Romaine River Hydro Project', *Towards Freedom* (4 July 2012).

204 '*school without limits*': Uapukun Mestokosho and Yenny Vegas Cárdenas, 'Recognizing the Legal Personhood of the Magpie River/Mutehekau Shipu in Canada', in *A Legal Personality for the St Lawrence River and Other Rivers of the World*, ed. Yenny Vega Cárdenas and Daniel Turp (Montreal: Les Éditions JFC, 2023), pp. 113–64, p. 120.

206 Sustained protests against the Romaine project . . .: see Alexis Lathem, 'Innu Continue to Protest the Plan Nord and Romaine River Hydro Project', *Towards Freedom* (4 July 2012).

206 *'Find their river and slit its throat'*: Natalie Diaz, *Postcolonial Love Poem*, p. 66.

206–7 *'I would have liked . . . our monuments to protect'*: Jean-Charles Piétacho, quoted in Philip Authier, 'Innu Chief Delivers Message of Caution as Romaine Hydro Complex is Inaugurated', *Montreal Gazette* (12 October 2023).

207 *Though employment levels rose significantly in the region*: for an in-depth assessment of the public health impacts of the Romaine Project, see *Summary Analysis of the Impact of the Romaine Hydroelectric Project on the Health of the Population: Monitoring the Situation in the Municipality of Havre Saint-Pierre*, Institut National de Santé Publique (July 2013).

211 *During his many moves over the past quarter-century*: Wayne has given me permission to adapt this from Wayne Chambliss, 'Fetishes (16)', *HiLoBrow.com* (17 May 2019).

215 *'a legal person with the right to live'*: Hélène Jouan, 'The Fight to Protect Canada's Magpie River, Now a "Legal Person with the Right to Live"', *Le Monde* (12 December 2022).

215 *'to exist and to flow . . . be preserved and protected'*: Innu Council of Ekuanitshit, 'Part 4: The Legal Foundations', in *Ekuanitshit Innu Council Resolution: Magpie River* (January 2021), p. 6.

215 *'Two-Eyed Seeing'*: see Cherlyn M. Bartlett, Murdena Marshall and Albert Marshall, Mi'kmaq Nation, 'Enabling Concepts within a Journey Guided by Trees Holding Hands and Two-Eyed Seeing', unpublished manuscript, Integrative Science Program (Nova Scotia: Cape Breton University, 2007), pp. 1–29.

215 *traditional ecological knowledge*: see Kimmerer, *Braiding Sweetgrass*, passim.

216 *'For Innu communities . . . deserve respect'*: Mestokosho and Cárdenas, in *A Legal Personality for the St Lawrence River and Other Rivers of the World*, p. 121.

216 *'profoundly inspired'*: ibid., p. 124.

216 *'the voice and the light . . . eyes of the world'*: ibid., p. 156.

217 *'WHEREAS since time immemorial . . . the Innu of Ekuanitshit'*: Innu Council of Ekuanitshit, in *Ekuanitshit Innu Council Resolution: Magpie River* (January 2021), p. 2, p. 6.

221 *'real silence . . . witness life'*: personal email from Rita Mestokosho to me, my translation (16 March 2024)

221–2 *'My people wrote while walking . . . geographies of forests'*: *Atik^U utei: Le cœur du caribou* (Montreal: Mémoire d'encrier, 2023), p. 35. My translation; all subsequent translations from Rita's French-language writing are by me and quoted with Rita's permission. Original French: 'Mon peuple écrivait en marchant [. . .] / il avait la bibliothèque de la terre avec lui // Mon peuple écrivait des millions de livres / éparpillés sur le territoire / des encyclopédies de rivières / des dictionnaires de montagnes / des géographies de forêts'.

222   *'speaks the language of hope'*: ibid., p. 33; 'parle la langue de l'espoir'.

222   *'grandmothers who have . . . learned to listen to it'*: ibid., p. 10; 'Grands-Mères qui ont marché près de l'eau et ont appris à l'écouter'.

222   *'The river plunges in my dreams'*: ibid., p. 63; 'la rivière plonge dans mes rêves'.

222   *'free . . . / to feel the water in my veins'*: ibid., p. 21; 'libre . . . / sentir l'eau dans mes veines'.

222   *'my heart is made of pine branches'*: ibid., p. 45; 'mon coeur est fait de branches de sapin'.

222   *'I will become salmon'*: ibid., p. 45; 'je deviendrai saumon'.

222   *'We all have a river who calls to us'*: ibid., p. 44; 'nous avons tous une rivière qui / nous appelle'.

223   *'I have crossed . . . borne me away'*: ibid., p. 69; 'j'ai traversé la dernière rivière / le torrent m'a emportée'.

230   *I remember the passage in* A River Runs Through It: see Norman Maclean, *A River Runs Through It* (1976; Chicago: University of Chicago Press, 2011).

236   *'We pay homage to our rivers . . . follow the current'*: Uapukun Mestokosho and Shanice Mollen-Picard, *Shipu*, documentary film (2017).

237–8   *'It seems crazy . . . connections in time and space'*: Lydia Mestokosho-Paradis, in interview with me on 6 October 2023, quoted here with her permission.

251   *'is now a story . . . to change Canadian law'*: Mestokosho and Cárdenas, in *A Legal Personality for the St Lawrence Rivers and Other Rivers of the World*, p. 126.

251   *'give legal capacity to the St Lawrence river'*: Canadian House of Commons, *Bill C-271: St Lawrence River Capacity and Protection Act*, Section 4.1a (May 2022), p. 2.

251   *'All things on the Earth . . . Quebec is not going to do it'*: Ross Montour, quoted in Mar Lalonde, 'AFNQL Recognizes Legal Personhood of St Lawrence River', *Penticton Herald* (4 May 2023).

251   *'We believe water and nature . . . under Indigenous law'*: Anellah Orosz and Deklan Orosz, quoted in Brian Banks, 'The Rights of Nature', *ON Nature* (Spring 2022), pp. 24–9; pp. 26–7.

251–2   *Dozens of communities in the United States . . .*: I'm grateful to Tzintzun Aguilar-Izzo and Blake Lavia for summarizing some of these initiatives and actions for me.

262   *'a gong-like humming'*: Algernon Blackwood, 'The Willows', in *The Listener and Other Stories* (1907; Blackmask Publishing, 2007), pp. 75–120; p. 111.

262   *'whirring of wings'*: ibid., p. 105.

262   *'We had strayed . . . close about us'*: ibid., p. 107.

262 '*the sound of their world . . . leaks through somehow*': ibid., p. 112.

262 '*Our thoughts make spirals . . . at all costs if possible*': ibid., p. 111.

263 '*the early feeling . . . other life was possible*': Algernon Blackwood, *Episodes Before Thirty* (London: Cassell & Company, 1923), pp. 32–3.

263 '*The Danube . . . with its* aliveness': Blackwood, 'The Willows', p. 77.

269 I could feel her echolocation through my whole body . . .: see *Whale with Steve Backshall*, Sky Nature (December 2023).

274 '*Angel of History*': see Walter Benjamin, 'Theses on the Philosophy of History' (1940), in *Illuminations*, ed. Hannah Arendt, trans. Harry Zohn (New York: Schocken Books, 1969), pp. 253–64; p. 257. I'm grateful to Wayne Chambliss for pointing out the affinity between Benjamin's angel and my profane posture on the wave.

288–9 '*The mad water rushes thro' . . . into one majestic Thing . . .*': Samuel Taylor Coleridge, letter to Sara Hutchinson, 25 August 1802, in *Collected Letters of Samuel Taylor Coleridge*, ed. Earl Leslie Griggs, Vol. II: 1801–1806 (1956; Oxford: Clarendon Press/Oxford University Press, 1966), pp. 853–4.

SELECT BIBLIOGRAPHY
AND RESOURCES

The literature of rivers is vast, ancient and wandering; the literature of the modern Rights of Nature movement is young, vigorous and extensive. This bibliography includes a selection of the books, essays and articles that I have read on these and associated subjects. Under-represented in terms of proportion to the number read are academic/journal articles about legal, ethical and regulatory aspects of the Rights of Nature; to include them all would have been roughly to double the length of the bibliography, so I have focused on those I felt to be most useful.

The entries asterisked below are those I found especially interesting or to which I am particularly indebted. Memories, thoughts and quote-splinters on the part of this book's narrator may be tested against the works cited here and in the Notes.

At the end of the Bibliography there is a small gathering of some of the many Acts, bills, declarations, judgments and resolutions arising from Rights of Nature actions and associated ideas/movements.

In terms of key resources: for UK readers wishing to know in considerable and practical detail how they might best take action on behalf of rivers in England and Wales, there is no better single document than the King's College London Legal Clinic's *A Rights of Nature River Toolkit: How to Protect Rivers in England and Wales* (2023), which is free to download at https://www.kcl.ac.uk/legal-clinic/assets/rights-of-nature-toolkit.pdf.

The Universal Rights of Rivers Declaration is downloadable and adaptable by any local group wishing to declare the rights of their river or rivers: https://www.rightsofrivers.org.

GARN – the Global Alliance for the Rights of Nature – is the hub of the world-wide movement: https://www.garn.org. Its website is rich with information, inspiration and resources, including a glossary, a reading list, an anthology of 'untold stories' and a global map of key Rights of Nature locations. It also includes an annually updated timeline of the modern Rights of Nature movement, 1972–present: https://www.garn.org/rights-of-nature-timeline/.

More Than Human Rights: An Ecology of Law, Thought and Narrative for Earthly Flourishing (New York: NYU Law/MOTH collective, 2024), ed. César Rodríguez-Garavito, is a freely downloadable book containing chapters by diverse contributors, which together discuss the philosophical, legal and scientific foundations of More-Than-Human rights, as well as its implications for ideas and practices in fields including law, human rights, ecology, music, politics and storytelling: https://mothrights.org/more-than-human-rights-an-ecology-of-law-thought-and-narrative-for-earthly-flourishing/.

Lastly, the Eco Jurisprudence Monitor is a database and tracker of 'Earth-centered laws that transcend anthropocentrism': https://ecojurisprudence.org. It includes a 'political map' showing countries and locations where ecological jurisprudence is advancing, and a 'physical map' that allows the user to explore these advances 'without human borders'.

~

Abram, David, *The Spell of the Sensuous: Perception and Language in a More-Than-Human World* (New York: Pantheon, 1996)

Adébísí, Folúkẹ́, *Decolonisation and Legal Knowledge: Reflections on Power and Possibility* (Bristol: University of Bristol Press, 2024)

Allen, Jessie, 'Property and More-than-Human Personhood', *University of Pittsburgh Legal Studies Research Paper No. 2023-34* (August 2023), 1–64

Alvaredo, Ana Cristina, 'Indigenous Leader Assassinated amid Conflict over Oil That Divided Community', *Mongabay News* (17 April 2023)

AMBER Consortium, *The AMBER Barrier Atlas: A Pan-European Database of Artificial Instream Barriers. Version 1.0* (29 June 2020)

AP News, 'New Zealand River's Personhood Status Offers Hope to Māori', *Independent* (15 August 2022)

Aravind, Sakshi, 'How to Write About Pipelines', *PPESYDNEY* (March 2021)

De Arriaga, Father Pablo Joseph, *Regulations for the Extirpation of Idolatry*, trans. L. Clark Keating (1621; Lexington, Kentucky: University of Kentucky Press, 1968)

Authier, Philip, 'Innu Chief Delivers Message of Caution as Romaine Hydro Complex is Inaugurated', *Montreal Gazette* (12 October 2023)

*Aves, Yuvan, *A Naturalist's Journal* (Chennai: Notion Press, 2017)

*——, 'A Tamil Animist: Gleaning Identity, Nativity, and Animate Wisdom from Tamil Culture', *Dark 'n' Light* (March 2022)

*——, *Intertidal: A Coast and Marsh Diary* (London: Bloomsbury, 2023)

~

Bacon, Francis, 'The Wisdom of the Ancients', in *The Essays* (1609; London: Penguin, 1985), pp. 264–76

——, *Novum Organum*, ed. Joseph Devey (1620; New York: P. F. Collier, 1902)

Baer, Terra, 'Constitutional Limitations and the Rights of Nature', *Common Dreams* (25 July 2022)

Bajpai, Shrishtee, 'Dialogue on Rights of Rivers (Report and Annexures)', *Vikalp Sangam* (28 April 2020)

*——, 'A Living Hill: Reflections on Animistic Worldviews, Stories, Resistance and Hope', *Heinrich Böll Stiftung* (10 September 2020)

——, 'River as a Living Entity', *Frontline* (14 October 2021)

——, 'Rivers and Rights: Rights of Nature and Systemic Transformations in India', *Global Assembly* (March 2023)

Bakan, Joel, *The Corporation: The Pathological Pursuit of Profit and Power* (London: Constable, 2005)

Bakker, Karen, *An Uncooperative Commodity: Privatizing Water in England and Wales* (Oxford: Oxford University Press, 2003)

——, *The Sounds of Life: How Digital Technology is Bringing Us Closer to the Worlds of Animals and Plants* (Oxford: Oxford University Press, 2022)

Banks, Brian, 'The Rights of Nature', *ON Nature* (Spring 2022), pp. 24–9

Baquero-Díaz, Carlos Andres, 'José Gualinga Montalvo: "The Jungle is a Living, Intelligent and Conscious Being"', *Sumaúma* (5 January 2024)

*Barnett, Rod, 'Utu in the Anthropocene', *Places Journal* (August 2021)

Barrenengoa, Mateo (dir.), *Let Things Rot* (2021)

Bartlett, Cherlyn M., Murdena Marshall and Albert Marshall, Mi'kmaq Nation, 'Enabling Concepts within a Journey Guided by Trees Holding Hands and Two-Eyed Seeing', unpublished manuscript, Integrative Science Program (Nova Scotia: Cape Breton University, 2007), pp. 1–29

Beer, Amy-Jane, *The Flow: Rivers, Water and Wildness* (London: Bloomsbury Wildlife, 2023)

Benjamin, Walter, 'Theses on the Philosophy of History' (1940), in *Illuminations*, ed. Hannah Arendt, trans. Harry Zohn (New York: Schocken Books, 1969), pp. 253–64

Bennett, Jane, *Vibrant Matter: A Political Ecology of Things* (Durham, North Carolina: Duke University Press, 2010)

Berry, Thomas, 'The Dream of the Earth: Our Way into the Future', *CrossCurrents*, 37:2/3 (1986), 200–215

——, 'A New Era: Healing the Injuries We Have Inflicted on Our Planet', *Health Progress*, 73:2 (1992), 60–63

——, *Evening Thoughts: Reflecting on Earth as Sacred Community* (San Francisco: Sierra Club Books, 1996)

———, *The Great Work: Our Way into the Future* (New York: Bell Tower, 1999)

——— and Thomas Clarke, *Befriending the Earth: A Theology of Reconciliation Between Humans and the Earth* (Mystic, Connecticut: Twenty-Third Publications, 1991)

Betasamosake Simpson, Leanne, 'Land as Pedagogy: Nishnaabeg Intelligence and Rebellious Transformation', *Decolonization: Indigeneity, Education & Society*, 3:3 (2014), 1–25

Blackstone, William, *Commentaries on the Laws of England, Volume II: On the Rights of Things* (1766; Chicago: University of Chicago Press, 1979)

Blackwood, Algernon, *Episodes Before Thirty* (London: Cassell & Company, 1923)

*———, 'The Willows', in *The Listener and Other Stories* (1907; Blackmask Publishing, 2007), pp. 75–120

*Bonnell, Jennifer L., *Reclaiming the Don: An Environmental History of Toronto's Don River Valley* (Toronto: University of Toronto Press, 2015)

Boreham, Steve, Julie Boreham and Lawrence Billington, 'A Flint Scatter at Nine Wells, Great Shelford', *Proceedings of the Cambridge Antiquarian Society*, 107 (2018), 7–14

Boulos, Guilherme, 'Ecocide Bill', quoted in 'Ecocide Bill Submitted to Congress in Brazil', *StopEcocideEarth* (June 2023)

Bourgeois-Gironde, Sacha, *Être la rivière: comment le fleuve Whanganui est devenu une personne vivante selon la loi* (Paris: Presses Universitaires de France, 2020)

Boyd, David, *The Rights of Nature: A Legal Revolution That Could Save the World* (Toronto: ECW Press, 2017)

Bridle, James, *Ways of Being: Animals, Plants, Machines and the Search for a Planetary Intelligence* (London: Penguin, 2022)

Brudenell, Matt, Anwen Cooper, Chris Green, Courtney Nimura and Rick Schulting, 'What Rivers Did: A Study of If and How Rivers Shaped Later Prehistoric Lives in Britain and Beyond', *Proceedings of the Prehistoric Society* (2024), 1–6

Brum, Eliane, *Banzeiro Òkòtó: The Amazon as the Centre of the World*, trans. Diane Whitty (London: Indigo Press, 2023)

~

*Cadena, Marisol de la, *Earth Beings: Ecologies of Practice Across Andean Worlds* (Durham, North Carolina: Duke University Press, 2015)

*Cárdenas, Yenny Vega, and Daniel Turp (eds), *A Legal Personality for the St Lawrence River and Other Rivers of the World* (Montreal: Les Éditions JFC, 2023)

Carver, Raymond, *Where Water Comes Together with Other Water* (New York: Random House, 1985)

Cayley, David, *Ivan Illich in Conversation* (Concord, Ontario: House of Anansi Press, 1992)

*Chambliss, Wayne, 'Fetishes (16)', *HiLoBrow.com* (17 May 2019)

Chao, Sophie, Karin Boldender and Eben Kirksey (eds), *The Promise of Multispecies Justice* (Durham, North Carolina: Duke University Press, 2022)

Chaturvedi, Hemendra, 'Environmentalist Seeks FIR for "Attempt to Murder" Yamuna River, Now a Living Entity', *Hindustan Times* (26 March 2017)

Chen, Cecilia, Janine MacLeod and Astrida Neimanis (eds), 'Introduction: Toward a Hydrological Turn?', in *Thinking with Water* (Montreal: McGill-Queen's University Press, 2013), pp. 4–22

Cohen, I. Bernard (ed.), *Isaac Newton's Papers & Letters on Natural Philosophy* (Cambridge, Massachusetts: Harvard University Press, 1958)

Correa, Rafael, 'Ecuador's Path', interview, *New Left Review*, 77 (September/October 2012), 88–104

Cullinan, Cormac, *Wild Law: A Manifesto for Earth Justice* (Totnes: Green Books, 2003)

~

Dark Matter Labs, 'Radicle Civics – Building Proofs of Possibilities for a Civic Economy and Society', *Medium* (14 August 2023)

Davis, R. M., 'The Nature of Mesolithic Activity at Selected Spring Sites in South-West England', unpublished doctoral thesis, University of Worcester (2012)

Dayton, Paul K., Mia J. Tegner, Peter B. Edwards and Kristin L. Riser, 'Sliding Baselines, Ghosts, and Reduced Expectations in Kelp Forest Communities', *Ecological Applications*, 8:2 (1998), 309–22

Deer, Jemma, *Radical Animism* (London: Bloomsbury Academic, 2020)

Diaz, Natalie, *Postcolonial Love Poem* (Minneapolis, Minnesota: Graywolf Press, 2020)

Downes, Liz, 'Neoliberalism versus Justice on Ecuador's Mining Frontier', *Chain Reaction: The National Magazine of Friends of the Earth Australia*, 137 (December 2019), 38–9

Durante, Francesco, Markus Kröger and William LaFleur, 'Extraction and Extractivisms: Definitions and Concepts', in *Our Extractive Age: Expressions of Violence and Resistance*, ed. Judith Shapiro and John Andrew McNeish (Abingdon: Routledge, 2021), pp. 19–30

~

Eliot, George, *Felix Holt, the Radical*, ed. William Baker and Kenneth Womack (1866; Peterborough, Ontario: Broadview, 2000)

Estes, Nick, *Our History is the Future: Standing Rock versus the Dakota Access Pipeline, and the Long Tradition of Indigenous Resistance* (London: Verso, 2019)

Esteva, Gustavo, 'The Time for Resistance and Solidarity', *Radio Zapatista* (September 2012)

Evans, Chris, 'Disappearance Beyond Recall: A Social Context for Bronze Age Aurochs Extinction in Britain?', *Proceedings of the Prehistoric Society* (September 2015), 1–17

~

Fisher, Mark, *Capitalist Realism: Is There No Alternative?* (Winchester: O Books, 2009)

Fisk, Harold Norman, 'Ancient Courses, Mississippi River Meander Belt, Cape Girardeau, Mo.-Donaldsonville, La.', *Geological Investigation of the Alluvial Valley of the Lower Mississippi River* (Vicksburg, Mississippi: Mississippi River Commission, 1945)

Foote, Robert Bruce, *The Foote Collection of Indian Prehistoric and Protohistoric Antiquities: Notes on Their Ages and Distribution* (Madras: Government Press, 1916)

Frankfort, Henriette, Henri Frankfort, John A. Wilson, Thorkild Jacobsen and William A. Irwin, *The Intellectual Adventure of Ancient Man* (Chicago: University of Chicago Press, 1946)

Freeman, Jody, and Chief Jean-Charles Piétacho, 'When is a River a Person? A Conversation with Chief Jean-Charles Piétacho', *Montréal Serai* (11 January 2023)

Fundación Pachamama, 'Experienca: Reconocimiento de los Derechos de la Naturaleza en la Constitucíon Ecuatoriana', *Iniciativa Ciudadanizando la Política Ambiental*, 6 (April 2010)

——, 'La Naturaleza también tiene derechos' (2011), https://www.youtube.com/watch?app=desktop&v=PfCszVQD_kU&t=129s

~

Gagné, Karine, *Caring for Glaciers: Land, Animals and Humanity in the Himalayas* (Seattle: University of Washington Press, 2019)

Galeano, Eduardo, 'La Naturaleza no es muda'/'Nature is not mute', *Seminario Brecha* (21 April 2008)

García-Antón, Katya, Harald Gaski and Guvnor Guttorm (eds), *Let the River Flow: An Indigenous Uprising and Its Legacy in Art, Ecology and Politics* (Oslo: Office for Contemporary Art Norway, 2020)

Gautham, Komal, 'It's Official: Chennai's Rivers are "Dead"', *Times of India* (18 January 2023)

*Ge, Krupa, *Rivers Remember: #Chennairians and the Shocking Truth of a Manmade Flood* (Chennai: Context, 2019)

George, Andrew, and Farouk Al-Rawi, 'Back to the Cedar Forest: The Beginning and End of Tablet V of the Standard Babylonian Epic of Gilgamesh', *Journal of Cuneiform Studies*, 66 (2014), 66–90

Georgescu-Roegen, Nicholas, *The Entropy Law and the Economic Process* (Cambridge, Massachusetts: Harvard University Press, 1971)

Ghosh, Amitav, *The Great Derangement: Climate Change and the Unthinkable* (Chicago: University of Chicago Press, 2016)

*——, *The Nutmeg's Curse: Parables for a Planet in Crisis* (Chicago: University of Chicago Press, 2021)

Gielse, Erica, 'What Does Water Want? Most Humans Seem to Have Forgotten', *Psyche* (15 November 2022)

Giraud, Eva Haifa, *What Comes After Entanglement?* (Durham, North Carolina: Duke University Press, 2019)

Godin, Mélissa, 'The Fight to Save Ecuador's Sacred River', *TIME Magazine* (25 October 2022)

Graham, Jorie, *[To] the Last [be] Human* (Manchester: Carcanet, 2022)

Greenfield, Patrick, 'Plans to Mine Ecuador Forest Violate Rights of Nature, Court Rules', *Guardian* (2 December 2021)

Griggs, Earl Leslie (ed.), *Collected Letters of Samuel Taylor Coleridge*, Vol. II: 1801–1806 (1956; Oxford: Clarendon Press/Oxford University Press, 1966)

Gualinga, Eriberto (dir.), *Helena from Sarayuka* (2022)

*Guha, Ramchandra, *The Unquiet Woods: Ecological Change and Peasant Resistance in the Himalaya* (1989; London: Permanent Black, 2013)

Le Guin, Ursula K., *The Dispossessed* (1974; London: Gollancz, 1991)

*——, *The Word for World is Forest* (1972; London: Gollancz, 2015)

——, in *Arts of Living on a Damaged Planet / Ghosts of the Anthropocene*, ed. Anna Tsing, Elaine Gan, Heather Swanson and Nils Bubandt (Minneapolis: Minnesota University Press, 2017), pp. 15–21

~

Hadot, Pierre, *The Veil of Isis: An Essay on the History of the Idea of Nature*, trans. Michael Chase (2004; Cambridge: Belknap Press, 2008)

Haniff, Jasmine, 'The Rights of Nature Movement', *Latin American Bureau* (12 January 2021)

Haraway, Donna J., 'Anthropocene, Capitalocene, Plantationocene, Chthulucene: Making Kin', *Environmental Humanities*, 6:1 (2015), 159–65

——, *Staying with the Trouble: Making Kin in the Chthulucene* (Durham, North Carolina: Duke University Press, 2016)

Hayden, Rebekah, 'Saving Los Cedros is "Case of the Century"', *Ecologist* (26 November 2020)

*Heath Justice, Daniel, *Why Indigenous Literatures Matter* (Waterloo, Ontario: Wilfrid Laurier University Press, 2018)

Heidegger, Martin, 'The Question Concerning Technology' (1954), in *The Question Concerning Technology and Other Essays*, trans. William Lovitt (New York: Harper & Row, 1977), pp. 307–42

*Helle, Sophus, *Gilgamesh: A New Translation of the Ancient Epic* (New Haven, Connecticut: Yale University Press, 2021)

Howard, Emma, 'Keep it in the Ground Campaign: Six Things We've Learned', *Guardian* (25 March 2015)

Hussain, Shumon T., and Harald Floss, 'Streams as Entanglement of Nature and Culture: European Upper Paleolithic River Systems and Their Role as Features of Spatial Organization', *Journal of Archaeological Method and Theory*, 23 (2016), 1162–218

Hydro-Québec, 'Declaration of Commitment to the First Nations and the Inuit Nation' (November 2021)

~

Illich, Ivan, *H₂O and the Waters of Forgetfulness: Reflections on the Historicity of 'Stuff'* (Berkeley: Heyday Books, 1985)

Ingold, Tim, *Being Alive: Essays on Movement, Knowledge and Description* (London: Routledge, 2021)

Institut National de Santé Publique, *Summary Analysis of the Impact of the Romaine Hydroelectric Project on the Health of the Population: Monitoring the Situation in the Municipality of Havre-Saint-Pierre* (July 2013)

~

Jabr, Ferris, 'The Social Life of Forests', *New York Times* (2 December 2020)

Jouan, Hélène, 'The Fight to Protect Canada's Magpie River, Now a "Legal Person with the Right to Live"', *Le Monde* (20 December 2022)

~

Kauffman, Craig M., and Pamela L. Martin, The Politics of Rights of Nature (Cambridge, Massachusetts: MIT Press, 2021)

Kemp, Martin, *Leonardo* (Oxford: Oxford University Press, 2011)

Kimbrough, Liz, 'Ecuador Court Upholds "Rights of Nature", Blocks Intag Valley Copper Mine', *Mongabay News* (31 March 2023)

*Kimmerer, Robin Wall, *Braiding Sweetgrass: Indigenous Wisdom, Scientific Knowledge and the Teachings of Plants* (Minneapolis, Minnesota: Milkweed Editions, 2013)

Klein, Naomi, *This Changes Everything: Capitalism vs. The Climate* (London: Penguin, 2015)

Klvana, Iva, *Coureur des Bois* (Paris: Transboréal, 2010)

Kohn, Eduardo, *How Forests Think: Toward an Anthropology Beyond the Human* (Los Angeles: University of California Press, 2013)

Kolbert, Elizabeth, 'A Lake in Florida is Suing to Protect Itself', *New Yorker* (18 April 2022)

——, 'Talk to Me: Can Artificial Intelligence Allow Us to Speak to Another Species?', *New Yorker* (4 September 2023)

Kothari, Ashish, Ariel Salleh, Arturo Escobar et al. (eds), *Pluriverse: A Post-Development Dictionary* (New Delhi: Tulika Books, 2019)

Kottke, Jason, 'Just Added! Jason Kottke Intros Two New Vintage Mississippi River Maps', 20x200.com (18 June 2019)

Kremer, Michael, and Seema Jayachandran, 'Odious Debt', *Finance & Development: A Quarterly Magazine of the IMF*, 39:2 (June 2002)

Krenak, Ailton, *Ancestral Future*, trans. Alex Brostoff and Jamille Pinheiro Dias (London: Polity, 2024)

Krishnamurti, Jiddu, 'Creative Discontent', in *Think on These Things* (New York: Harper & Row, 1964), pp. 38–44

——, *Krishnamurti's Journal* (San Francisco: Harper & Row, 1982)

Kuhar, Francisco, Giuliana Furci, Elisandro Ricardo Drechsler-Santos et al., 'Delimitation of Funga as a Valid Term for the Diversity of Fungal Communities: The Fauna, Flora & Funga Proposal (FF&F)', *IMA Fungus*, 9:2 (2018), A71–A74

~

Lalonde, Mar, 'AFNQL Recognizes Legal Personhood of St Lawrence River', *Penticton Herald* (4 May 2023)

Landry, Christopher (dir.), *Joanna Macey and the Great Turning* (2014)

Lathem, Alexis, 'Innu Continue to Protest the Plan Nord and Romaine River Hydro Project', *Towards Freedom* (4 July 2012)

Laville, Sandra, 'UN Expert Condemns UK Crackdown on Environmental Protest', *Guardian* (23 January 2024)

Lears, Jackson, *Animal Spirits: The American Pursuit of Vitality from Camp Meeting to Wall Street* (New York: Picador USA, 2023)

Lee, Darlene, 'Earth Law Means Rights for All (Including Humans)', *Earth Law Center* (August 2017)

Lem, Stanisław, *Solaris*, trans. Joanna Kilmartin and Steve Cox (1961; London: Faber, 2016)

Levine, Alice (ed.), *Byron's Poetry and Prose* (New York: W. W. Norton, 2010)

Liboiron, Max, *Pollution is Colonialism* (Durham, North Carolina: Duke University Press, 2021)

Lindqvist, Sven, *Exterminate All the Brutes* (London: Granta, 2002)

*Linton, Jamie, *What is Water? The History of a Modern Abstraction* (Vancouver: University of British Columbia Press, 2010)

*Lopez, Barry, *Arctic Dreams: Imagination and Desire in a Northern Landscape* (1986; London: Vintage, 2014)

——, *Embrace Fearlessly the Burning World: Essays* (New York: Random House, 2022)

*Lorde, Audre, 'The Master's Tools Will Never Dismantle the Master's House', in *Sister Outsider: Essays and Speeches* (1984; Berkeley: Crossing Press, 2007), pp. 110–14

*Los Cedros Reserve, 'Los Cedros and the Rights of Nature', https://loscedros reserve.org

Lovejoy, Arthur O., *The Great Chain of Being: A Study of the History of an Idea* (1936; Cambridge, Massachusetts: Harvard University Press, 2001)

Lovejoy, Thomas, 'Foreword', in Adrian Forsyth and Ken Miyata, *Tropical Nature: Life and Death in the Rain Forests of Central and South America* (1984; New York: Touchstone Editions, 1995)

~

McGee, William John, 'Water as a Resource', in *Annals of the American Academy of Political and Social Science*, 33:3 (1909), 37–50

Maclean, Norman, *A River Runs Through It and Other Stories* (Chicago: University of Chicago Press, 1976)

MacLeod, Finlay, *The Chapels and Healing Wells of the Western Isles* (Stornoway: Acair, 2018)

McNeill, J. R., and Peter Engelke, *The Great Acceleration: An Environmental History of the Anthropocene since 1945* (Cambridge, Massachusetts: Harvard University Press, 2016)

Macpherson, Elizabeth, Axel Borchgrevink, Rahul Ranjan and Catalina Vallejo Piedrahíta, 'Where Ordinary Laws Fall Short: "Riverine Rights" and Constitutionalism', *Griffith Law Review*, 30:3 (2021), 438–73

Macy, Joanna, and Molly Young Brown, *Coming Back to Life: Practices to Reconnect Our Lives, Our World* (Gabriola Island, British Columbia: New Society Publishers, 1998)

Magan, Manchán, *Listen to the Land Speak* (Dublin: Gill, 2022)

Magnason, Andri Snær, *On Time and Water: A History of Our Future*, trans. Lytton Smith (2020; London: Serpent's Tail, 2021)

Mainwaring, G. B., *Dictionary of the Lepcha-Language*, rev. Albert Grünwedel (Berlin: Unger Brothers, 1898)

Maisonnave, Fabiana, Teresa de Miguel and André Penner, 'Indigenous Leader Inspires an Amazon City to Grant Personhood to an Endangered River', *AP News* (7 August 2023)

Marcuse, Herbert, *One-Dimensional Man: Studies in the Ideology of Advanced Industrial Society* (1964; Oxford: Routledge, 2002)

Martuwarra River of Life, and Anne Poelina, Donna Bagnall, Michelle Lim, 'Recognizing the Martuwarra's First Law Right to Life as a Living Ancestral Being', *Transnational Environmental Law*, 9:3 (2020), 541–68

Marx, Karl, *Capital: A Critique of Political Economy*, trans. Ben Fowkes (1867; New York: Vintage, 1977)

Mestokosho, Mathieu, and Serge Bouchard, *Caribou Hunter: A Song of a Vanished Life* (Vancouver: Greystone Books, 2005)

*Mestokosho, Rita, *Née de la pluie et de la terre* (Paris: Éditions Bruno Doucey, 2014)

*——, *Atik^U utei: Le cœur du caribou* (Montreal: Mémoire d'encrier, 2023)

Mestokosho, Uapukun, and Shanice Mollen-Picard (dir.), *Shipu* (2017)

Mills, Aaron, 'The Lifeworlds of Law: On Revitalizing Indigenous Legal Orders Today', *McGill Law Journal*, 61:4 (June 2016), 847–84

Mills, Kenneth, *Idolatry and Its Enemies: Colonial Andean Religion and Extirpation 1640–1750* (Princeton: Princeton University Press, 1997)

Miranda, Beatriz, ' "We Can't Hunt or Fish": The Villages in Ecuador Surrounded by Abandoned Explosives', *Guardian* (18 April 2024)

Mitchell, Stephen, *Gilgamesh: A New English Version* (London: Profile, 2005)

Miyazaki, Hayao (dir.), *Nausicaä of the Valley of the Wind* (1984)

Morizot, Baptiste, *Ways of Being Alive*, trans. Andrew Brown (London: Polity, 2022)

Morris, James D. K., and Jacinta Ruru, 'Giving Voice to Rivers: Legal Personality as a Vehicle for Recognising Indigenous Peoples' Relationships to Water?', *Australian Indigenous Law Review*, 14:2 (2010), 49–62

Mustil, Tom, *How to Speak Whale: A Voyage into the Future of Animal Communication* (London: William Collins, 2022)

~

Nagendra, Harini, and Seema Mundoli, *Cities and Canopies: Trees in Indian Cities* (Delhi: Penguin Random House India, 2019)

Nakkeeran, *Neer Ezhuthu* (Chennai: Crow's Nest, 2019)

Naturvation.eu, 'Munich: The Restoration of the Isar River', https://naturvation.eu/sites/default/files/munich_snapshot.pdf

Neimanis, Astrida, 'Hydrofeminism: Or, On Becoming a Body of Water', in *Undutiful Daughters: Mobilizing Future Concepts, Bodies and Subjectivities in Feminist Thought and Practice*, ed. Henriette Gunkel, Chrysanthi Nigianni and Fanny Söderbäck (New York: Palgrave Macmillan, 2012), pp. 85–99

*Nerberg, Susan, 'I am Mutehekau Shipu: A River's Journey to Personhood in Eastern Quebec', *Canadian Geographic* (April 2022)

Nevin, Claire, 'Rights of Nature in Ireland – Towards a Living Island or Rights-Bearing Communities: Submission to the Irish Citizens' Assembly on Biodiversity Loss', *Lawyers for Nature* (30 September 2022)

Newton, Isaac, *Isaac Newton's Papers & Letters on Natural Philosophy*, ed. I. Bernard Cohen (Cambridge, Massachusetts: Harvard University Press, 1958)

Nijhuis, Michelle, 'Rights for Rivers: Fighting for the Legal Rights of Nature', *Yes Magazine* (6 July 2021)

*Nixon, Rob, *Slow Violence and the Environmentalism of the Poor* (Cambridge, Massachusetts: Harvard University Press, 2011)

~

PA Media, 'Environment Agency "Letting River Wye Go into a Death Spiral"', *Guardian* (8 February 2024)

Pandey, Siddharth, 'Emplacing Tasks of Magic: Hand, Land, and the Generation of Fantasy Taskscape in Terry Pratchett's Tiffany Aching Series', unpublished doctoral thesis, University of Cambridge (submitted 2020)

——, *Fossil* (Tasmania: A Published Event, 2021)

Paramasivan, Tho, *The Sweet Salt of Tamil*, trans. V. Ramnarayan (Chennai: Navayana, 2023)

Pauly, Daniel, 'Anecdotes and the Shifting Baseline Syndrome of Fisheries', *Trends in Ecology and Evolution*, 10:10 (1995), 430

Peck, Mika (dir.), 'Paraecologists for the Rights of Nature' (30 August 2022)

——, M. Desselas, S. Bonilla-Bodoya, G. Redín et al., 'The Conflict between Rights of Nature and Mining in Ecuador: Implications of the Los Cedros Cloud Forest Case for Biodiversity Conservation', *People and Nature*, 6:3 (June 2024), 1096–115

Plumb, Jessica (dir.), *Return of a River* (2014)

*———, 'A River Reawakened', *Orion Magazine* (2021), https://orionmagazine. org/article/a-river-reawakened/

*Poelina, Anne, Alessandro Pelizzon, Afshin Akhtar-Khavari, Cristy Clark et al., 'Yoongoorrookoo: The Emergence of Ancestral Personhood; Martuwarra River of Life', *Griffith Law Review*, 30:3 (2021), 505–29

———, Alessandro Pelizzon and Erin O'Donnell, 'Australia's Rivers are Ancestral Beings', University of Melbourne, *Legal Affairs* (18 October 2021)

Powers, Richard, *The Overstory* (2018; London: Vintage, 2019)

Prynne, Jeremy, 'The Glacial Question, Unsolved', first published in 1969; collected in *Poems* (Northumberland: Bloodaxe, 2005), pp. 65–7

~

*Raman, Bhavani, 'The Curious Disappearance of the Ennore Creek', *Wire* (13 November 2017)

Ramírez-Barahoa, Santiago, and Luis E. Eguiarte, 'The Role of Glacial Cycles in Promoting Genetic Diversity in the Neotropics: The Case of Cloud Forests during the Last Glacial Maximum', *Ecology and Evolution*, 3:3 (2013), 725–38

Rancière, Jacques, *Le Partage du Sensible: Esthétique et Politique* (Paris: La Fabrique, 2000)

Rangeley-Wilson, Charles, *Silt Road: The Story of a Lost River* (London: Chatto and Windus, 2013)

Revkin, Andrew C., 'Thomas Berry, Writer and Lecturer with a Mission for Mankind, Dies at 94', *New York Times* (4 June 2009)

———, 'Peeling Back Pavement to Expose Watery Havens', *New York Times* (16 July 2009)

*Riofrancos, Thea, *Resource Radicals: From Petro-Nationalism to Post-Extractivism in Ecuador* (Durham, North Carolina: Duke University Press, 2020)

*Rodríguez-Garavito, César (ed.), *More Than Human Rights: An Ecology of Law, Thought and Narrative for Earthly Flourishing* (New York: NYU Law/MOTH collective, 2024)

Rogge, Malcolm (dir.), *Under Rich Earth* (2008)

*Rose, Deborah Bird, 'Double Death', *The Multispecies Salon*, https://www. multispecies-salon.org/double-death/

———, 'What If the Angel of History Were a Dog?', *Cultural Studies Review*, 12:1 (2006), 67–78

———, 'Multispecies Knots of Ethical Time', *Environmental Philosophy*, 9:1 (Spring 2012), 127–40

——, *Shimmer: Flying Fox Exuberance in Worlds of Peril* (Edinburgh: Edinburgh University Press, 2022)

Ruru, Jacinta, 'Who are Your Waters?', *e-flux* (26 July 2019)

~

Safi, Michael, 'Murder Most Foul: Polluted Indian River Reported Dead Despite "Living Entity" Status', *Guardian* (7 July 2017)

Salvidge, Rachel, 'How Clean are England's Rivers?', *Guardian* (25 September 2020)

Sands, Philippe, Dior Fall Sow et al., 'Independent Expert Panel for the Legal Definition of Ecocide: COMMENTARY AND CORE TEXT', Stop Ecocide Foundation (June 2021)

Scalercio, Mauro, 'Dominating Nature and Colonialism: Francis Bacon's View of Europe and the New World', *History of European Ideas*, 44:8 (2018), 1076–91

*Schama, Simon, *Landscape and Memory* (London: HarperCollins, 1995)

Schmelzer, Matthias, Andrea Vetter and Aaron Vansintjan (eds), *The Future is Degrowth: A Guide to a World Beyond Capitalism* (London: Verso, 2022)

*Scott, James C., *Seeing Like a State: How Certain Schemes to Improve the Human Condition Have Failed* (New Haven, Connecticut: Yale University Press, 1998)

Serres, Michel, *The Natural Contract*, trans. Elizabeth MacArthur and William Paulson (1992; Ann Arbor: University of Michigan Press, 1995)

Shah, Priya, 'Language, Discipline, and Power: The Extirpation of Idolatry in Colonial Peru and Indigenous Resistance', *Voces Novae: Chapman University Historical Review*, 5:7 (2013), 101–24

Sheldrake, Merlin, *Entangled Life: How Fungi Make Our Worlds, Change Our Minds and Shape Our Futures* (London: Vintage, 2021)

Shepherd, Nan, *The Living Mountain* (1977; Edinburgh: Canongate, 2011)

Simard, Suzanne, 'Net Transfer of Carbon Between Ectomycorrhizal Tree Species in the Field', *Nature*, 388 (1997), 579–82

Singh, Manvir, 'It's Time to Rethink the Idea of the "Indigenous"', *New Yorker* (February 2023)

Skelton, Richard, *Stranger in the Mask of a Deer* (London: Penned in the Margins, 2021)

*Solnit, Rebecca, *Hope in the Dark: Untold Histories, Wild Possibilities* (2004; Edinburgh: Canongate, 2016)

*Soto, Daniela Paz, 'The Energy Transition and Lithium Extraction in Chile: Decolonising Resource-making in the Salar de Atacama Basin', unpublished doctoral thesis, University of Sussex (submitted 2023)

Sparrow, Josie, 'Against the New Vitalism', *New Socialist* (10 March 2019)

Standing, Guy, *Plunder of the Commons: A Manifesto for Sharing Public Wealth* (London: Pelican, 2019)

Stegner, Wallace, 'Wilderness Letter', in *The Sound of Mountain Water* (New York: Doubleday, 1969), pp. 145–56

*Stone, Christopher D., '"Should Trees Have Standing?"': Towards Legal Rights for Natural Objects', *Southern California Law Review*, 45 (1972), 450–501

*——, *Should Trees Have Standing?: Law, Morality, and the Environment*, 3rd edn (1972; New York: Oxford University Press, 2010)

Stowell, Laurel, 'Songs, Tears as Bill Passes First Reading', *Whanganui Chronicle* (26 May 2016)

Strang, Veronica, *Water Beings: From Nature Worship to the Environmental Crisis* (London: Reaktion, 2023)

Surma, Katie, 'A Thousand Miles in the Amazon, to Change the Way the World Works', *Inside Climate News* (9 October 2022)

~

Talbot-Jones, Julia, and Jeff Bennett, 'Implementing Bottom-up Governance through Granting Legal Rights to Rivers: A Case Study of the Whanganui River, Aotearoa New Zealand', *Australasian Journal of Environmental Management*, 29:1 (2022), 64–80

Tuck, Eve, and K. Wayne Yang, 'Decolonization is Not a Metaphor', *Decolonization: Indigeneity, Education & Society*, 1:1 (2012), 1–40

~

Vaillant, John, *Fire Weather: A True Story from a Hotter World* (London: Sceptre, 2023)

*Vandergrift, Roo, D. S. Newman, B. T. M. Dentinger et al., 'Richer than Gold: The Fungal Biodiversity of Reserva Los Cedros, a Threatened Andean Cloud Forest', *Botanical Studies*, 64:17 (2023), 1–22

~

*Walsham, Alexandra, *The Reformation of the Landscape: Religion, Identity, and Memory in Early Modern Britain and Ireland* (Oxford: Oxford University Press, 2011)

Warne, Kennedy, 'A River Calls My Name', *E-Tangata* (12 May 2019)

Weber, Andreas, *Enlivenment: Toward a Poetics for the Anthropocene* (Cambridge, Massachusetts: MIT Press, 2019)

——, Aküm Longchari, Ash Narain Roy et al., *Sharing Life: The Ecopolitics of Reciprocity* (Delhi & Berlin: Heinrich Böll Stiftung, 2020)

Whitehead, Alfred North, *Process and Reality: An Essay in Cosmology, Corrected Edition*, ed. David Ray Griffin and Donald W. Sherburne (1929; New York: Free Press, 1978)

Whyte, Kyle, 'Indigenous Climate Change Studies: Indigenizing Futures, Decolonizing the Anthropocene', *English Language Notes*, 55:1 (2017), 153–62

Williams, Terry Tempest, 'I am Haunted by What I Have Seen at Great Salt Lake', *New York Times* (25 March 2023)

Williams Walsh, Mary, 'Looking for Inexpensive Photo Processing? Try Lake Ontario', *Los Angeles Times* (13 November 1990)

Wilson, Edward O., 'Beware the Age of Loneliness', *The Economist* (18 November 2013)

Wilson, Elouise, Mary R. Benally, Ahjani Yepa and Cynthia Wilson, 'Women of Bears Ears are Asking You to Help Save It', *New York Times* (25 April 2021)

Wormald, Mark, *The Catch: Fishing for Ted Hughes* (London: Bloomsbury, 2022)

Wright, Alexis, *The Swan Book* (Penrith: Giramondo, 2013)

*——, 'We All Smell the Smoke, We All Feel the Heat: This Environmental Catastrophe is Global', *Guardian* (18 May 2019)

*——, 'The Inward Migration in Apocalyptic Times', *Emergence Magazine* (26 October 2022)

Wulf, Andrea, *The Invention of Nature: The Adventures of Alexander von Humboldt, Lost Hero of Science* (London: John Murray, 2015)

Wurundjeri Woiwurrung Cultural Heritage Aboriginal Corporation, *Nhanbu narrun ba ngargunin twarn Birrarung – Ancient Spirit and Lore of the Yarra* (2019)

~

Yarina, Lizzie, 'This River is a Model', *Places Journal* (February 2024)

Yunkaporta, Tyson, *Sand Talk: How Indigenous Thinking Can Save the World* (New York: Harperone, 2020)

~

Zimmermann, Erich, *World Resources and Industries* (New York: Harper & Row, 1951)

Zorrilla, Carlos, 'How to "Stop Mining Before It Starts"': interview with Liz Kimbrough, *Mongabay* (4 April 2024)

~

Acts, Bills, Declarations, Judgments, Resolutions

Amazon Forest, Sarayaku Territory, Ecuador: the Kichwa Indigenous People of Sarayaku, Ecuador, 'Kawsak Sacha – The Living Forest. A Living and Conscious Being: The Subject of Rights' (2012/2018)

Atrato River, Colombia: Constitutional Court of Colombia, 'The Atrato River as a "Subject of Rights"', Decision T-622/16 (10 November 2016)

Birrarung/Yarra River, Australia: Australian Government and the Wurendjeri Council, 'Yarra River Protection (Wilip-gin Birrarung murron) Act 2017', Act No. 49/2017 (1 December 2017)

Ganga and Yamuna Rivers, Uttarakhand, India: Uttarakhand High Court, India, 'Mohammad Salim vs State of Uttarakhand & others', PIL 126 of 2014 (20 March 2017)

Ganga and Yamuna Rivers, their glacial sources and watersheds, Uttarakhand, India: Uttarakhand High Court, India, 'Lalit Miglani vs State of Uttarakhand and Others', PIL 140 of 2015 (30 March 2017)

Great Lakes, USA: State of New York, 'Bill of Rights for the Great Lakes', 4344 of 2022–23 regular sessions (14 February 2023)

Lake Erie, USA: Toledo Residents, 'Lake Erie Bill of Rights' (26 February 2019)

Los Cedros cloud-forest, Ecuador: Constitutional Court of Ecuador, 'Los Cedros Protected Forest', Judgment No. 1149-19-JP/21 (10 November 2021)

Mutehekau Shipu, Nitassinan/Magpie River, Quebec: Conseil des Innu de Ekuanitshit, 'Ekuanitshit Innu Council Resolution: Magpie River', 919-082 (18 January 2021)

Pachamama, Ecuador: Constitution of the Republic of Ecuador (2008)

River Ouse, Sussex, England: Councillor Matthew Bird, 'Motion – Rights of the River', Lewes District Council Meeting (20 February 2023)

St Lawrence River, Canada: Parliament of Canada, House of Commons, 'An Act to give legal capacity to the St Lawrence River and to provide for measures respecting its protection', Bill C-271 (5 May 2022)

Snake River, Idaho, USA: Nez Perce Tribal Nation, 'Snake River Resolution', SPGC20-02 (June 2020)

State of Tamil Nadu, India: Madras High Court, India, 'A. Periyakaruppan vs The Principal Secretary to Government, Revenue Department & The Additional Chief Secretary and Commissioner of Revenue Administration', W.P. (MD) Nos. 18636 of 2013 and 3070 of 2020 (19 April 2022)

Whanganui River, Aotearoa New Zealand: Aotearoa New Zealand Parliament, 'Te Awa Tupua (Whanganui River Claims Settlement) Act 2017', Public Act 2017 No.7 (20 March 2017)

ACKNOWLEDGEMENTS
AND AFTERMATHS

Across ten previous books and more than twenty years of writing, I have never before known a subject with the urgency of this one. The process of research and fieldwork has been thrilling and unnerving: like wading upstream, chest-deep in a torrenting river – unsure of footing at times, but always following the clear, strong path of the moving water. Several times I have been taken right to the limits of my language and my beliefs – and then taken beyond them.

This intensity of encounter proceeded right up to the day I sent the book off to be typeset. That afternoon in Cambridge I spoke with a fascinating man from the state of Odisha in eastern India, Devidas Mishra – whose commute for the majority of his working life as a headteacher in a deprived rural school, where he taught predominantly Dalit and Adivasi women, involved three hours' travel each way, each day (on bicycle, motorcycle, boat and bus). By the side of a pond in the city which is filled by the same spring-water that rises near my home, Devi unpromptedly told me a seven-minute-long cosmogony story for the sacred rivers of India, which began with an account of a song so beautiful that it melted the bones of a *god* – and turned them into running water. It was a wonderful note to end on.

A book has one name on its cover but hundreds within and behind its pages. Many people have shaped the course and flow of *Is a River Alive?* I want to thank first and above all the six people whose voices, visions and ways of being in the world are central to this book, who have allowed me to travel, speak and think with them, and then to write about them as I have – and who have all become dear friends and inspirations: Yuvan Aves, Wayne Chambliss, Giuliana Furci, Rita Mestokosho, César Rodríguez-Garavito and Cosmo Sheldrake. I trust you know how vital you have been to this book; you *animated* it. I thank also the rivers, forests, mountains, creatures, plants and fungi without whom I could not have written this book, who are named in its pages and who – especially the rivers – are truly its co-authors.

Then: deep thanks to those others who were variously my guides, companions, illuminators and interviewees over the miles and years, and shared their knowledge, skills, stories and perceptions: Alberto Acosta, Yogeshwaran Amarneethi, Ramiro

Acknowledgements and Aftermaths

Ávila Santamaría, Shrishtee Bajpai, José Cueva, Cormac Cullinan, Josef DeCoux, Natalia Greene, Patricia Gualinga, Agustín Grijalva Jiménez, Raju KK, Ilya Klvana, Margaret Lawrence, Lydia Mestokosho-Paradis, Claudia Narváez Vásconez, Martín Obando, Danny Peled, Bhavani Raman, Raphael St-Onge, Monse Vásquez, Yenny Vegas Cárdenas and Arun Venkatraman. Gratitude is also due for various forms of contribution and assistance along the way to Uapukun Mestokosho, Shanice Mollen-Picard, Julienne Piétacho and Sylvain Roy. A small number of names, details and identifying characteristics have been changed for political or personal reasons; some dialogue has been recreated from memory rather than from notebook or recording.

Two people who crossed the river too early, Roger Deakin (1943–2006) and Barry Lopez (1945–2020), have stayed by my side, providing both stars on the horizon to steer by, and touches on the tiller to correct my course.

Parts of this book were researched and written in the unceded Innu homeland of Nitassinan; I am very grateful to Rita Mestokosho and Lydia Mestokosho-Paradis for their trust and encouragement there and afterwards. Where I quote Indigenous voices arising from personal encounter, I do so with full permission of those speaking, and do not presume to speak for them.

In terms of specialists (in addition to those already named), I'm thankful for the generous sharing of research, reflection, support and experience to: David Abram on language and the living world; Marlene Creates on northern forests; Tony Eva on Cambridgeshire chalk streams and Nine Wells Wood; Chris Evans on the archaeology of south Cambridge; Ramchandra Guha on India and Chipko; Amina Khan on Islam and the living world; Smriti Mahesh, Sarah Mohan and Meyyappan Saravanan on animism and the Rights of Nature in Indian contexts; Ananya Mishra on Adivasi resistance movements and the rivers of Odisha, and many points beyond; Paul Powlesland on UK law, activism and river guardianship; Charles Rangeley-Wilson for our annual in-a-river-walk, for his exceptional chalk-stream and river-restoration expertise, and for teaching me the word 'hyporheic'; and Wasté Win Young on the Dakota Access Pipeline and the life-long, lived nature of resistance more broadly.

Many collectives and organizations have been generative of information, support and ideas: I thank above all the members of the MOTH (More Than Human Rights) collective, of which I have been a part since its inception; also Boreal River Adventures; the Chennai Climate Action Group; the Fungi Foundation; the inspirational GARN/the Global Alliance for the Rights of Nature (led by Natalia Greene); Grasshopper Geography with its river-centric maps; HOWL; Rainforest Concern; Tom Wolff and Revive the Northern Rivers; all at the UK Rights of Nature group; Rights of Rivers South Asia; the River Dôn Project; the South Asia Network on Dams, Rivers and People; Tzintzun Aguilar-Izzo and Blake Lavia at the wonderful

Talking Wings; and the hive-mind kindness of many friends and strangers on Twitter/X and Instagram.

Is a River Alive? could not have been written without the support of the Philip Leverhulme Trust in the form of a year-long research fellowship, which allowed me to undertake the three extended periods of fieldwork/travel that were necessary. I am very grateful to the Trust. Thanks also to colleagues in the Faculty of English and Emmanuel College, Cambridge, where I have been lucky enough to teach year after year of brilliant students for more than two decades; and to the Cambridge Humanities Research Grant Scheme and Emmanuel College for their support in the substantial form of small grants.

I wrote this book not in secrecy but in privacy: no one had read more than a handful of paragraphs until I finished a full first draft, some three and a half years after beginning work. At that point, I benefited from the outstanding editorial eyes and ears of my friends Phoebe Campion, Rob Cowen, Nati Greene, Jedediah Purdy and Jessica Woollard; my troika of legendary editor-publisher-friends, Anne Collins, Simon Prosser and Matt Weiland, who were meticulous and wise in all they did to help me streamline the river to its fastest form; my parents, John and Rosamund Macfarlane; and of course those who feature significantly in the book, and who underwent the not-always-easy experience of meeting themselves in another's pages. I was the beneficiary of responses that ran athwart the first draft's flow, as well as those which were carried by its currents: both were valuable. Phoebe was more widely superb in the expertise and referencing assistance she provided in the final four months of the book's making; without her I could not have brought it to copy-edit on time. Wayne read the whole book once and the opening twice (once aloud), bringing his lynx eyes relentlessly to bear, and he also kindly allowed me to adapt and absorb comments and messages from him into the book's voice – as Jed has also done.

I wish to thank my friend Julith Jedamus, who also read the book in first draft and then in revised form. Julith – a poet, memoirist and novelist – has now been among the first and most trusted readers of all my 'big' books since *The Wild Places*. She's a remarkable reader at the levels of the sentence, large-scale arcs and structures of feeling. Julith: so many thanks for all the pencil-marks, the letters and messages of first response and the unfailing friendship.

To dear friends who have companioned, supported and encouraged me along the way, and who have not yet been named, my gratitude: Julie Brook, Horatio Clare, Peter Davidson, Aly Derby, Johnny Flynn, Michael Hurley, Raphael Lyne, Leo Mellor, Jackie Morris, Clair Quentin, Siddharth Pandey, Rob Petit, Corinna Russell, Jan-Melissa Schramm, Merlin Sheldrake, Rebecca Solnit, James Wade, Kelcey and Edward Wilson-Lee and Alexis Wright.

Then: thanks are also due – for many kinds of assistance, information, influence, inspiration and kindness over these river-years – to: Oscar Aldred, Nicholas Allen, Akila Balu, Carlos Andrés Baquero-Díaz, Joslyn Barnes, Amy-Jane Beer, Tim Bell, Prerna Singh Bindra, Amber Massie Blomfield, Jennifer Bonnell, Pier-Olivier Boudreault, Eve Bowen, James Bradley, Joanna Braniff, Lindsay Bremner, Garnette Cadogan, Yenny Vega Cárdenas, Alicia Carey, Melanie Challenger, Stefan Collini, Adrian Cooper, Rory Cox, Cormac Cullinan, Mary Ann Cullinan, Tim Dellow, Bathsheba Demuth, Liz Downes, Laurence Edwards, Olafur Eliasson, Sophie Erlund, Christopher Evans, Gareth Evans, David Farrier, Charlie Foran, Xésus Fraga, Gavin Francis, Jacqueline Gallant, Mark Goodwin, Arnie Guha, Keshava Guha, Ramchandra Guha, Henessa Gumiran, Flore Gurrey, Safet HadžiMuhamedović, Milo Harries, Alexandra Harris, Nick Hayes, Rebecca Henson, Daniela Soto Hernandez, Julia Hofmann, Michael Hrebeniak, Nick Hunt, Alex Jeffrey, Bob Jellicoe, Emily Jones, James Keay, Anjana Khatwa, Sahil Kher, Robin Wall Kimmerer, Louis Klee, Ashish Kothari, Simone Kotva, Niko Kristic, Tom Kruse, Arati Kumar Rao, Nomisha Kurian, Jessica Lee, Sam Lee, Hester Lees-Jeffries, Patrick Limb, Thomas Linzey, Rogelio Luque Lora, Thelma Lovell, Anneke Lubkowitz, Simon McBurney, Jim, Claudia, Iona and Sam Macfarlane, April McIntyre, Finlay MacLeod, Andri Snær Magnason, Claire Marshall, Gary Martin, Nick Measham, Anne Michaels, Inigo Minns, Cristian Moreno, Ali Naulls, Helen Needham, Susan Nerberg, Rob Newton, Alastair Vere Nicoll, Joseph Nizeti, Oke Odudu, Alejandra Olguín, Ruth Padel, Donald Peck, Jen Peedom, Nicola Peel, Fiona Perez, Cameron Petrie, Max Porter, Sita Reddy, Fiona Reynolds, Malcolm Rogge, Ian Rosa, Sanjan Sabherwal, Rob St John, Lydia Samuels, Chris Sandbrook, Philippe Sands, Ruth Sapsed, Paul Scully, Mark Seow, Feargal Sharkey, Neha Sharma, Geoff Shipp, Ariel Sim, Brendon Sims, Neha Sinha, Dylan Stirewalt, Hayden Thorpe, Phoebe Tickell, David Trotter, Mary Evelyn Tucker, Jack Turner, Roo Vandegrift, Christie Van Tinteren, Bhaskar Vira, Jim Warren, Jeff Wasserstrom, Tom Wells, Ross Wilson, Jane Wolff, Mark Wormald, Jeremy Wyatt, Lewis Wynn, Marine Yzquierdo and Carlos Zorrilla.

My agent of more than twenty years is also one of my friends of more than twenty years: the already mentioned Jessica Woollard. Thank you, dear Jess, for all of it. I am also unfailingly supported by Jim Rutman in the US, and all my friends at DHA: Ilaria Albani, Giulia Bernabe, Esme Bright, David Evans, Sophia Hadjipateras, Emma Jamison, Sam Norman, Emmanuel Omodeinde and Georgie Smith.

I am very fortunate in my long-term translators, several of whom have become friends: in particular, Nico Groen, Patrick Hersant, Andreas Jandl and Frank Sievers.

At Hamish Hamilton/Penguin Random House I continue to work with the best team of people, all outstanding at what they do, and now old friends: Simon Prosser, of course, and the great Anna Ridley and Hermione Thompson. Ellie Smith has seen several of my books through production with tremendous patience and attention, and Caroline Pretty is simply the finest copy-editor any writer could hope to have. My thanks also to Ruby Fatimilehin, Annie Underwood, Sarah Coward, Elisabeth Merriman, Pat Rush, and my indexer, Ben Murphy.

Lastly, of course, I turn (as ever) to my family: to dearest Julia, to whom the book is dedicated, and to our children, Lily, Tom and Will, who feature in it; and to my parents, Rosamund and John, who have, as throughout my life, been unfailingly interested and lovingly supportive of what I do, and who have made space and taken weight at vital stages in the process.

~

For the granting of textual permissions, I am grateful to the following: Natalie Diaz for excerpts from 'The First Water is the Body' and 'exhibits from The American Water Museum' from *Postcolonial Love Poem*, copyright © 2020 by Natalie Diaz, reprinted with permission of The Permissions Company, LLC (on behalf of Graywolf Press, graywolfpress.org), and Faber and Faber Limited. | Johnny Flynn for lines from 'The Water', copyright © 2010 by Johnny Flynn, reprinted with the permission of Blue Raincoat and Transgressive Records. | Rita Mestokosho for excerpts from *Atik^U utei: Le cœur du caribou*, copyright © 2023 Rita Mestokosho, reprinted with permission of Mémoire d'encrier and Copibec.

~

The images prefacing and within the main sections of the book are all mine and the copyright lies with me. The portrait images of Giuliana Furci and Yuvan Aves are also mine. The portrait image of Rita Mestokosho is © Christian Fleury. I'm grateful to Christian for permission to reproduce this image. For expertise in creating the three maps which preface the three main sections, I'm hugely grateful to Iqtedar Alam, archaeologist-architect-cartographer extraordinaire. The copyright in these maps lies with me, and they were made using open-source data.

~

Even in the relatively short time (at the moment of writing) since these journeys were completed, there have been numerous aftermaths. Here are a few of them.

Josef DeCoux – the courageous, cantankerous, unbudgeable protector of Los Cedros – died suddenly of complications from his cancer in May 2024. This book is in part dedicated to his memory. Soon afterwards, the mining vultures began to circle the cloud-forest once again. But José Cueva and Monse Vásquez, among others, quickly took over the protection of Los Cedros and its rivers, in liaison with the wider network of anti-mining resistance in the Intag Valley. Giuliana, Cosmo and I have joined the Board of Directors of the Los Cedros Fund, dedicated to the indefinite support and protection of the cloud-forest and all that it holds. César, Agustín, Ramiro and our MOTH Rights group have worked tirelessly to produce both a monitoring programme for Los Cedros and a plan for ensuring the implementation of Agustín's ruling, as well as working to fortify the Rights of Nature basis of its ongoing defence. Giuliana and Bryn's discoveries of new fungi species in the forest have added substantively to the biological case for Los Cedros's rights to flourish and evolve. Thanks to Giuliana and César's wider efforts, as well as those of Ecuadorian ethnomycologists, fungi are moving decisively towards the centre of future Rights of Nature cases in Ecuador and other jurisdictions, functioning as indicators and protectors of the right to life. Giuliana named the first of the new species she and Bryn identified as *Psilocybe stametsii*, in honour of Paul Stamets, who in 1996 wrote *Psilocybin Mushrooms of the World*, and who has been pivotal in the advancement and appreciation of mycology worldwide. Multiple significant Rights of Nature cases have been fought and won in Ecuador in a matter of months, many of them river-focused, including a July 2024 ruling that the rights of the Machángara River, who flows through Quito, had been violated by chronic pollution, and requiring the government to make reparation and restore the river's health. There is a real sense of momentum building in Ecuador, in terms of the judicial system giving evolving form and force to the rights of nature in the country. Indigenous and local activists remain central to this progress, and the inter-braiding of human and natural rights is increasingly tight.

On the anniversary of Giuliana's father's death, she wrote to César, Cosmo and me. 'I've realized that when I think back now to those weeks,' she said, 'the first sensation is of Los Cedros. I think of his death, and I see and feel forest. I don't take this at all lightly, as I was feeling cracked and scared when I landed in Quito.'

In India, Yuvan and his friends continue to fight for the well-being of Chennai's wounded waterbodies, and those through whom they flow. Like the mongoose, they dart and nip opportunistically, consequentially. Among their several recent victories is that, in the course of only three days, they managed to get a court to rule against a highway expansion programme which would have run a four-lane highway directly through Odiyur Lagoon, a vital wetland to the south of Chennai. They continue to work closely with the fisherfolk of the Pulicat region, north of Chennai, to resist the planned massive expansion of the Adani port into Kattupalli, which would devastate life and livelihoods on that coast, and would likely destroy Pulicat Lagoon itself: the second-largest saltwater lake in India. The arduous process of restoring a 'good' Ennore Creek continues, in all its complexity. Yuvan and I are in touch most days; he is writing a book about insects called *Inscendence*, and he sends me WhatsApp messages with photographs of insect esoterica, with accompanying notes like this one:

This is a chalcid wasp I saw on a cluster fig tree today, Rob. That egg-shaped thing you see is the pupa of an ichneumon wasp, which has punctured a banyan tussock moth caterpillar and laid its egg in it. The wasp larva ate the caterpillar inside out and fashioned a pupa. The chalcid wasp, however, is a hyperparasitoid and is now puncturing the ichneumon wasp pupa to lay its eggs inside. Its larvae will now devour it and form a pupa out of the pupa.

These messages make me very happy.

Yuvan visited me in England – his first time outside India – and within two days was far better than me at IDing British birds from appearance and song. During our time together, we followed the path of flowing water from the centre of Cambridge for two miles, uphill and against the current, until it led all the way back to the clear pools where springs rise from the chalk in a little copse near my home known as Nine Wells Wood. . .

Shortly after Wayne and I reached the silvery mouth of the Mutehekau Shipu at the Gulf of St Lawrence, we returned to Ekuanitshit. As we pulled up in the car park outside the Innu House of Culture, Rita was standing there. 'I've been expecting you,' she said, wholly unsurprised at our arrival – though there was no way she could have known which day we would appear, let alone which minute. I gave her the water I'd collected from William Napess's hunting grounds at her request, the bag of Labrador tea leaves I'd gathered for her, and a river-smoothed stone I'd found for her. We tumbled out an account of our time on the river: the fasting, the question, the discovery of the sacred tree, the encounter at the Gorge. She nodded calmly throughout our narrative, as if all of this had been predicted – which of course it had. Then she set me and Wayne to work, assisting her with the preparations for a healing ceremony for the women of the village. Under Rita's supervision, Wayne and I gathered gallons of river water, then built and tended a spruce-wood pyre in which we heated forty rounded river stones until they glowed red. Rita, to our surprise, invited us to join the ceremony – and so we did. I have promised not to speak or write of the hours that followed, so will only say here that they were among the most moving and perspective-shifting of my life. My friendship with Rita has flourished: we maintain a close correspondence of notes and photographs. 'Greetings to my distant brother, who speaks to the sacred tree,' she wrote to me a few weeks after my return from Nitassinan, 'thank you for your friendship. Life flows peacefully here; the first snowflakes have appeared as if by magic, and this has calmed autumn. May the Great Spirit protect you!' A week later, to my joy, Rita won the Governor General's Award for Poetry for her magnificent collection *Atik^U utei: Le cœur du caribou.* The following spring Rita and I met up in Montreal, where we walked and talked in the streets of that city as the last of the winter snows were melting and a pro-Palestine encampment was being set up on the grounds of McGill

University. For now, the Mutehekau Shipu remains alive and undammed. On 28 September 2023, the river was formally designated as an 'Aire du patrimoine autochtone et communautaire', an internationally recognized designation for the conservation of Indigenous lands and territories, which among its criteria requires evidence of a deep-running relationship between the landscape and the local and Indigenous communities, and a local system of governance which assures the conservation of the territory. The declaration of the nine rights, aliveness and 'personnalité juridique' of the river in 2021 was seen as a central pillar of this recognition. It is the first region to be thus designated in Canada. Nevertheless, Hydro-Québec refuses explicitly to rule out future damming of the river, and the provincial and national governments have declined to give the river absolute protection, so its status as an asset for potential future hydro-development remains open. If Hydro-Québec does move forwards with damming plans, however, the resistance will be huge – and it will come from all over the world.

In a house in Austin, Texas, and in a caldera in Naples, Italy, Wayne continues to experiment with ways of recreating and re-encountering Paul's eidolon. Elsewhere he is extending his geonautic experiments in burial to extreme levels, fathoming the outer limits of the human body beneath the full weight of the subterrane. Now and then I receive a sequence of 'inhumation' images from him: a 'before' photograph of Wayne snapping on a pair of swimming goggles and fitting a specially extended snorkel into his mouth; a 'during' photo of flattened earth with the little black plastic O of the snorkel's tip – Wayne's lifeline – just visible; then an 'after' photograph of Wayne having been dug up minutes or hours later, standing wild-eyed, yellow and punk-haired with dirt, as if he has just surfaced from another world, which he has. He has become a Jacques Cousteau of the Earth's crust; an envelope-pushing explorer of the viability of life in the boundary layer, downwards. I was recently pleased to be able to introduce him to Grand Commander's banging 2021 track 'fuck you i'm going underground'.

Oh, and the bracelet of red cloth that Rita tied around my right wrist, and which 'only time or the river, which are the same things, can remove', is still there.

~

Three water-songs have arisen from the writing of this book.

The first is the 'Song of the Cedars', which Cosmo, Giuliana, César and I wrote with the forest and river of Los Cedros, and the genesis of which is described in the Ecuador section. We have deliberately placed this song under a Creative Commons licence, in order to extend the domain of the commons rather than that of private property. The song is presently also the focus of a well-advanced attempt to make legal history by bringing the Constitutional Court in Ecuador to recognize the moral rights of the Los Cedros forest in the co-creation of the song. This would be the first time anywhere in the world that the creative authorship of a natural entity has been recognized in law. As such, the case might address a minor aspect of the vast injustice of what Karl Marx once called 'the free gift of nature to capital'.

The second song is 'Night-Swimmer', which is based on the ghazal Yuvan and I wrote together for the Olive Ridley sea turtles who come to nest on Chennai beach, and which I briefly describe us speaking aloud to the ocean late in the India section of the book. The song was beautifully set by composer Lydia Samuels, and sung by HOWL, the nine-person female and non-binary vocal ensemble of which Lydia is also a part. You can hear this song in all the usual places and ways online; best of all is to visit the HOWL Bandcamp site: https://howlsingers.bandcamp.com/album/night-creatures.

The third song is emerging as I write these Acknowledgements: it is a 'Spring Song', and is a collaboration between me, Lydia Samuels and Johnny Flynn. It is a song to be sung at a spring site who is at risk of drying up, or over a stream or river who is dying; a song that begins as one voice only, but which voice after voice then joins, as tributaries swell a stream into a river.

I listened to a great deal of music while researching, writing and travelling for this book. Much of it has been rivery or watery; I now have a very long 'river' play-list/mix-tape, which I won't inflict on the reader here. I will say that among the artists whose work I've listened most to while writing *Is a River Alive?* are: Big Thief, Joshua Burnside, Johnny Flynn, P. J. Harvey, King Creosote, Anna Mieke, Alexi Murdoch, Agnes Obel, the Pixies, Cosmo Sheldrake, This Is The Kit, Hayden Thorpe, Tiny Ruins – and Wet Leg when I needed a pick-up. Thanks to them all for what they make. I will name eleven river songs that I've listened to often while working on some aspect of this book: Chelsea Carmichael's 'Bone and Soil' (Shabaka Hutchings remix; all the shivers when the lyrics kick in . . .); Nick Drake's 'Riverman'; Florence + The Machine's 'What The Water Gave Me'; Johnny Flynn's 'The Water'; Keeley Forsyth's 'Bring Me Water'; Julie Fowlis, Éamon Doorley, Jim Molyneux, Laura Jane Wilkie, Rachel Newton and Nan Shepherd's 'The Hill Burns (River Dee)'; Marika Hackman's 'I Follow Rivers'; Ibeyi's 'River'; Bassekou Kouyate and Ngoni ba's 'The River Tune'; Oddfellows Casino's 'Carp, Lamprey, Perch and Bream'; and Richard Skelton's 'Threads Across the River'.

~

The cover image is by my long-time friend and collaborator Stanley Donwood. Stanley has now provided the art for the covers of seven of my books, among them two that we have co-created (*Holloway*, with Dan Richards; and *Ness*). Stanley's incandescent acrylic painting *Nether* (2013) became the cover image of *Underland*, which caught the eyes and imaginations of readers around the world. This new cover art stands in sibling relationship to that of *Underland*, and emerged out of conversations between us around the temporal forms of rivers – how they wander, meander and remember across centuries and millennia. Both Stanley and I are admirers of Harold Fisk's celebrated 1944 series of 'Meander Maps' of the Mississippi (discussed in Part II of the book); we both felt that the meander is the most striking single visual embodiment of the vitality, intentions and presence of rivers through time – and so that became the basis for the blazing art, beginning as large linocuts incised by Stanley's 'little chisel', then scanned, monoprinted and coloured. Richard Bravery at Penguin Random House is the design genius behind this and several of 'our' other covers.

~

Lastly, I was closely watched throughout the process of writing this book. My watcher stands in front of me as I write these sentences. It is a wooden carving, perhaps a foot and a half high, of a waterbird: a 'brolga' – also known as *Antigone rubicunda*, the Australian crane and the 'companion bird'. Brolga comes from *burrulga*, the bird's name in Gamilaraay, the language of the Gamilaraay (Kamilaroi) people of what is now called south-eastern Australia.

The brolga was carved by Arthur Kirby and sent to me by my friend Alexis Wright, whose novels, essays and wider corpus will be known to many people reading this, and whose words provide one of the opening epigraphs to *Is a River Alive?* Alexis is a writer, land activist and member of the Waanyi nation of the southern highlands of the Gulf of Carpentaria, in Australia's far north. Alexis and I have been friends and correspondents for years now, to my happiness, and she has encouraged me in this book from its inception. Early in my writing of *Is a River Alive?*, she sent me the brolga, which had previously watched over the writing of her novel, the epic *Praiseworthy* (2023).

The brolga is a bird of floodplains, marshes and rivers: a grey-feathered, black-wing-tipped, red-headed bird, both elegant and gregarious. I could not have wished for a better companion to write about water. I kept the brolga close to me, and found that it regarded me with a watchful eye which, uncannily, seemed always to be fixed upon me, wherever I stood or sat in relation to it. It reminded me, when I needed it, that there was a serious responsibility to the task undertaken.

During Australia's devastating series of floods and wildfires in 2019–20 – the floods creating an immense inland sea, and drowning half a million cattle; the fires ravaging traditional lands and, in a brutal alchemy, transforming billions of trees and around a billion animals into 434 million metric tons of atmospheric carbon dioxide – Alexis wrote an anguished, piercing essay called 'We All Smell the Smoke,

We All Feel the Heat'. 'How do you find the words to tell the story of the environmental emergency of our times?' she asked there. By way of an answer, she described how, after the Darling River fish die-off – in which around a million fish died as a result of river mismanagement – Aboriginal elders travelled from different parts of the river system to gather in the high country known as Walgalu, in New South Wales, where several of Australia's major rivers are born. There, Alexis wrote, they performed a water ceremony, a 'Narjong', which invoked 'the sacred duty of caring for the river systems, a tribal responsibility for thousands of years'. The elders 'called the rivers – their relative, their relation – by their traditional names', addressing them, 'speaking to them gently'. For Alexis, this ancient practice had echoes in contemporary acts of guardianship, protest and protection – including the modern Rights of Nature movement, the ideas of which she sees as beginning 'with Ecuador's 2008 constitutional acknowledgement of the Rights of Nature *to exist, persist, maintain and regenerate its vital cycles'*.

In an extraordinary essay written two years later, 'The Inward Migration in Apocalyptic Times', Alexis wrote a paragraph that I printed out and kept to hand:

> The world desperately needs powerful storytellers to help us make sense of the unfathomable events taking place. And while sitting in eternity, the very old ones will be impressing into the minds of these future writers a way of figuring out how to bring life back into the laws of the creative beings in the sand desert and the seas; how to bring life back into the waters, the mountains and skies, the flatlands and plains, back into the bushlands, the forests, the thunder and winds, back into the trees, and the animals.

Those words have stayed close by me, and the brolga Alexis sent has fixed me with its scouring, staring eye. Together, they've been the best kind of conscience I could have asked for. I know that what I've written here falls far short of the demands and possibilities Alexis outlines above, but I also know that I've tried as hard as I can 'to bring life back'.

Giuliana Furci

Yuvan Aves

Rita Mestokosho

INDEX

Page references in *italics* indicate images.
RM indicates Robert Macfarlane.

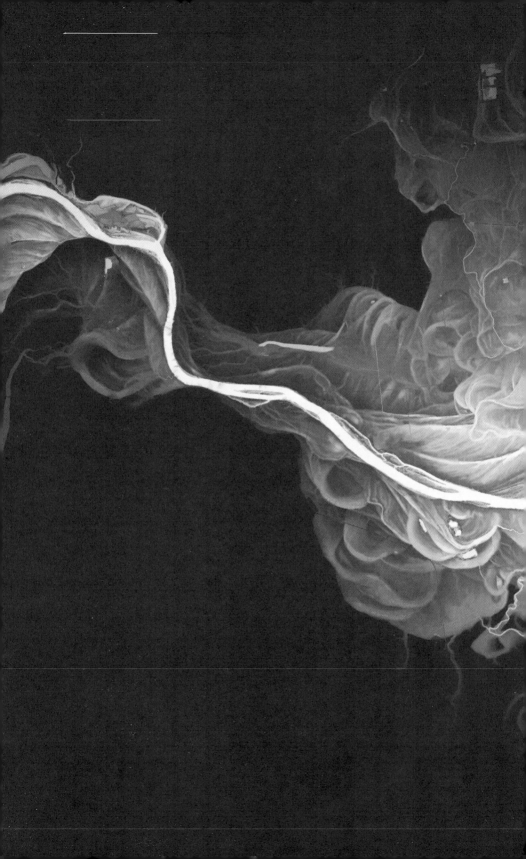